Routledge Library Editions

JAPANESE CULTURE

ANTHROPOLOGY AND ETHNOGRAPHY

Routledge Library Editions
Anthropology and Ethnography

SOCIAL AND CULTURAL ANTHROPOLOGY
In 16 Volumes

I	Social Anthropology and Language	*Ardener*
II	The Relevance of Models for Social Anthropology	*Banton*
III	The Social Anthropology of Complex Societies	*Banton*
IV	Other Cultures	*Beattie*
V	Social Anthropology	*Evans-Pritchard*
VI	Meaning in Culture	*Hanson*
VII	The Social Anthropology of Radcliffe-Brown	*Kuper*
VIII	History and Social Anthropology	*Lewis*
IX	The Social Context of Violent Behaviour	*Marx*
X	Seasonal Variations of the Eskimo	*Mauss*
XI	Socialization	*Mayer*
XII	Egyptian Religion	*Morenz*
XIII	The Foundations of Social Anthropology	*Nadel*
XIV	Japanese Culture	*Smith & Beardsley*
XV	Taboo	*Steiner*
XVI	Social Life of Early Man	*Washburn*

JAPANESE CULTURE

Its Development and Characteristics

EDITED BY ROBERT J SMITH
AND RICHARD K BEARDSLEY

LONDON AND NEW YORK

First published in 1963

Reprinted in 2004 by
Routledge
2 Park Square, Milton Park, Abingdon, Oxon OX14 4RN

Simultaneously published in the USA and Canada by Routledge
711 Third Avenue, New York, NY 10017

First issued in paperback 2013

Routledge is an imprint of the Taylor & Francis Group, an informa business

© 1962 Wenner-Gren Foundation for Anthropological
Research, Inc.

*Reprinted from 'Japanese Culture', Robert J Smith and Richard K Beardsley (eds),
Viking Fund Publications in Anthropology No 34, New York, by permission of the
Wenner-Gren Foundation for Anthropological Research Inc., New York, New York*

All rights reserved. No part of this book may be reprinted or
reproduced or utilized in any form or by any electronic, mechanical,
or other means, now known or hereafter invented, including
photocopying and recording, or in any information storage or retrieval
system, without permission in writing from the publishers.

The publishers have made every effort to contact authors/copyright
holders of the works reprinted in *Routledge Library Editions –
Anthropology and Ethnography*. This has not been possible in every case,
however, and we would welcome correspondence from those
individuals/companies we have been unable to trace.

These reprints are taken from original copies of each book. In many
cases the condition of these originals is not perfect. The publisher has
gone to great lengths to ensure the quality of these reprints, but wishes
to point out that certain characteristics of the original copies will, of
necessity, be apparent in reprints thereof.

British Library Cataloguing in Publication Data
A CIP catalogue record for this book is available from the British Library

Japanese Culture
ISBN 978-0-415-33039-8 (hbk)
ISBN 978-0-415-86927-0 (pbk)

Miniset: Social and Cultural Anthropology

Series: Routledge Library Editions – Anthropology and Ethnography

JAPANESE CULTURE
Its Development and Characteristics

edited by
ROBERT J. SMITH *and* RICHARD K. BEARDSLEY

METHUEN & COMPANY LIMITED,
36 Essex Street London WC2

This volume comprises one of a series of publications on research in general anthropology published by the Wenner-Gren Foundation for Anthropological Research, Incorporated, a foundation created and endowed at the instance of Axel L. Wenner-Gren for scientific, educational, and charitable purposes. The reports, numbered consecutively as independent contributions, appear at irregular intervals.

First Published in Great Britain 1963
Copyright © 1962 by
WENNER-GREN FOUNDATION FOR ANTHROPOLOGICAL RESEARCH, INC.
Printed in the United States of America
Catalogue No. 2/2705/10

PREFACE

ALL the essays collected in this volume originated as papers comprising six sessions of the Tenth Pacific Science Congress, held in Honolulu, Hawaii, from August 21 to September 6, 1961. The way these six sessions came into being exemplifies a fresh step of development in studies of Japanese society and culture, happily evidenced on other recent occasions as well, and the temptation is strong to record this step in its historical context as the papers of this segment of the Congress go to press.

The new trend referred to is one of explicit collaboration between Japanese and American scholars in Japanese studies, important because it promises to relieve one-sidedness and enrich the field as a whole. It will be evident from the list of contributors to this volume that Japanese participated in the six Congress sessions in almost equal numbers with Americans. Each session, moreover, had Japanese and American co-chairmen and was organized under mutual consultation. In certain cases, joint participation in the session was the sequel to a period of collaborative research, though such close relationship has not yet become the rule. This joint organization and participation, a mere organizational detail in itself, gathers significance when placed against its proper background, the development of the study of Japanese society. Japanese studies have evolved through two or more stages, and we venture to point to intensified collaboration in research and reporting, evidenced to a modest degree in the present papers, as a primary feature of the stage now commencing. A glance at the past and present situations will point to such an outcome.

For a very long time after Japan first renewed her contact with the outside world in the middle nineteenth century, she remained the mysterious island nation of the Orient, best known for a few quaint customs and delicate arts—her geisha, haiku poems, woodblock prints, and embroidered kimono. Social science study remained rather casual, with exceptions in the fields of economics, politics, and archeology. John Embree's admirable community study, *Suye Mura: A Japanese Village* (Chicago, 1939), was an outstanding exception to the exoticism that tended to prevail even on the eve of World War II. His clear-eyed depiction of local organization presaged an era of close examination of details of Japanese society, an era that was hastened by the wartime imperative to acquire intelligence about all aspects of Japan.

After peace returned to the Pacific, Japan was revealed to be an area of extraordinary interest to social scientists of every hue. Some scholars have been lured to study her prodigious economic growth over the last century, or her accompanying rapid and extreme social change, with cities developing into top-rank metropolitan giants, where life of ultra-modern aspect can be viewed side by side with persisting patches of traditional living and attitudes. Because feudal patterns flourished so recently in Japan, persons with historical interests are beginning to study feudal institutions not for their sake alone but for structural comparison with European feudal conditions and with neighboring but non-feudal traditional societies. Still others are attracted to a much more recent period, the Occupation period of 1945–52, having in mind its relevance to general problems of applied social science and directed culture change. The democratization policies to which the Occupation authorities dedicated their effort provide an instance of social experiment on a massive scale hard to match except in Russia and China under Communist regimes, neither of which is readily available for study. For all these reasons and others, the wartime surge of interest in Japanese social phenomena tended to gain momentum in postwar years. This postwar period, thus, was characterized by systematic and intensive investigation of Japanese society and culture quite unprecedented in prewar years.

Nevertheless, the access of outsiders to knowledge of Japanese society has been far from ideal. Not only does Japan remain at an awkward geographic distance from America or Europe, being halfway around the world even in an age of jet travel, but, more importantly, communication has been difficult between two distinct bodies of scholars at work on the same subject matter: the Japanese themselves and outsiders. As any student of social sciences knows, a considerable body of Japanese social scientists has delved into corners of Japanese society and culture as yet untouched by outsiders, making discoveries and formulating interpretations by paths of thought often quite different from those of foreign scholars. It has not been easy to merge all this into one common body of knowledge, however. The Japanese language and script, though perhaps no more difficult inherently than English, for historical reasons form a barrier that sequesters a wealth of material published annually in this highly literate nation. Few outsiders find apertures through this barrier, which has consequently confined the enlightened discourse of even the most articulate Japanese scholars mainly to a Japanese audience. Under such circumstances, it is not surprising that the two groups, Japanese and outsider, have found themselves sometimes talking past each other on those rare occasions when the barrier to discourse has been temporarily raised.

Thus, there is something of a triumph in recent occasions that have brought together Japanese and foreign social scientists to discuss common problems in mutually shared terms before a common audience. The Pacific Science Congresses have provided such a common forum, each successive Congress, at four-year intervals, giving evidence of closer rapport and fuller communication. Co-ordination for the sessions at the Tenth Pacific Science Congress was unprecedently close, bringing about a program with over-all coherence that was shared throughout by Japanese and Americans.

The successful conjoining of Japanese and others at Honolulu required more than a spirit of mutuality. Practical logistical problems had to be overcome. On the American side, acknowledgment is due Dr. Harold J. Coolidge, Secretary-

General of the Congress, for his untiring effort to facilitate the participation of Japanese scientists in all fields. The National Science Foundation put generous grants for travel funds at the disposal of organizers of the Congress, while on the Japanese side the National Science Council underwrote the travel costs of several participants in the sessions from which this volume of papers is derived.

The sequence of arrangements that led to the co-ordinated program on the Development of Japanese Culture may be simply narrated. Fred Eggan, as chairman of the Organizing Committee for Anthropology and Social Sciences, requested Richard K. Beardsley to form a convening committee charged with securing the fullest possible participation of Japanese scholars. After some preliminary liaison, a similar committee was formed under Allen Smith to pull together research on the Ryukyu Islands. Japanese ethnological and archeological subjects were tentatively scheduled, and a Japanese scholar was requested to serve as counterpart organizer together with each American in charge of a session. Only one of the sessions that were initially contemplated failed to materialize despite considerable interest: Overseas Japanese Migrants to North and South America. With this exception, the papers of the six sessions presented in this volume provide a fair sampling of current research interests and findings in the various fields of cultural anthropology, including culture and personality.

Appreciative acknowledgment is due the chairmen of the respective sessions for scrupulously carrying out the principle of joint organization and joint participation. Serving as chairmen on behalf of the Japanese were: Eiichiro Ishida, Tadashi Fukutake, Yuzuru Okada, and Takeo Doi. On behalf of Americans, they include, besides the present editors: Gordon T. Bowles and William J. Caudill, Jr.

The editors, having assembled and arranged the groups of papers, express their appreciation to the Pacific Science Congress Commission for a grant, received through the University of Hawaii Press, in partial subsidization of publishing cost, and to the Viking Fund and Sol Tax, Editor of the Viking Fund Papers in Anthropology, for facilitating publication.

Since biographical materials on Japanese scholars is almost inaccessible to the American reader, brief identification of each Japanese contributor is offered here:

DOI, TAKEO, M.D.
: Born 1920. Psychiatrist-in-chief, St. Luke's International Hospital, Tokyo. A graduate of Tokyo University, he also received training in the United States at the Menninger School of Psychiatry and at the San Francisco Psychoanalytic Institute. Author of two books and various papers on psychiatric theory and techniques.

EGAMI, NAMIO
: Born 1906. Professor, Institute for Oriental Culture, Tokyo University. A graduate of Tokyo University. Specialist on East Asian culture history and archeology, he has made field trips to Inner Mongolia and to the Near East. He is a director of the Japanese Ethnological Society, a standing committee member in the Far Eastern Prehistory Association, and member of the Japanese Historical Society. He is the author of several books and many articles on Eurasian and Far Eastern ethnic history.

FUKUTAKE, TADASHI
: Born 1917. Professor, Department of Sociology, Tokyo University. A graduate of

Tokyo University, he has done field research in China and various localities of Japan, specializing in community study problems. He is a director of the Japanese Sociological Society. His books cover studies of Chinese village society; Japanese rural communities; social sciences and value judgments; and the intriguing study of reverse acculturation, "America-village," dealing with the influences exerted on their home village by emigrants to Canada.

Ishida, Eiichiro

Born 1903. Professor, Department of Cultural Anthropology, Tokyo University. With a doctorate from the University of Vienna, he has pursued research both in folklore and in cultural anthropology, with field research among the Tungus, Mongols, and Ainu, as well as in many parts of Japan. He is a member of the American Anthropological Association and the Japanese Ethnological Society, Folklore Society, Anthropological Society, Sociological Society, Archaeological Society, and Oriental Society and has served as president or director of several of these societies. His books include texts in general cultural anthropology and Japanese culture history as well as folklore monographs and textbooks.

Kitano, Seiichi

Born 1899. Professor of Sociology, Faculty of Letters and Institute of Industrial Labor Relations, Osaka University. A graduate of Tokyo University, he is a Director of the Japanese Sociological Association and member of the Executive Committee, Humanistic Sciences Commission, Ministry of Education. His works include a village life study in south China and field work studies as well as methodological and theoretical works on Japanese village life. Particularly well known is his early study of Shirakawa, a village with large extended family organization.

Koyama, Takashi

Born 1900. Professor, Department of Anthropology, Tokyo Municipal University. A graduate of Tokyo University. A director of the Japanese Sociological Society. Based on field work in various parts of Japan, his publications deal mainly with family organization as related to economy and to modernizing influences.

Ono, Susumu

Born 1919. Assistant Professor, Yamaguchi University. A graduate of Tokyo University and specialist in linguistics, his published books have been on the ancient use of *kana*-syllabary script and on the origin of the Japanese language.

Yawata, Ichiro

Born 1892. Lecturer at Tokyo University, Yokohama Municipal University, and Nippon University, he was until recently curator of archeology at the National Museum in Tokyo. He is a graduate of Tokyo University and is a member of the Japanese Archaeological Society and the Ethnological Society. His field work has taken him to Melanesia and Southeast Asia as well as throughout Japan. He is the author of books on Southeast Asian culture, on the Neolithic cultures of Japan, and on prehistoric art.

Robert J. Smith
Richard K. Beardsley

CONTENTS

PREFACE v

I. ORIGINS

NATURE OF THE PROBLEM OF JAPANESE CULTURAL ORIGINS 3
    Eiichiro Ishida, University of Tokyo

PREHISTORIC EVIDENCE FOR JAPANESE CULTURAL ORIGINS 7
    Ichiro Yawata, University of Tokyo

LIGHT ON JAPANESE CULTURAL ORIGINS FROM HISTORICAL ARCHEOLOGY AND LEGEND   11
    Namio Egami, University of Tokyo

THE JAPANESE LANGUAGE: ITS ORIGIN AND ITS SOURCES 17
    Susumu Ono, Yamaguchi University

II. SOCIAL STRUCTURE

STABILITY IN JAPANESE KINSHIP TERMINOLOGY: THE HISTORICAL EVIDENCE . . . 25
    Robert J. Smith, Cornell University

CORPORATE EMPHASIS AND PATTERNS OF DESCENT IN THE JAPANESE FAMILY . . . 34
    Harumi Befu, University of Missouri

"DŌZOKU" AND "IE" IN JAPAN: THE MEANING
OF FAMILY GENEALOGICAL RELATIONSHIPS 42
    Seiichi Kitano, Osaka University

CHANGING FAMILY STRUCTURE IN JAPAN 47
    Takashi Koyama, Tokyo Metropolitan University

NOTES ON PRIMOGENITURE IN POSTWAR JAPAN 55
    Y. Scott Matsumoto, Atomic Bomb Casualty Commission, Hiroshima

III. VILLAGE ORGANIZATION

COMMON-INTEREST ASSOCIATIONS IN RURAL JAPAN 73
    Edward Norbeck, Rice University

VILLAGE COMMUNITY ("BURAKU") IN JAPAN AND ITS DEMOCRATIZATION 86
    Tadashi Fukutake, University of Tokyo

THE EMERGENCE OF A SELF-CONSCIOUS ENTREPRENEURIAL CLASS IN RURAL JAPAN . 91
    Erwin Johnson, University of Buffalo

SOCIAL AND TECHNOLOGICAL CHANGE IN RURAL JAPAN:
CONTINUITIES AND DISCONTINUITIES 100
    Iwao Ishino, Michigan State University

IV. CULTURE AND PERSONALITY

PATTERNS OF EMOTION IN MODERN JAPAN 115
    William Caudill, National Institute of Mental Health, Bethesda

"AMAE": A KEY CONCEPT FOR UNDERSTANDING JAPANESE PERSONALITY STRUCTURE   132
    L. Takeo Doi, University of Tokyo

ENTRANCE EXAMINATIONS AND EMOTIONAL DISTURBANCES
IN JAPAN'S "NEW MIDDLE CLASS" 140
    Ezra F. Vogel, Harvard University

DEVIANCY AND SOCIAL CHANGE: A PSYCHOCULTURAL EVALUATION
OF TRENDS IN JAPANESE DELINQUENCY AND SUICIDE 153
    George A. De Vos, University of California, Berkeley

REFLECTIONS ON DEPENDENCY PHENOMENA AS SEEN
IN NISEI IN THE UNITED STATES 172
    Charlotte G. Babcock, University of Pittsburgh

INDEX 189

I. Origins

NATURE OF THE PROBLEM
OF JAPANESE CULTURAL ORIGINS

EIICHIRO ISHIDA

1

BEFORE discussing the problem of Japanese cultural origins I should like to define what we mean by "Japanese culture." Japanese culture is, of course, the culture of the Japanese people throughout history. The concept of a people (or *Volk* in German) is not biological but cultural. The Japanese appeared on the Japanese archipelago at a particular time in history as a unified ethnic group with a common language called Japanese and with a common traditional way of life. The unity and the "we-feeling" of the Japanese must have been further strengthened by political unification as a Japanese nation and by their subsequent common history and destiny. However, something that is as difficult to change as the core personality of an individual, once it is established, does exist in the case of a people and its culture, and it is just the origins of this sort of Japanese culture that we are now going to discuss.

Hence, the problem will not necessarily correspond to that of the racial origins of the Japanese but is very close to the problem of the origin of the Japanese language that Professor Ono takes up in his paper. The commonness of language is at least a dominant factor, if not the only factor, in the formation of a people, with its unique pattern of culture and national character.

2

The first question to ask is whether the higher civilization of the continent, which was introduced into Japan by the Yamato dynasty about the fifth century A.D., played any decisive role in creating basic Japanese culture. Indeed Buddhism and Chinese civilization exerted as powerful an influence on Japanese culture as Christianity and the Graeco-Roman legacy did on Western civilizations. But just as the basis of Germanic cultures had been built up before the introduction of Christianity and the civilization of the Roman Empire, so the core of Japanese culture that carries over even into the twentieth century was already in existence when the Yamato dynasty introduced through Korea Buddhist sutras and the Analects of Confucius together with Chinese characters. What we are concerned with is when, where, and how this pre-Buddhist and pre-Chinese core or basis of Japanese culture was formed and brought the Japanese people as an ethnic unit into being.

The second question to raise is: Was the founder of the Yamato dynasty one of the local powers on the Japanese islands or a conqueror from abroad? In this connection, the theory propounded by Professor Egami is worth thorough examination. Against the broad perspective of Oriental history, Professor Egami postulates that the Yamato dynasty was founded by one of the horse-riding Tungus tribes that, during the age of disunion and turmoil on the Chinese continent after the collapse of the great Han empire, swept over the Korean peninsula from the northeast and established the so-called "Three Kingdoms" of Korea. Around the turn of the fifth century, so he asserts, a well-equipped military group of these horse-riders crossed the Tsushima strait, invaded Kyushu, conquered the local chiefdoms of the autochthonous Wa people mentioned in Chinese chronicles, and finally founded a centralized state of Yamato in western Japan. This opinion of Professor Egami would account for the fact that, while the funeral gifts of the early Tomb period consist largely of objects for ceremonial use, such as mirrors and jades, the mound tombs of the late Tomb period contain large quantities of armor, helmets, horse-trappings of iron and gold, and gorgeous personal fittings, which in the words of an archeologist "give a vivid image of continental monarchs clad from tip to toe in costumes of brilliant golden color." The striking similarities that exist between the mythical narrative about the founding of the Korean dynasties and that of the ancestor of the Japanese imperial family descending from the Plain of High Heaven, as well as the accounts of the eastward expedition of conquest of the first Emperor Jimmu from Kyushu, will also bear out this very intriguing view.

3

However, if one assumes that the Japanese language, with its Altaic structure, appeared only after the conquest by the horse-riding invaders from the continent, this presumption contradicts the general opinion of the linguists that the Wa people in the Yayoi and early Tomb periods, so far as we can guess from the Chinese sources about the Japan of the third century, were already speaking the same Japanese language as after the Nara period. It is not merely a matter of language. We have sufficient grounds to believe that the basic patterns of Japanese culture, centering on rice cultivation and ranging from technology to Weltanschauung, were set in the Yayoi period, i.e., from about the third century B.C. to about the third century A.D. The Wa people of the subsequent early Tomb period, divided quite probably into small local states with magicoreligious leaders, were the same farming population as that of the Yayoi period. If, then, a horse-riding Altaic tribe really established the Yamato dynasty, it must have been a comparatively small group of warriors who ultimately came to be absorbed and assimilated among the native Wa both in language and physical characteristics.

Here I should like to point out the possibility of an alternative to the theory of a horse-riders' conquest. The origin of the state does not always presuppose a conquest of agrarian societies by a nomadic people, as Oppenheimer and Schmidt once assumed. In the New World we have examples enough of the political and military capacity of agricultural peoples to create well-organized and large-scale states. According to Chinese chronicles, the Wa people from the later Yayoi to the early Tomb periods had established the Yamatai realm under Queen Himiko as a powerful confederation of local lords. Why could such a Wa kingdom not rise to hegemony dominating other regional powers? In this case, too, however, we should take into account the southward movement of horse-riding peoples through Korea and their contact with the Wa, who most likely occupied also the southernmost part of the peninsula. If one of the Wa chiefdoms of the early Tomb period developed into the Yamato state of the late Tomb period, it must have owed its success to cavalry, which was a new military technique imported from the continent.

4

At any rate, whether the first emperor of the Yamato dynasty was an Altaic conqueror or not, basic Japanese culture undoubtedly took shape in the Yayoi period, and the formation of the Japanese people was complete by the fifth century. Who then, one may ask, were the people of the preceding Jomon period? Were they not the same Japanese as in the Yayoi period? This question is all but unanswerable at our present level of knowledge. Some physical anthropologists in Japan argue that the present-day Japanese are direct descendants of the Jomon people merely on the grounds that the difference of skeletal remains of the Yayoi and later periods from those of the preceding Jomon period can be adequately explained from the changes in the way of life. But if the mixture of heterogeneous races provides an equally satisfactory explanation of the very same difference, this logic fails, and we shall have to turn to archeological, ethnological, and linguistic data for the final conclusion.

On this score Professor Ono's hypothesis about the origins of the Japanese language, advanced after examining the results of physical-anthropological, archeological, and ethnological studies, and combining with them the findings of his own linguistic and dialectological research, is exceedingly stimulating. He presumes that in western Japan the people of the Jomon period spoke a language of southern origin with a phonetic system like that of present-day Polynesian, while a language with grammatical system and vowel harmony like the Altaic was introduced with Yayoi culture and spread eastward from northern Kyushu along with rice cultivation, metal implements, the art of weaving, and so on. Thus he accounts for the Japanese language with an Altaic structure and a non-Altaic vocabulary that is at least partly of Malayo-Polynesian origin.

5

On the other hand, Professor Beardsley once offered a tentative suggestion that the Jomon culture was a local variant of non-agricultural but pottery-making culture relying on fishing and hunting, which very slowly diffused from west to east along the stream networks of the coniferous forest zone covering the vast territory of boreal Eurasia and North America. This suggestion should be taken into serious consideration, especially as regards the northeastern half of Japan and the earlier periods of Jomon culture. At the same time we must keep the following two facts in mind: first, that the so-called Jomon culture lasted for thousands of years, possibly consisting of diverse waves of different nature; second, that even from the pre-Jomon, non-ceramic period throughout the whole of prehistoric and historic times up to the present, the Japanese archipelago has been divided into two great provinces, with an unmistakable dividing line running north-south in central Honshu. Professor Beardsley mentioned this division concerning the Jomon culture, and Professor Ono and many other Japanese anthropologists have discussed it in detail in connection with blood types, fingerprints, social structure, archeological and ethnographical materials, and (most conspicuously) the two major dialects of the Japanese language. I suspect that this sharp contrast between eastern and western Japan will remain an outstanding problem, whose solution will throw new light on the origins of Japanese culture.

6

In the foregoing, we do not touch on the Ainu problem, one of the most favored and most difficult topics of anthropology. It is fair to say, however, that the participation of the Ainu was relatively insignificant in the ethnic formation of the Japanese people. If the Ainu were the bearers of at least a part of the Jomon culture in eastern Japan, they must have been driven to the north by the Wa people with whom the Yayoi and Tomb cultures spread from southwest to northeast. Even if racial mixture occurred between the two, the Ainu have remained until the twentieth century a distinctive ethnic unit with their own racial, linguistic, and cultural characters.

PREHISTORIC EVIDENCE FOR JAPANESE CULTURAL ORIGINS

ICHIRO YAWATA

A DEFINITION of our concept of "Japanese culture" seems called for at the outset. Is it the indigenous Japanese culture centered on the emperor concept, or is it rather the culture that has Buddhism as one of its focal points and that entered from the continent in successive waves? All this, to be sure, is Japanese culture, but a still different concept that leads yet farther back into the past comprises all the manifestations of human activity from the time man first populated the Japanese archipelago. It has fallen to me to review the first and most ancient part of human activity on these islands, namely the so-called "stone age." I will deal with its distribution and time span and, where feasible, with its affinities.

PRECERAMIC PERIOD

Research during the last décade has established beyond serious doubt that Japan was inhabited during the Pleistocene period. The inhabitants left cultural remains consisting of chipped-stone implements in loam strata of Upper Pleistocene date. The period in question corresponds roughly to the end stages of the European third interglacial and includes the whole fourth glacial period. However, fossilized human or mammal bones have not yet been found in association with artifacts. The chipped implements of this period can be divided into four typological groups. The first group consists of shale core implements that are sometimes defined as "hand axes" and were identified as Mousterian by Dr. Maringer. The second group comprises flaked shale and obsidian implements that are somewhat reminiscent of the European Upper Paleolithic flake industries. The third group consists mainly of spearheads that may possibly be identified with the European Solutrean. The fourth group is formed by blade implements; their proportion of microlithic specimens progressively increases.

The stratigraphic position of these four groups is as yet unclear. It seems, however, that the first, or "hand axe" group, is the most ancient and the fourth, or blade group, is the newest.

JOMON CULTURE

Overlying the loam layer is a layer of black alluvial soil 30–100 centimeters in depth. This alluvium contains cultural deposits from Jomon times upward.

The cultural material from the lowest part of this layer is characterized by pottery, chipped and sometimes edge-ground stone implements, and bone and antler implements as well. In Hokkaido, pottery, together with blade points, has recently been confirmed in the lowest part of the humus layer. In Siberia, identical blade points have been found, in some cases associated with pottery. On the one hand, these blade points furnish us with a link between the most ancient artifacts and Jomon culture; on the other hand, they provide some indication for the origin of Jomon culture.

Jomon culture is generally subdivided into five periods: earliest, early, middle, late, and latest phases. The earliest Jomon phase is characterized by conoid pottery with pointed base. Ornamentation of this kind of pottery in the northeast differs from that in the southwestern half of Japan. Whereas we cannot at the moment find outside parallels to the southwestern variety, the northeastern variety shows distinct affinities with Siberia. Not only are arrowheads found in association with this pottery, but there are also completely polished greenstone axes shaped by abrasion. Nephrite implements polished by the same technique are well known from Siberia. Finally, fishhooks and harpoons made of antler complete the typical find inventory of this layer. Leaving southwestern Japan out of account, we can say that the earliest Jomon stage of northeastern Japan has distinct affinities with Siberia.

The pottery of the second, or early, phase is of cylindrical form and is characterized by a fibrous temper. The whole surface of these flat-bottomed vessels is ornamented by cord marks. The southwestern variety is also flat-bottomed but of varied form, lacking cord marks and fibrous temper. Therefore, the same clear distinction as before between northeastern and southwestern Japan characterizes the second Jomon phase.

The third, or middle, phase witnesses the emergence of three cultural subareas: northeastern, central, and southwestern. The central area is considered the product of southwestern contact imposed on the second northeastern phase. The middle phase of the Jomon culture presents a multitude of problems. To mention but one: the gorgeously decorated Jomon ware found together with a profusion of various types of polished stone implements in the inland regions of the central subarea was accompanied by some practices that in the opinion of many scholars nurtured the natural plant cycle. Human clay figurines, especially female ones, though found occasionally in earlier Jomon phases, flourish in the third stage. However, it seems premature to identify them all as fecundity symbols and infer the existence of agriculture from their presence.

In the fourth, or late, phase the three formerly distinct subareas are uniformly blanketed by cord-marked pottery that is gray or black, well-fired, and thin-walled. This pottery comes, moreover, in a multitude of forms. A tendency toward polishing it after firing anticipates Yayoi techniques. Other trends of the same period include tracing incisions on the pottery or ornamenting it with cinnabar or ocher paint and working stone with improved techniques. This type of culture is mainly found along the seashore. It is further characterized by extremely well-developed fishing techniques. The toggle-head harpoon suddenly appears in northeastern Japan. It is typologically and technically very like an Eskimo harpoon.

In the fifth, or final, Jomon stage local subareas emerge once again. A culture (Okhotsk) that is sometimes considered to be outside the Jomon tradition spreads over Hokkaido. Southwestern Japan, especially northern Kyushu, is characterized by development eventually leading to the emergence of the Yayoi culture. It is the result of periods of mutual fertilization among various local centers combined with outside influence. The stone implements of this period show numerous and elaborate specializations of uncertain function. The burial grounds tend to become extremely large, sites yielding two to three hundred skeletons sometimes being encountered.

One of the questions arising from consideration of the five Jomon sequential stages concerns the switchover from a food-gathering to a food-producing type of economy. Leaving this problem aside, we might say that this entire period of Jomon culture conforms in general type to the northeastern Asiatic Neolithic.

YAYOI CULTURE

The earliest appearance of Yayoi culture can be traced to northern Kyushu, where it manifests itself in undecorated ware in a number of standard, specialized forms, namely, jars, urns, and dishes on stands or pedestals. The predominantly polished-stone implements of this period link up with the stone implements of the Korean peninsula, Manchuria, and northern China. But the chipped implements that accompany Yayoi pottery and polished stone belong to the cultural heritage of the Jomon period. Examples are arrowheads and knives. Together with the polished implements, small numbers of bronze and iron halberds, daggers, and mirrors seem to have entered from the continent.

The presence of rice cultivation can be attested from the very first appearance of Yayoi culture in Japan. As already mentioned, the stone implements of this period link up with northern China, thereby following the northern orientation of the previous Jomon culture. Yet rice cultivation was not in evidence in northern China at this stage of development, so Yayoi rice gives notice of a decisive cultural impulse from the south for the first time. The method of disposing of the dead provides another interesting subject, for northern Kyushu is an area of urn, dolmen, and stone cist burials. From northern Kyushu the rice-cultivating Yayoi culture spread along the shores of the Inland Sea and culminated in the formation of a great cultural center in south-central Honshu. Its further expansion to the east and north was extremely rapid, the process being characterized by progressive incorporation of local cultural elements encountered en route. In this way Yayoi pottery acquired cord marking through contact with a strong Jomon tradition in central Japan, whereas it completely lacked this feature originally. The well-known bronze bells are distributed also through the central Japanese area.

Whereas rice cultivation expanded all over Japan, together with other features of Yayoi culture, the special methods of disposing of the dead mentioned before remained limited to northern Kyushu. It is to be wondered in what relation they stand to the Burial Mound or Tomb culture that emerges in the central area. Considering the fact that Yayoi culture, generally dated from 300 B.C. to A.D. 300, is roughly contemporaneous with the Han empire in China, we suggest that the subsequent cultural developments in Japan may be due to rice-cultivating immigrants from southern China, driven out from the continent in the course of Han expansion.

LIGHT ON JAPANESE CULTURAL ORIGINS FROM HISTORICAL ARCHEOLOGY AND LEGEND

NAMIO EGAMI

I

JAPANESE history rises mistily out of the period known to archeologists as the Tomb or Tumulus period. During this important period Japan was unified under the imperial court of Yamato and became intimately involved with South Korea, pathway for many cultural elements of continental origin into Japan. Writing was one such element. Japan began to have historico-legendary records of its own and gradually moved from its protohistoric to the historic period.

During the protohistoric Tomb period, hundreds of tumuli (tomb mounds) were built all over Japan except for part of Tohoku and all of Hokkaido. Among them, the most characteristic are called *"zempō-kōen"* or "square in front and round in the rear"; the English term derived from their ground plan is "keyhole-shaped" tomb. Some are larger than the pyramids of Egypt, a feature that speaks for the enormous power of the Japanese ruling class of that time to mobilize people to work for them.

The Tomb period, though still viewed by some Japanese scholars as one continuous period, must be divided into two subperiods. The early and late subperiods are quite different in both cultural content and character. The culture of the early Tomb period developed somewhere in the Kinki district (around modern Osaka), rising out of Yayoi culture. Its span was from the late third through the middle fourth century A.D. It retained many elements of Yayoi origin, especially high esteem for swords, mirrors, and jewels as ritual objects. Burial customs of this subperiod were tinged with much religious symbolism and mysticism. Strange objects, the exact use or meaning of which is unknown, often accompanied the dead. It is unlikely that the people of Japan in the early Tomb period changed essentially from those of the Yayoi period; they were peaceful, religious people marked by the magical beliefs mentioned above, though there appeared a differentiation of classes, which had been almost unknown during the Yayoi period.

During the late Tomb period, on the contrary, the people—or at least their ruling class buried in tumuli—seem to have been very warlike. They made common use of weapons and horse equipment of continental origin, paralleled especially in northern Asia. Their iron weapons and horse equipment included swords with pommel in dragon or phoenix design, whistling arrows, horse masks, decorated saddles, and pendants with floral, dragon, and sometimes animal designs. Their graves contain quantities of pottery, weapons, horse equipment, personal ornaments, and other objects that they thought were necessary to the dead in the next world. They even made clay models for many things, such as quivers, saddled horses, houses, ships, warriors, beasts, men, and women. These clay *haniwa* were set in or on the tombs perhaps as substitutes for the real things to serve the dead in the next world. The remains suggest warlike and worldly orientations for the ruling class of the late Tomb period quite at variance with the peaceable and mystical character of the people preceding them.

The cultural reorientation perceived in archeology corresponds with a great social and political change recorded in history, namely, the unification of Japan under the imperial court in Yamato. To perceive this correspondence between archeology and history, however, does not answer all our questions about the period. We must look outside Japan, for the garments, personal ornaments, and armor of the new ruling class, while rarely linked with ways of the earlier period, are intimately related with those of the continent. The design elements first mentioned above parallel those known in Korea, Manchuria, northern China, central Asia, and even in southern Russia and Hungary. Such elements in northern Asia particularly fall between the third through the fifth century A.D. In these centuries states in northern China, Manchuria, and Korea were being established or taken over by warlike horsemen of northern Asiatic origin, who had cultures so similar to that of the late Tumulus period in Japan. So the establishment of the Japanese state by the imperial court in Yamato, coinciding as it does with the introduction of continental culture elements, must be treated in the wider context of eastern Asiatic archeology and history.

II

At the outset, let us suggest a hypothesis to conform with the history of eastern Asia during the third and fourth centuries A.D. As we have noted, during this turbulent period various militant pastoral tribes from central and northeastern Asia came to head kingdoms in northern China, Manchuria, and Korea. In northern China, the T'opa Wei and, in eastern Manchura and North Korea, the Kokuli (Koguryo) were especially powerful. In South Korea, Kudara (Paekche) was founded by a royal family of the Fuyu tribe out of northern Manchuria during the first half of the fourth century A.D. Thus it is reasonable to suppose that the founding of the Japanese state by the imperial court in Yamato in turn resulted somehow from these movements of militant horse-riding tribes in eastern Asia during the third and fourth centuries.

Next, we may try to support this hypothesis by comparing certain historico-mythological traditions of Japan with others of Korea and China. Let us consider several themes selected from these traditions: (1) the outside origin of Japan's imperial house; (2) details of the eastward conquest by Jimmu to found the empire in Yamato; (3) possible identity of Jimmu and Sujin, traditionally regarded as tenth emperor succeeding Jimmu; (4) early Japanese claims to reign over South Korea; and (5) evidence for the conquest of the Wa, or autochthonous Japanese. All these lend support to the argument that early Japanese kings were sovereign over South Korea as well as Japan, that they had come from there to Japan, and that they had arrived in Korea as conquerors out of the pastoral zone of Asia.

1. Japanese mythology distinguishes two categories of deities, the heavenly gods (Amatsu-kami) and the native or territorial gods (Kunitsu-kami). Some myths represent the heavenly deities as descending to the land of Japan to conquer or rule its autochthonous deities. The myth of land transfer in Izumo is one instance. Two generals of the heavenly gods were dispatched to Izumo to demand of O-Kuninushi, chief of the native gods and master of the territory of Japan, that he hand over sovereignty to the heavenly gods. A second instance is the myth of the eastward conquest of Jimmu. This myth tells of the Grand Goddess of the Sun, chieftainess of the heavenly gods, ordering one of her progeny to descend to the summit of Mount Takachiho, in Kyushu, to rule Japan. His descendant was Jimmu, who moved from Kyushu eastward to conquer Japan and establish the imperial court in Yamato. One might suggest that the so-called heavenly deities in either of these traditions represent foreign conquerors, while the native gods represent the chieftains of aboriginal tribes in Japan, particularly after examining further details.

The second myth cited here comprises three motifs: (1) by divine order, Japan is to be ruled by descendants of the chieftainess of heavenly deities; (2) Prince Ninigi, offspring of the chieftainess, descends from heaven through thick clouds, wrapped within a mattress; (3) he alights on the peak called Kushifuru or Kushihi or Sohori, of Mount Takachiho in Kyushu. Now, Korea offers many traditions parallel to the myth of a person descending from heaven to found a state, notably the tradition of the Six Kaya Kingdoms in South Korea whose territories included Mimana (to be discussed below). The annals of these kingdoms related that in ancient times there was a strange voice from the heavens asking the name of the place; when people answered saying the place was called Kushi, the voice announced, "I shall descend, then, being ordered by the heavenly god to rule here and make new kingdoms," whereupon gold eggs wrapped in red cloth came down. From them appeared six children who grew up within ten days. Each became king of one of the Six Kaya Kingdoms.

The Korean and Japanese myths both reveal a divine order to establish new kingdoms. In each, the divine rulers-to-be descend from heaven wrapped in a mattress or cloth. Their arrival is at a place of very similar name: Kushi or Kushihi or Kushifuru (note that Korean *furu* means village). The variant name in Japan, Sohori, is easily explained through Korean, where Sohori and Soburu meant "capital" in the Silla dialect of the south, as present-day Seoul represents "capital" farther north. Furthermore, the Korean myth shares motifs not only with Japan but elsewhere as well. Similar myths of a divine ruler coming out of an egg and growing up to found a kingdom are recorded for the South

Korean kingdoms of Kudara and Kinkan and for the Manchurian kingdoms of Fuyu and Kokuli. Thus, the myths may have spread from somewhere in northeastern Asia, a variant arriving in Japan by way of South Korea.

2. In his eastward conquest, according to Japanese tradition, Jimmu departed from Tsukushi, the northern part of Kyushu. He went east to Aki and to Kibi on the shore of the Inland Sea. There he met a winged person who was riding on the back of a tortoise and fishing. Jimmu called to him, asking who he was. He answered that he was a god of the region, Utohiko. Jimmu then asked if he knew the way by sea, and he replied that he knew it very well. So Jimmu took Utohiko aboard to guide the way and went on to found the new kingdom in Yamato. Now, widely distributed among ancient peoples of northeastern Asia are traditions about the founder of a new state who crossed a river on the back of a large tortoise to a land where he founded his state. The kingdoms of Fuyu and Kokuli in Manchuria had this tradition.

Furthermore, the legendary founders of Kokuli and Kudara, both of Fuyu tribal origin, are supposed to have been sons of a heavenly god and a river goddess, a motif that is closely paralleled in the Japanese legend of Jimmu, son of a heavenly god and the sea goddess. We may see the river goddess of continental tradition transformed into the Japanese sea goddess, perhaps in an environment of islands surrounded by the sea. Allowing this transformation, then, we have a second important motif from traditions about the founders of kingdoms in northern Manchuria contained also in the Japanese tradition of Jimmu's eastward conquest.

3. In the Japanese historico-mythological records Jimmu is called *hatsukuni-shirasu-sumera-mikoto* ("Emperor who is first ruler of the land"). But the same title of "first ruler of the land" is also given to a later emperor, Sujin, who is particularly known for dispatching four great generals in four directions from Yamato to conquer and rule the land. Sujin had a second title or proper name, "Prince of Mima Castle." Tradition locates this castle by relating it to a local name, Mimana, a district in southern Korea that became territory of Nippon at a period that is not precisely known but must have been close to the time of Sujin, who lived in perhaps the first half of the fourth century A.D. Many scholars have come to suppose that Sujin was the real first ruler of Japan and that all alleged predecessors, including Jimmu, were completely fictitious. It is significant, then, that his name is linked with a local district name in South Korea known to have become territory of Nippon at about the date of his reign. Perhaps the double title suggests that Sujin, the "first ruler of Japan," had his original royal castle in Mima-na, in southern Korea, and so was called "Prince of Mima Castle."

4. Turning to Chinese historical works, we find it recorded that five kings of Japan in the fifth century, one after another, dispatched envoys to the imperial court of China to petition recognition of their title as sovereigns of both Japan and South Korea. They asked, further, that recognition be extended backward to the period of the Three Kingdoms in Korea, that is, preceding the fourth century

A.D., a date which would be prior to the establishment of the Japanese imperial court in Yamato. Why should their request embrace South Korea and reach back to a prior date?

The so-called Three Kingdoms of Korea were three Han tribes of the third century, Mahan (Bakan), Chinhan (Shinkan), and Pyonhan (Benkan). Each embraced various South Korean tribelets not yet unified within a kingdom. Yet a certain ruler, the king of Chin, dwelt among the Mahan and reigned also over twenty-four tribes of Chinhan and Pyonhan. He was said to have been of foreign birth, raised to the throne by the people of Mahan, and his throne could be inherited from generation to generation only by consent of all the Mahan tribes. One may speculate that the "king of Chin" was originally a *chin-jen*, a person identified with the Chinese and other intrusive cultures. At any rate, succession to his throne stayed in his line through the third century. But in the first half of the fourth century a royal house of Fuyu origin out of northeastern Manchuria took over, establishing the kingdom of Kudara in Mahan. Later in the same century, Chinhan fell to the lineage that founded the kingdom of Silla (Shiragi). Thus the fourth century brought great political and social change to South Korea.

Somewhere about this time, in the kingdom of Pyonhan, whose early history is almost unknown, Mima-na came into being. There is some historical suggestion that the displaced king of Chin, moving out of Mahan before A.D. 280, occupied Pyonhan as his own territory, whereupon it became Mima-na. A Korean paleographer suggests that Korean *Nin-na*, "the king's territory," became in Japanese *Mima-na*, a synonym for *Miya-ke*, "royal territory." However this may be, Mimana may well have been founded a bit before the end of the third century by a king of Chin; the last king of Chin may then have been Sujin, "Prince of Mima Castle," who began the conquest of Japan by moving his capital to Tsukushi in Kyushu or Yamato in Honshu at the opening of the fourth century.

The founding of Mimana may, then, very well be linked to the claim laid by each of the five Japanese sovereigns who wanted the Chinese imperial court to sanction their titles. These interesting titles mention existing kingdoms: Wa (Japan proper) Mimana, Kudara, and Silla. They go on to mention entities that had perished before their time: Chinhan and Mahan. Though most scholars have dismissed this as mere boasting of a wide domain by adding safely obsolete names, one must ask why five rulers in succession repeated the same extravagance and, moreover, significantly omitted extinct Pyonhan. My supposition is that they named all the lands for which they wanted sanction of their present sovereignty (Japan and Silla, Kudara, and Mimana in South Korea) and other lands for which they wanted sanction of their former sovereignty (Mahan, Chinhan), but that they omitted Pyonhan from the latter list because they still occupied it as Mimana.

5. Other Chinese records distinguish Nippon (Erh-pen) from the land of Wa, describing it as a separate tribe of the Wa people. A separate account in the same record gives the report that Nippon was formerly a small land but there-

after occupied all the land of Wa. Since these accounts came into the Chinese historical records either as reports by Japanese envoys dispatched from the Yamato court to the T'ang court of China or as reports by Chinese envoys sent to the Yamato court to return Japanese visits in the seventh century, they should not be undervalued. This date still precedes the compilation of the Nihon-shoki and Kojiki in the eighth century in Japan, historico-mythological accounts embodying the doctrine that the imperial household originated anciently within Japan, to become sole dynasty and to rule the land forever. The Chinese account, on the contrary, tends to support the idea that the Japanese imperial household was of foreign origin and established itself by conquest of Japanese territory.

III

Thus our account ends with a survey of the archeological material and a scrutiny of mythological history bearing on the origin of the Japanese imperial household. We suggest that the imperial ancestors came out of northern Asia, possibly from among the Fuyu of northeastern Manchuria. They became the kings of Chin in South Korea up into the late third century A.D. In the early fourth century they moved from Mimana to Japan, were thus the conquerors of the land of Wa, and founded the imperial court in Yamato. Their titles suggest that they ruled united kingdoms of Japan and South Korea. This hypothesis, that a militant pastoral tribe from northeastern Asia became the ruling class over the aborigines, who were peaceful and religiously oriented, accounts for a dualistic quality notable in Japan's ancient mythology, religion, social structure, and customs, which has been pointed out by Professor Oka and his colleagues.

THE JAPANESE LANGUAGE:
ITS ORIGINS AND ITS SOURCES*

SUSUMU ONO

RELATIONSHIP between languages is demonstrated by correspondence in (1) grammatical structure and (2) vocabulary, as corroborated by phonetic law. With respect to grammar, Japanese is quite unlike Chinese, Austroasian, and Austronesian. But it has structural similarities with the Altaic group, which are puzzling because the vocabulary presents very few instances of correspondence. Korean and Japanese, however, share many points of grammar, including an ancient use of vowel harmony, and share about two hundred vocabulary cognates as well.

Japanese linguistic data, at most, go back to the third century A.D. and become abundant only after the ninth century. Data on neighboring languages are in yet poorer state, so their comparison with ancient Japanese is difficult even without reckoning the problem imposed by the agglutinative morphology of Japanese, which reduces the number of purely grammatical forms.

In view of these difficulties, it seems justifiable to venture outside linguistic materials proper and use anthropometric, archeological, and ethnological approaches to Japanese cultural history, not to solve problems of language relationship, but to suggest fruitful lines of comparison.

Among the data of physical anthropology are clear indications of somatic variation along a cline running from northeastern to southwestern Japan (excluding the Ainu, who fit no point along these clines). In blood types, the ratio of A to B is higher in northeastern Japan and decreases toward the southwest—similarly with the ratio of whirls to loops in fingerprints. Among archeological remains, also, a similar division is foreshadowed in stone implements of the Preceramic period and becomes much clearer in the remains of the succeeding, long Jomon period and the still later Yayoi period. Thus, an important division of Japan into two ethnic and cultural zones, northeast and southwest, meeting in central Honshu, is suggested by somatic and archeological data. We may look for its linguistic reflection.

A corresponding dialect division is clear in the evidence from the Nara period

---

* Professor Ono's paper read at the Tenth Pacific Science Congress appeared in essentially similar form in the KBS (Kokusai Bunka Shinkokai) Bulletin, No. 44, September–October, 1960, pp. 1–6. Both because this source is not readily available in the United States and in order to preserve the full coverage of matters important to Japanese origins as they were presented at the Congress, a summary is offered here.—THE EDITORS.

(late seventh–eighth centuries A.D.). The earliest collection of poems, the Manyoshu, distinguishes poems from the eastern provinces as "Azuma-uta"; these contain words at variance with the dialect of the Yamato district of western Japan, including not a few that represent original examples of the modern differences between eastern and western dialects today: E. *shiroku* ("white," adj.), W. *shirou;* E. *miro* ("look," imper.), W. *mii;* E. *ikanai* ("don't go"), W. *ikan;* E. *haratta* ("have paid"), W. *harouta;* E. *ame da* ("it rains"), W. *ame ya*.

As of the Nara period, western Japanese culture was stronger and more sophisticated than that of eastern Japan. Similar predominance is evident as far back as the period of Yayoi culture, between 300 B.C. and A.D. 300, when rice agriculture and the use of metal implements by Yayoi people characterized southwestern Japan, while hunting and gathering Jomon cultures persisted in the northeast. Yayoi decorative designs remind one of typical ornaments in the Altaic-speaking areas of continental Asia, so it may be conjectured that Altaic languages first made contact with western Japan in the Yayoi period.

What evidences of similarity link Japanese to Altaic languages? One is vowel harmony, a phenomenon characterizing Turkish, Tungus, Manchu, Hungarian, and Finnish and anciently known in Korean. Vowels in these languages fall into two groups, usually back vowels (*a, o, u*) and front vowels (*e, ö, ü*), in such a fashion that vowels of only one group normally appear in any single word. The vowel *i* is neutral and may appear in words with vowels of either group, whereas, for example, *a* accompanies *o* or *u* but never *e, ö, ü* either in the root or in the suffix of a word. Japanese today has five vowels but has changed since antiquity. In the eighth century, according to studies of *Manyo kana* (syllabic script) by Shinkichi Hashimoto, the vowel system was:

back	*u*	*o*	*a*
mid	(*ï*)	*ö*	(*ë*)
front	*i*		(*e*)

Parenthesized vowels seem derived from diphthongs as follows: *ï < ui, ï < oi, ë < ai, e < ia*. Of the remaining vowels (*u, o, a, ö, i*), the first three combined primarily with each other or with *i*, whereas *ö* combines usually only with itself, as demonstrated by Arisaka and Ikegami. Examples follows:

fato ("pigeon")   *kökörö* ("mind")
fako ("box")   *tökörö* ("place")
tuka ("mound")   *sökö* ("bottom")
fafa ("mother")   *kötö* ("thing")
taka ("high")   *kötö* ("Japanese harp")
kusa ("grass")   *töki* ("time")
matu ("pine")   *aki* ("autumn")
kozo ("rubbing sound")   *kita* ("north")
  itö ("thread")

Besides this patterned similarity with Altaic vowel harmony, other features are shared:

1. No sharp distinction exists between singular and plural.
2. There is no distinction between masculine, neuter, and feminine.
3. There are no articles.
4. Postpositions are used.
5. The distinction between nouns and the stems of adjectives is not clear.
6. There are no comparative or superlatives of adjectives.
7. Basic forms of verbs are used as nouns and imperatives of verbs.
8. There is no expression in the passive form.
9. There are no relative pronouns.
10. Adjectives and adverbs come before nouns and verbs.
11. An interrogative sentence is formed by placing an interrogative word at the end.

However, despite these morphological resemblances, there seems to be no cognate vocabulary. Vowel harmony ceased in Japanese in the ninth century, and it is further distinguished from both the Altaic group and Korean by its characteristic word ending with an open syllable. If we turn to vocabulary, some two hundred cognates, of which a sample is presented here, appear between Japanese and Korean even though notable morphological similarities are lacking:

Japanese		Korean
kama	("kiln")	kama
kasa	("bamboo hat")	kat
kata	("hard")	kut
ki	("wooden pestle")	ko
kura	("saddle")	kirəma
kumo	("cloud")	kurum
susu	("soot")	sus
sökö	("bottom" or "back")	sok
sima	("island")	syöm
sisi	("deer")	sasəm
sade	("net")	sadul
satu	("arrow")	sal
taba	("bundle")	tabal
tapi	("sea bream")	tomi
turu	("crane")	turumi
tuma	("nail")	top
taku	("paper mulberry")	tak
nata	("hatchet" or "sickle")	nat
namari	("lead")	nap
napa	("rope")	no
na	("vegetables")	mamul
niko	("ripe")	nik
nupu	("to sew")	nupi
numa	("swamp")	nop
na	("i")	na
natu	("summer")	nyörəm
nöru	("to tell")	nil
pari	("pin")	panil
paru	("to paste")	pari

pata	("field")	pat
pösi	("star")	pyöl
potaru	("firefly")	pantoi
pëmi	("snake")	pəiyam
paru	("spring")	pom
ipu	("to say" or "mouth")	ip
pidi	("elbow")	p'əl
puku	("lung")	puxua
para	("abdomen")	pai–pəri
pako	("box")	pakoni
pata	("outside")	pas
yörö	("ten thousand")	yörö
kötö	("thing")	köt
ömö	("mother")	ömi
öpu	("to carry on one's back")	öp
öru	("to weave")	örk ("to bind")
;ö	("it")	cö
önö	("self")	nö
kosi	("loin")	xöri
kötö	("same")	köt
öröka	("fool")	ör

What inferences can be drawn from the foregoing comparisons? Before developing a conjecture, we should note ethnological parallels in a direction not yet considered: with the Pacific Islands and Indonesia. Most Japanese mythology has Indonesian analogues; tooth-blackening, tattooing, and other customs are parallel. If culture contact is assumed to have brought about these parallels, it should date from a period prior to Yayoi culture on the reasoning that prevailing orientations thereafter would have made adoption of these customs in Japan difficult at a later period. But the assumption of culture contact leads us to seek linguistic parallels, which can be identified as follows between Heian period Japanese (A.D. 794–1185) and Polynesian or Malayan:

1. Polynesian also has five distinctive vowels.
2. Polynesian words also regularly end with an open syllable.
3. When two vowels come in succession, one is often dropped in Polynesian.
4. Cognate words exist for parts of the body, in Polynesian or Malayan, e.g., *ma* ("eye"), *kutsu* ("mouth"), *hara* ("abdomen"), *hoso* ("naval"), *hoho* ("cheek"), etc.

The following reconstruction attempts to account for the linguistic, cultural, and somatic parallels noted up to this point. Through Jomon times a language of southern origin with a phonetic system like that of present-day Polynesian was widespread through western Japan. About 300 B.C., along with rice cultivation, use of metals, weaving, and (eventually) tumuli that distinguished Yayoi culture, a new language of northern derivation with grammar and vowel harmony of Altaic character arrived and spread south and east from northern Kyushu. This language extended as far as the Kinki (Osaka) area rather soon but did not readily cross the cultural boundary already in existence. It spread meanwhile to the Ryukyu Islands. Eventually as rice cultivation and metal working penetrated eastward, so did the language, but without obliterating the line of division.

Blood types, in which the Japanese patterns differ greatly from the values recorded in various parts of Korea, do not permit the assumption that migrants from South Korea whose influence was made manifest in Yayoi culture came in any great numbers or exterminated the aboriginal population. If such migrants were few, this fact may account for the weakening of vowel harmony and its disappearance in the ninth century, for the reworking of word endings into open-syllable form, and for the survival of a vocabulary of southern origin for body parts.

It cannot be insisted that South Korean migrants actually spoke Altaic. Considering the probable southerly origin of rice culture, it may be that the pattern suggested here for Japan had already emerged in Korea, producing Altaic grammatical features in association with a southerly, non-Altaic vocabulary. Had such speech existed in South Korea, vocabulary resemblances between Korean and Japanese that are *not* discovered in Altaic need occasion no surprise.

In historical times, Chinese contacts began after the fifth century and intensified after the seventh century, bringing a large quota of vocabulary borrowings from Chinese, in addition to a basic writing system out of which the Japanese eventually devised *katakana* and *hiragana* syllabaries.

II. Social Structure

STABILITY IN JAPANESE KINSHIP TERMINOLOGY: THE HISTORICAL EVIDENCE*

ROBERT J. SMITH

ALTHOUGH there exists a substantial literature on the Japanese kinship system in Western languages,[1] very little attention has been paid to the history of the development of kin terminology. Japanese scholars have been more interested in the questions raised by the extensive documentation available and have given us discussions of the early Chinese influence on legal codes dealing with kin relations, the history of the definitions of degrees of relationship, changing concepts of inheritance, and the varying emphases given throughout Japanese history to the horizontal and vertical fluctuations of the genealogical chart. The work of Nakata (1926, 1929) and Toda (1937) is an essential starting point for any student of the history of Japanese kin terms, and there are valuable papers by a number of Japanese sociologists, anthropologists, historians, and legal historians.[2]

No attempt will be made in this paper to deal with the full range of Japanese literature from which information about kin-term usages could be culled. Terms of reference as well as terms of address are, of course, to be found in the earliest written sources, the *Kojiki* (A.D. 712) and the *Nihon Shoki* (A.D. 720), and could be traced through literary sources up to the present time. I have limited this paper, however, to a consideration of the sources that deal explicitly with kin reckoning, that is, vocabularies, various legal codes, handbooks, and commentaries on customary usages. These sources are given in Table 1.

* The author is indebted to the following sources of funds: The Faculty Research Grants Committee and the Social Science Research Center, both of Cornell University; the Social Science Research Council (Grant-in-Aid, Summer, 1961); the Public Health Service, National Institute of Mental Health (Research Grant M-4161). The author wishes to acknowledge the extensive assistance of his wife, Kazuko S. Smith, without whose help the investigation could not have been undertaken.

1. See particularly Morgan (1871), Embree (1939, pp. 86–88), Spencer and Imamura (1950), Cornell (1956, pp. 159–62), Befu and Norbeck (1958), Beardsley, Hall, and Ward (1959, pp. 219–47). The present writer's article "Japanese Kinship Terminology: The History of a Nomenclature," will appear in the journal *Ethnology*. In it, an attempt is made to relate the stability of this terminology to discussions by the evolutionists of the correlation of kin terms and level of cultural development.

2. Of great value are the studies of Ishii (1948), Makino (1928), Naitō (1954), Takayanagi (1937), and Takeuchi (1954a, 1954b).

TABLE 1
PRIMARY AND SECONDARY DOCUMENTS FOR THE HISTORICAL STUDY
OF THE DEVELOPMENT OF JAPANESE KIN TERMS*

718 A.D. (Taihō 1)	Yōrō-ryō Gisei-ryō Sōsō-ryō Fuku-ki-ryō	Yōrō Code Regulation of Ceremonies Code Funerals and Mourning Code Mourning Code
931–936 A.D. (Shōhei 1–6)	Wamyō-ruijūshō	Collection and Classification of Japanese Words
1235 A.D. (Bunryaku 2)	Taiza-ryō	Withdrawal Code
Early 15th century	Ji-pen-chi-yü (Nihon-kigo)	A Japanese vocabulary
1597 A.D. (Keichō 2)	Ekirin-bon Setsu-yōshū	"Ekirin's Book of Principles"
1684 A.D. (Jōkyō 1)	Fuku-ki-ryō	Mourning Code
1693 A.D. (Genroku 6)	Genkō-ryō Fuku-ki-ryō	Current Legal Code Mourning Code
1736 A.D. (Gembun 1)		Supplement to above
1725 A.D. (Kyōhō 10)	Dazai Shundai "Shinzoku-shōmyō"	DAZAI SHUNDAI "Correct Terms for Relatives"
Early 18th century	Itō Chōin (Tōgai) "Shaku-shin-kō"	ITŌ CHŌIN (TŌGAI) "Commentary on Relatives"
1809–22 A.D.	Takai Hangan "Nōka Chōhōki"	TAKAI HANGAN "Handbook for Farm Households"
1882	Meiji Keihō	Meiji Criminal Code
1890/98	Meiji Mimpō	Meiji Civil Code
1947	Kaisei Mimpō	Revised Civil Code

* Excluding family registers of all periods.

Not included in the table are the famous family registers (*koseki keichō*) in the Imperial Repository at Nara. The establishment of these registers was required by the Taika Reform of A.D. 645, and the oldest extant are dated A.D. 702 (Taihō 2). They come from the province of Mino, now part of Gifu Prefecture (Ariga, 1948, pp. 111–12; Joüon des Longrais, 1958, pp. 444–45; Sano, 1958, p. 9; Toda, 1937). These registers list the residents of households by their relationship to the house head, but, since they do not represent a systematic consideration of relationships, they will not be discussed here. They are only the earliest of a long series of such registers preserved in various parts of Japan.

Let us turn now to the sources given in the table:

1. The Yōrō Code. The first systematic treatment of terms of relationship was undertaken in the Regulation of Ceremonies Code (*Gisei-ryō*) and the Mourning Code (*Fuku-ki-ryō*) of the Funerals and Mourning Code (*Sōsō-ryō*) of the no longer extant Taihō Code (*Taihō-ryō*) of A.D. 701 and its minor revision of A.D. 718, the Yōrō Code (*Yōrō-ryō*). The Yōrō Code itself was preserved through two later commentaries, the *Ryō-no-gige* of A.D. 833 (Tencho 10) and the more extensive *Ryō-no-shuge* of A.D. 920 (Engi 20). While all these early laws reveal heavy Chinese influence, it is nevertheless true that the mourning codes show unmistakable traces of repeated revision intended to bring them closer to Japanese mourning practices. It is for this reason that they are generally taken to be the earliest trustworthy evidence for kin reckoning in Japan (Sansom, 1943, p. 158–59). They specify, for the different degrees of relationship, the required periods of mourning.

2. The *Wamyō-ruijūshō* ("Collection and Classification of Japanese Words"). Between A.D. 931 and 936 (Shōhei 1–6), at the command of a daughter of the Emperor Go-Daigo, an official named Minamoto-no Shitagau undertook this compilation of Japanese words and their Chinese written forms. It contains much material of great interest to the student of Japanese culture and society. The best-known edition was published in A.D. 1617 (Genna 3) and reissued in 1648 (Keian 1), 1667 (Kambun 7), and 1688 (Genroku 1) in editions that were reprinted frequently thereafter (Aston, 1892/93; Goh, 1892/93; Takeuchi, 1954*b*; Toda, 1937). The contents of the work are listed under such headings as "Section on Clothing"; the one that concerns us here is that called the "Section on Relatives" (*Shinseki-bu*). What Minamoto did was to put down common nouns, for the most part, using Chinese characters, beside most of which he placed an entry in Japanese syllabary as a guide to pronunciation. These syllabary entries are not found consistently in the "Section on Relatives" for the very good reason that many of the Chinese written forms never became incorporated into spoken Japanese. They existed in literary Japanese, as some still do, but they simply have no equivalents in the spoken language.

3. The *Taiza-ryō*. In A.D. 1231 (Jōei 1) appeared one of the best-known legal codes of medieval Japan, the *Goseibai Shikimoku Shō*, known also as the "*Jōei* Formulary" (*Jōei Shikimoku*) for the name of the era in which it was first promulgated (Hall, 1906; Sansom, 1943, 1958). A supplement to the Formulary, which appeared in A.D. 1235 (Bunryaku 2, more usually called Katei 1), is the Withdrawal Code (*Taiza-ryō*). Its name refers to its intent, which was to specify the degree of relationship that could obtain between a judge and a plaintiff before his court. If the relationship was closer than that permitted by the code, the judge was to withdraw from the case (Satō and Ikeuchi, 1955; Takeuchi, 1954*a*). This attempt to prevent miscarriages of justice by reason of a prejudiced court is useful in tracing the reckoning of kinship in the Kamakura period. Several versions of the *Taiza-ryō* are known, some applying to courts in the capital, others to the district courts in other cities. They differ only in minor particulars (Takeuchi, 1954*a*).

4. *Ji-pen-chi-yü* (*Nihon-kigo*). This curious work is a Chinese-Japanese word list, apparently dating from the early fifteenth century. It was done by Chinese who seem to have obtained the Japanese vocabulary from Japanese informants of limited educational attainment (Edkins, 1882; Satow, 1882) and represents a strange mixture of insight and misunderstanding on the part of the recorders. Of the several hundred entries, twenty-six are kin terms, many of which are in error. The errors themselves are instructive, however, for they demonstrate the great difficulty experienced by the recorders in making sense of the Japanese system.

5. *Ekirin-bon Setsu-yōshū* ("Ekirin's Book of Principles"). This neglected work sheds some light on kin reckoning in mid-Muromachi Japan. Written in A.D. 1597 (Keichō 2), its two thin volumes list "nouns and compounds," categorizing entries in much the same way as that chosen by the compiler of the *Wamyō-ruijūshō*. There are sections on the parts of the body, on morals, and on kin terms. Since it is not a legal document but presents terms in general use in Ekirin's day, the work is of special value, and its utility is enhanced by the apparent care with which he attempted to record the pronunciation of late sixteenth-century Japanese.

6. *Fuku-ki-ryō*. The first Mourning Code (*Fuku-ki-ryō*) of the Tokugawa era appeared in A.D. 1684. Based on earlier funeral and mourning codes (*Sōsō-ryō*), it underwent numerous revisions. The first was in 1686 (Jōkyō 3), reflecting an effort, as in earlier periods, to bring the code into line with actual practice. It was revised again in 1688 (Genroku 1) and once more in 1693 (Genroku 6) as a part of the more extensive Current Legal Code (*Genkō-ryō*). This code was itself repeatedly revised, and a supplement commenting on its provisions was added in 1736 (Gembun 1) (Takayanagi, 1937).

7. *Shinzoku Shōmyō*. About A.D. 1725 (Kyōhō 10) the Confucian scholar Dazai Shundai (1680–1747) produced a work entitled *Shinzoku Shōmyō* ("Correct Terms for Relatives"). By "correct" he meant in part "Chinese," and the book exhibits nicely the unhappiness of the Confucianists at the failure of Japanese kinship terminology to conform to the Chinese system. Dazai doggedly lists a very large number of Chinese terms, notes their Japanese pronunciations where they exist at all, and comments at length on the insufficiencies of the Japanese system. For the more remote terms of relationship in Chinese, he remarks upon occasion that unfortunately "this country's barbaric system" contains no such term or that "this poor country's" usages are such that this relationship has no word in Japanese. While his list is rendered somewhat theoretical by his Confucian bias, he nevertheless appears to have stayed within the bounds of the Japanese system as he knew it to operate. His invective is a delight (Toda, 1937, pp. 295–98).

8. *Shaku Shin Kō*. Another scholar, Itō Chōin (1670–1736), known also as Itō Tōgai, writing about the time at which the "Correct Terms for Relatives" appeared, compiled a volume called *Shaku Shin Kō* ("Commentary on Relatives"). It is far less useful than Dazai's volume, primarily because Itō was less inclined

to restrain himself when faced with an instance of lack of congruence of the Chinese and Japanese systems. He invented terms, stretched meanings, and reinterpreted relationships, but his book stands as an impressive example of continued failure to find significant Chinese influences in Japanese terminology.

9. *Nōka Chōhōki* ("Handbook for Farm Households"). Written by Takai Hangan between 1809 and 1822, this three-part work is a kind of agricultural handbook and deals with a wide variety of topics relating to farm and village life. Among the miscellaneous entries is a "Section on Relatives" (*Shinrui-no Koto*), which is in fact a haphazard rendering of the more official mourning codes of the Tokugawa period. Owing to its many omissions and several misplacements of terms, the book is not as useful as the researcher would wish.

10. Criminal and Civil Codes. Since the Meiji Restoration in 1868, a number of legal definitions of degrees of relationship have been offered in the criminal and civil codes. These have been attacked by reformers as insufficiently faithful to contemporary kinship relations and by conservatives as less traditional than they ought to be. They are an untrustworthy guide to practice but are useful for the terminology that they contain.

There are other sources, although the major ones have been discussed above. The available material covers about twelve hundred years, and, as far as can be ascertained, there is nothing before the early eighth century that is of use in tracing the development of kin terminology in Japan. There are two general types to be distinguished among the documents referred to above, (1) those using only Chinese characters, with no guide to the Japanese pronunciation, and (2) those having both the Chinese characters and a guide to the Japanese reading, where these exist. Obviously, it is the latter that are of the most direct relevance to a study of stability and change in Japanese kinship terminology.

Perhaps a word of explanation is in order here. Even in contemporary written Japanese it is possible to write the word for "aunt" (*oba*) in at least two ways, one referring to the elder sister of one's father and mother, the second referring to the younger sister of one's father and mother. No matter which pair of characters is used, it is read *oba*. That is, while the borrowed (and modified) writing system offers a terminological distinction among aunts, spoken Japanese makes no such distinction. In using this group of old documents, this distinction must always be kept in mind, for a perusal of the Chinese characters alone will lead to entirely mistaken conclusions. This is, perhaps, one of the most intriguing features of the Japanese kinship system, for it means that there have been two systems in operation in that country for centuries, one written, the other spoken. This is perhaps less remarkable than the fact that the two belong to completely different types of kinship system—the former a modified version of the Chinese, the latter very much like the Yankee system. If kin terms are intimately related to behavior, the Japanese ought by rights to have had a difficult time of it in their efforts to rationalize their two systems.

Let us return to the question that gave this paper its title: To what extent does the record reveal stability in Japanese kinship terminology? Table 2 draws upon two of the sources described above, the *Wamyō-ruijūshō* of the early tenth century and the *Shinzoku Shōmyō* of the early eighteenth. Both contain pronunciation guides, and it is these *kana*-syllabary entries that are transcribed in the table. The third source, for contemporary usage, is field work conducted by the writer in 1960.

TABLE 2
JAPANESE KIN TERMS OF REFERENCE IN THE TENTH, EIGHTEENTH, AND TWENTIETH CENTURIES

English	A.D. 936	A.D. 1725	A.D. 1960
Father	chichi	chichi	chichi
Mother	haha	haha	haha
Elder brother	konokami	ani	ani
Younger brother	oto-uto	otōto	otōto
Elder sister	ane	ane	ane
Younger sister	imo-uto	imōto	imōto
Son	(not given)	musuko	musuko
Daughter	(not given)	musume	musume
Husband	(not given)	(not given)	otto
Wife	(not given)	(not given)	tsuma
Uncle	ochi	oji	oji
Aunt	oha	oba	oba
Nephew	ohi	oi	oi
Niece	mehi	mei	mei
Grandfather	oho-chi	ōji	ojī
Grandmother	oo-oha	ōba	obā
Great-uncle	oho-(chi)-ochi	ō-oji	ō-oji
Great-aunt	oho-oha	ō-oba	ō-oba
Grandnephew	mumako-ohi	oi-mago (mata-oi)	(no term)
Grandniece	mumako-mehi	(not given)	(no term)
Great-grandfather	oho-oho-chi	hi-ōji	hi-ojī
Great-grandmother	oho-oha	hi-ōba	hi-obā
Great-great-grandfather	(not given)	hihi-ōji	(no term)
Great-great-grandmother	(not given)	hihi-ōba	(no term)
Great-granduncle	oho-oho-chi-ochi	(not given)	(no term)
Great-grandaunt	(not given)	(not given)	(no term)
Cousin	itoko	itoko	itoko

Table 2 is a complete listing of the terms given in the *Wamyō-ruijūshō* and *Shinzoku Shōmyō*. Nothing has been omitted, and the romanization is a literal rendering of the *kana*-syllabary in the originals. Several commentaries mention the probable error in the *Wamyo-ruijūshō* term for "great-uncle," and I have put the middle *chi* in parentheses to indicate that it may have been a copyist's mistake.

What are the characteristics of the Japanese kinship system at these three points in time? The most striking finding is, of course, that for approximately one thousand years it has been essentially a "Yankee" system, differing crucially from contemporary terminology in the United States only in that it makes an age distinction among siblings. A second less important difference is that contemporary Japanese terminology is even more restricted than the American, lacking terms for "great-great-grandparents" and for "great-granduncle" and "great-grandaunt."

Throughout the period, parents are distinguished from uncles and aunts, siblings from cousins, grandparents from their siblings, and Ego's grandchildren from the grandchildren of his siblings. In these and other features, the Japanese system is very different from the Chinese, in spite of the frequent intensive contact between the two societies and the enormous impact of Chinese culture on virtually every aspect of Japanese life. Although some alternate terms have been adopted—for example, "grandfather" and "grandmother" are *sofu* and *sobo* from the Chinese, as well as *oji* and *obā*—even the borrowed terms are used for the parents of both Ego's father and Ego's mother without distinction.

There is no evidence to suggest that the Japanese have, within the last twelve hundred years, had any but an Eskimo kinship nomenclature. Their contact with China, even if they had borrowed the Chinese system wholesale, would certainly not have given them one. They have retained this system, with little alteration, through centuries of religious, social, political, economic, and legal change. Sweeping revisions of household organization and demographic structure have done little to alter the kinship terminology insofar as terms of reference are concerned. Kin behavior is another question entirely, and, if terms of address for early periods were available, some light might be shed on the question of connections between the systems. For the moment we have established only a very long-term stability of a terminological system in the face of vast social change in Japan.

BIBLIOGRAPHY

ARIGA, KIZAEMON
1947 "Dōzoku to shinzoku" ("Dōzoku and Relatives"), *Nihon Minzokugaku-no Tame-ni*, 2:1–70.
1948 "Nihon kodai kazoku" ("The Family in Ancient Japan"). In: H. TANABE (ed.), *Shakaigaku Taikei: Kazoku* ("Outline of Sociology: the Family"), pp. 103–50. Tokyo.

ASTON, W. G.
1892/93 "The Family and Relationships in Ancient Japan," *Trans. & Proc. Jap. Soc., London*, 2:160–76.

BEARDSLEY, RICHARD K., JOHN W. HALL, and ROBERT E. WARD
1959 *Village Japan*. Chicago: University of Chicago Press.

BEFU, HARUMI, and EDWARD NORBECK
1958 "Japanese Usages of Terms of Relationship," *Southwestern J. Anthrop.*, 14:66–86.

CORNELL, JOHN B.
1956 "Matsunagi: The Life and Social Organization of a Japanese Mountain Community." In ROBERT J. SMITH and JOHN B. CORNELL, *Two Japanese Villages*, pp. 113–232. Ann Arbor: University of Michigan Press.

DE BECKER, J. E.
1921 *The Principles and Practice of the Civil Code of Japan.* Yokohama: Kelly & Walsh.

EDKINS, JOSEPH
1882 "A Chinese and Japanese Vocabulary of the Fifteenth Century, with Notes, Chiefly on Pronunciation," *Trans. Asiatic Soc. Jap.*, 10:1–14.

EMBREE, JOHN F.
1939 *Suye Mura: A Japanese Village.* Chicago: University of Chicago Press.

GOH, DAIGORO
1892/93 "The Family Relations in Japan," *Trans. & Proc. Jap. Soc., London*, 2:117–56.

HALL, JOHN CAREY
1906 "Japanese Feudal Law: The Institutes of Judicature. Being a Translation of 'Go Seibai Shikimoku': the Magisterial Code of the Hojo Power Holders," *Trans. Asiatic Soc. Jap.*, 34:1–44.

ISHII, RYŌSUKE (ed.)
1948 *Nihon hōsei-shi gaisetsu* ("Legal History of Japan"). Tokyo: Kōbundō
1959 *Japanese Legislation in the Meiji Era.* Trans. WILLIAM J. CHAMBLISS. Tokyo: Pan-Pacific Press.

JOÜON DES LONGRAIS, F.
1958 *L'Est et L'Ouest: Institutions du Japon et de l'Occident Comparées.* Tokyo: Maison Franco-Japonaise.

MAKINO, TATSUMI
1928 "Nisshi shintō-sei no hikaku" ("Comparison of the Japanese and Chinese Kinship Systems"), *Minzoku*, 3:43–60.

MINZOKUGAKU KENKYŪ-SHO
1955/56 *Minzokugaku taikei* ("Encyclopedia of Folklore"). Vol. 5: *Sōgō nihon minzoku goi* ("Vocabulary of Local Terms"). Tokyo: Heibonsha.

MORGAN, LEWIS HENRY
1871 *Systems of Consanguinity and Affinity of the Human Family.* (Smithsonian Contributions to Knowledge 218.) Washington, D.C.: Smithsonian Institution.

MURDOCK, GEORGE PETER
1957 "World Ethnographic Sample." *Amer. Anthrop.*, 59:664–87.

NAITŌ, KANJI
1954 "Shinzoku" ("Relatives"). In: JAPANESE SOCIETY OF ETHNOLOGY (ed.), *Nihon shakai minzoku jiten* ("Social and Ethnographic Dictionary of Japan"), 2:733.

NAKATA, KAORU
1926 *Hōsei-shi ronshū* ("Papers on the History of Law"). Vol. I. Tokyo: Iwanami shoten.
1929 "Nihon kodai shinzoku kō" ("Thoughts on Relatives in Ancient Japan"), *Kokka Gakkai Zasshi*, 43:1–18.

SANO, CHIYE
1958 *Changing Values of the Japanese Family.* Washington, D.C.: Catholic University of America Press.

SANSOM, GEORGE B.
1932 "Early Japanese Law and Administration," *Trans. Asiatic Soc. Jap.*, 2d ser., 9:67–110.
1934 "Early Japanese Law and Administration," *ibid.*, 11:117–50.

1943 *Japan: A Short Cultural History*. New York: Appleton-Century-Crofts.
1958 *A History of Japan to 1334*. London: Cresset.

Satō, Shin-ichi, and Ikeuchi Yoshisuke (eds.)
1955 *Chūsei hōsei shiryō shū* ("Collection of Laws of the Medieval Period"). Vol. I: *Kamakura bakufu hō* ("Laws of the Kamakura Shogunate"). Tokyo: Iwanami shoten.

Satow, Ernest
1882 "Notes on Dr. Edkins' Paper 'A Chinese-Japanese Vocabulary of the Fifteenth Century,'" *Trans. Asiatic Soc. Jap.*, 10:15–35.

Sebald, W. J.
1934 *The Civil Code of Japan*. Kobe: Thompson.

Smith, Robert J.
1962 "Japanese Kinship Terminology: The History of a Nomenclature," *Ethnology*, 1:349–59.

Spencer, Robert F., and Imamura Kanmo
1950 "Notes on the Japanese Kinship System," *J. Amer. Orient. Soc.*, 70:165–73.

Steiner, Kurt
1950 "Postwar Changes in the Japanese Civil Code," *Washington Law Rev.*, 25:286–312.

Takayanagi, Shinzō
1937 "Tokugawa jidai no hōken hō ni okeru shinrui no kōsei to igi" ("The Structure and Meaning of *Shinrui* in Tokugawa Feudal Law"). In: Ishii Ryōsuke (ed.), *Nihon hōsei–shi gaisetsu* ("Legal History of Japan"), pp. 1–118. Tokyo: Kōbundō.

Takeuchi, Toshimi
1954a "Shinzoku" ("Relatives"). In: Japanese Society of Ethnology (ed.), *Nihon shakai minzoku jiten* ("Social and Ethnographic Dictionary of Japan"), 2:733–35.
1954b "Shinzoku shōko" ("Kinship Terminology"), *ibid.*, pp. 735–37.

Toda, Teizō
1937 *Kazoku kōsei* ("Structure of the Family"). Tokyo: Kōbundō.

CORPORATE EMPHASIS AND PATTERNS OF DESCENT IN THE JAPANESE FAMILY

HARUMI BEFU

IN JAPAN the traditional rule of descent has been and remains patrilineal and primogenitural; that is, the oldest son in the family is supposed to succeed to the status of the family head and inherit the family property. It is true that the postwar constitution has legally abolished the status of the family head and requires an equal division of property among the children. Nonetheless, the tendency even now in most of Japan, particularly in the typically more conservative rural areas, is toward primogeniture in the succession of the family headship and inheritance of property.[1]

In concrete cases, however, this ideal of patrilineal descent manifests a variety of exceptions, the result not so much of postwar legal requirements as of the practical exigencies of situations in which the principle of primogeniture simply cannot function.[2] Such situations consequently require solutions that, although deviating in one way or another from the ideal, are not haphazard—certain situations are resolved through particular arrangements.

A careful analysis of these deviations and their bases suggests theoretical interpretations of Japanese kinship organization. In interpreting the Japanese kinship system, we should clearly distinguish between the family as a kinship unit and as a corporate unit. The first concept stresses the genetic continuity in the family from father to oldest son, whereas the latter emphasizes the perpetuity of the family name and occupation. The two need not be coterminous, that is, a blood line may be continued even after the family name and occupation have been changed and, conversely, the family name and occupation may be continued not by the oldest son but by someone else. It is proposed here that the primary emphasis in the Japanese family system is not so much on the continuity of the "blood" from father to oldest son as on the perpetuation of the family as a corporate group through its name and occupation.

---

1. A 1949 survey of thirteen farming, mountain, and fishing communities showed that 70–80 per cent of those interviewed favored primogenitural succession and inheritance (Koyama, 1952, pp. 178–79).

2. This is not to deny the effects of the postwar constitution upon the Japanese family system. With democratization of the family system in the new constitution, the great tradition no longer sanctions the superiority of male over female members of the family and of parents-in law over their daughters-in-law. Postwar surveys have shown complex patterns of the impact of this change in the great tradition upon family practices (Fukutake and Tsukamoto, 1954; Fukutake [ed.], 1961).

Let us first examine some of the situations that require deviation from the patrilineal or primogenitural rules and then the solutions to these situations. In this analysis we shall focus our attention on the problem of succession to the headship of the family rather than the inheritance of family property, and on the consequent assumption of the family occupation.[3]

There are various reasons why the oldest son does not succeed to the headship of a family. He may die before reaching maturity, or he may be judged physically too weak, mentally incapable, or otherwise incompetent to assume this position. Or, he may be perfectly capable but may decide to leave home and establish an independent family elsewhere, as when a farmer's oldest son goes to an urban center, with or without his father's consent, to pursue a non-agricultural career.[4] In any of these situations, if there is a younger son in the family, he would probably take over its headship and occupation. The solution here is relatively simple.

A different problem arises when the oldest son is simply too young at the time of his father's death or retirement to assume the position of headship. There are then two alternative solutions. The wife of the deceased or retired head may take over the family headship and occupation until the son is ready to assume this responsibility. This is a very common solution when the oldest son is already adolescent and can take over the family headship and occupation in a short time, before his mother becomes too old to perform these functions.

The alternative, if the son is still an infant when his father dies or retires, would be for the mother or parents to adopt a male substitute known as a *mukoyōshi* ("groom foster-son"). At the time of his adoption a *mukoyōshi* marries a woman of his adopter's choice. He takes the surname and Buddhist sect of his adopter, worships the latter's ancestors, and prepares to take over the family occupation. The problem of succession may be resolved in the same way when there is no son in the family or when the only son dies, or is judged incompetent of assuming the responsibility of headship, or leaves home.[5]

If a family without an appropriate male heir happens to have a daughter of marriageable age, she is likely to become the bride of an adopted son. Although some pressure will be exerted upon a daughter to marry an adopted son, her unwillingness to do so is no drastic hindrance to the arrangement, nor, for that

---

3. Succession to the family headship is chosen for illustration because it is far more important in the traditional Japanese family system than inheritance of family property; the Japanese family may exist without any property to speak of, but it cannot exist without a head (Toda, 1944, pp. 146–47).

4. This particular type of deviation from the primogenitural rule has increased in the postwar years, no doubt partly as a result of the legal changes in the structure of the family. It was by no means absent in the prewar days, however, as Nojiri's analysis of 277 rural communities clearly shows (1942, p. 489). Of all the oldest sons between twelve and eighteen years of age who finished their elementary-school education between 1929 and 1933, 31 per cent left their native villages for one reason or another.

5. The last situation—of the only son leaving home—is rather rare. Social sanction disapproves an only son's forsaking his responsibility to his family, and direct pressure is brought to bear on him to induce him to stay. Nonetheless, some sons do leave the family home.

matter, is the lack of a marriageable daughter. In either case a bride will be brought in to marry the adopted son. This bride may or may not be a blood relative of either the present family head or the prospective *mukoyōshi*.

It is obvious that when neither the bride nor the groom has kinship ties with the family in which they have obtained membership, a condition that is neither unusual nor in violation of the cultural norms, there can be no genetic continuity of the family as a kinship unit. Yet childlessness in Japan is no deterrent to the perpetuation of the family line. The family referred to here is, of course, a corporation embodying the family name and occupation, not necessarily a group of individuals related by blood.

If the head of the family is still young enough to carry on its headship and occupation for some time and young enough to raise a child but sees no prospect of fathering one, he may adopt a boy of any suitable age, who will assume his surname and be ready to take over these functions by the time of his death or retirement. Although this practice may help foster a stronger bond between the child and his foster-father than the adoption of a fully mature *mukoyōshi*, it is not necessarily the preferred practice. This is because there is a risk in not knowing whether a young boy will develop the ability, aptitude, and desire to carry on the family occupation when he becomes mature, a risk that is minimized when a *mukoyōshi* is adopted. An alternative solution here, which also minimizes the risk, is to adopt a young girl instead of a boy and to find a *mukoyōshi* as her husband when she reaches maturity.

A prospective *mukoyōshi*, of course, must be single. Another important criterion for his selection is his capacity to carry on the family occupation.[6] For rural occupations this capacity may be no more than good health and industry. But in more specialized occupations, such as business involving complex managerial and entrepreneurial skills or the pursuit of arts and crafts, candidates become increasingly rare. In these occupations the usual practice, in default of an heir, is for a man to adopt one of his most capable apprentices or disciples. Often, in order to insure the success of the family occupation, a man may resort to the adoption of a qualified *mukoyōshi* if his own son has not demonstrated the talent necessary to carry on the family occupation (Takeuchi, 1959, p. 1538).

As has been indicated, an adoptive son's blood relationship to the head of the family is of little consequence. There is, to be sure, some slight preference of kinsmen to non-kin. This preference, however, seems to be based, at least partly, on practical convenience rather than on overconcern about blood continuity. Since a man generally has more intimate ties with his kinsmen than with non-relatives, and is therefore better acquainted with their personalities, backgrounds, and capabilities, it is often easier for him to find an appropriate candidate for adoption among them. It should be noted that the kinsman adopted need not be patrilineally related to the head of the family but may be any

---

6. The importance of other criteria of selection, such as a *mukoyōshi*'s ability to get along with members of the family, is not denied; but these are not of primary concern here.

person related through blood and/or marriage. For kinship is utilized here merely as a practical means of securing an appropriate *mukoyōshi* rather than for the continuity of the patrilineal line. The adoption by a childless man of a brother fifteen or twenty years younger (Embree, 1939, p. 83; Norbeck, 1954, p. 53) also seems to be dictated not by the necessity of continuing the blood line but by the advantage of such a relationship as conducive to effecting a smooth succession to the status of the headship. Again, the primary reason is that of practical expediency rather than blood continuity.

Being a *mukoyōshi* is not an enviable status, particularly if the adopted son was not originally a relative or familiar with members of the family that he enters. He faces the same problem of adjustment to his in-laws as a bride in an ordinary marriage. A woman marrying into a family and assuming the low status of a bride, however, receives support from the value system of the society, which rewards a woman who meekly accepts her lowly position. A *mukoyōshi* receives no such support. Instead, he suffers the humiliation of assuming a status equivalent to that of a bride in a society in which men generally enjoy a much higher status than women. The old saying, "as long as you have three *gō* (about one pint) of rice bran, do not become an adopted husband," well summarizes the society's attitude toward *mukoyōshi*.

What is significant is that, in spite of the disagreeable status of adopted son, adoption is very common in Japan, accounting for about one-fourth of successions in the communities noted below. The significance lies in the fact that the society attaches important value to the continuity of the family, and, because of the compelling nature of this societal value, some men must give up their privileged status.

Succession to the family headship by a younger son, the wife of the deceased head, or an adopted son, entailing the obligation of continuing the family name and carrying on the family occupation with all the implied rights and duties, has been reported from many parts of Japan. In a rural community in northern Honshū, studied in 1959 by Norbeck and the author (Befu, 1962), of the sixty-six families that had lasted for two or more generations, eight were headed by younger sons, eleven by wives of the deceased heads, and seventeen by adopted sons.[7] Thus the practice in more than one-half of the sixty-six families deviated from the ideal of primogeniture.

Figures for succession provided by Beardsley and others (1959, p. 238) for a community in southwestern Japan are equally striking. Of the thirty successions investigated, seven were solved by adoption, six by junior sons, and the remaining seventeen, or a little over half, by oldest sons. These seventeen account for only 70 per cent of the twenty-four oldest sons in the community, the rest having emigrated, been adopted out, or judged incompetent.[8]

---

7. Families recently established by the present heads through branching, which are thus in the first generation branch families, are established and headed by younger sons. Inclusion of these families, therefore, would bias our figures.
8. See Takeuchi (1959, p. 1537) for additional figures that are equally suggestive.

In reviewing these deviations from the ideal pattern of descent and observing their frequency, we note a significant feature of the Japanese descent practices, namely, the relative lack of concern over actual genetic continuity from father to oldest son. While the cultural ideology of primogeniture requires succession from father to oldest son, a younger son, a woman, or even a non-relative may be substituted. Such substitutions are not regarded by the Japanese as "cheating" but instead are seen as entirely legitimate means of coping with the actual exigencies (Suzuki and Kitano, 1952, p. 144).

This, incidentally, is in marked contrast to the Chinese practice. In China, too, family continuity through patrilineal descent is imperative. But the emphasis among the Chinese is not so much on the perpetuation of the family as a corporate unit as on perpetuation of the patrilineal blood line. If a man, therefore, has no son, he invariably adopts the next of kin, the father's brother's son (Yang, 1945, p. 83). As Levy states (1949, p. 127), there is in China an aversion to a change of surname, which interferes with the adoption of a non-relative or, for that matter, of anyone except a patrilineal kinsman.

It should be clear by now that what lies behind these varied practices of descent in Japan is the primary emphasis placed on the perpetuity of the family as a corporate unit, compared with which, continuity of the blood line is of only secondary importance. Thus the "unbroken line of descent," of which old Japanese families are so proud, refers not to the genetic continuity but rather to the succession of the family name and occupation.

It is this emphasis on the corporate family in Japan that gives rise to the practice of the "restoration" or "re-establishment" (*saiken, saikō,* or *fukkō*) by a complete stranger of a family that has been discontinued for many generations. Another expression of this emphasis is the practice of *kaiyōshi* ("buyer-adoptive son"), in which a man on the verge of bankruptcy sells his entire property to a total stranger who is willing to take over the family occupation and adopt and continue its name[9] (Takeuchi, 1959, p. 1538).

A critical factor in the perpetuation of the Japanese family, as we have seen, is the continuation of its occupation.[10] It is for this reason that the ability to carry out the family occupation is an important consideration in the selection of an heir. The lack of concern over the blood tie between the head of the family and the man to be adopted no doubt gives a wider range of choice and makes possible the selection of a more qualified individual. This situation, again, differs from the Chinese practice of requiring a patrilineal tie between a man and his foster-child. This requirement of the Chinese makes it difficult to adopt a boy of good promise (Levy, 1949, p. 127).

---

9. This practice of *kaiyōshi* differs from the ordinary adoption of a *mukoyōshi* in that, upon the completion of the transaction, the seller leaves his home and thereafter has no contact with the adoptive son who has bought his property.

10. This should not give the reader the impression that continuity of the family occupation is an overwhelming concern in every Japanese family. In urban families whose heads are salaried employees of business firms, succession to the head's occupation by a family member is a rare occurrence.

Patrilineal descent in Japan is a means of continuing the corporate group called "family." It is practiced in Japan because it is more efficient than other rules of descent in carrying on the family occupation and thus guaranteeing the continuity of the corporate family. The primacy of the perpetuation of the family as a corporation over the continuity of the blood line is seen in the very fact that the structural rule of descent readily gives way to other practices when this rule cannot meet the requirement of the perpetuation of the family.

This corporate primacy over blood line finds its expression also in the well-known *dōzoku* system. The classical *dōzoku* group (Ariga, 1943; Kitano, 1940; Nagai, 1953; Okada, 1952) consists of several patrilineally related families, which are organized hierarchically, with the oldest (main) family at the apex and newly founded branches occupying successively lower ranks. These families constitute a corporate group in the functional sense (Befu and Plotnicov, 1962) in that the hierarchical structure of the kin group serves political functions, with the main family acting as the political leader. Furthermore, the group shares a strong sense of solidarity through such practices as ancestor worship. What is significant for us about this *dōzoku* system is that a large number of families incorporated in it are not related to the main family, and yet they constitute a vital element for the continuity of the group. This cultural provision, which allows the incorporation of non-kin into the *dōzoku*, is indicative of the primacy of corporate continuity over genetic continuity of the *dōzoku* group.

To understand the theoretical implication of the Japanese system of descent, we can first look to the distinction made by Firth (1954) between social structure, which is the abstracted "model" of social action, and social organization, which is the concrete social activity ordered in reference to socially defined ends. In the Japanese context, we may regard the rules of patrilineal descent and primogeniture as representing the social structure and the variable, concrete practices of succession to the family headship as representing social organization. Some of these practices conform to the model, while others deviate from it. Whatever the practical solution adopted, it is determined with reference to the specific end of continuation of the corporation called "family."

These phenomena can also be analyzed in terms of the distinction that Bennett and Despres make between ideology and activity (1960). These authors define ideology as a category consisting of certain rules and values. These norms may or may not be adhered to in the course of social life (1960, p. 257). Bennett and Despres do not specifically define activity, but they do enumerate several examples—economic, political, and religious. Ideology and activity, these authors maintain, may be exact replicas, or they may vary independently.

Ideology in the context under discussion is patrilineal descent and primogenitural succession, while activity is continuation of the family and its name and occupation. What we observe is the primacy of the instrumental activity over the cultural ideology, the latter being only a means for organizing the former. Thus the ideal rule of succession is followed only insofar as it helps maintain the family and its occupation. If it does not help to accomplish this end, it is readily dropped in favor of other rules.[11]

A curious fact about the variability of descent practices in Japan discussed here is the element of universalism that is discernible in this primarily particularistic setting of the family. That is, the role of the family headship is not defined entirely in particularistic terms, and its status is not always ascribed. The very act of judging a son as being incapable of assuming the status of family headship on the basis of ill health or inadequate performance is a manifestation of a universalistic element in the definition of the role of the family head. On a more positive side, in the decision as to which of the "deviant" means of succession should be adopted in default of a son or a competent son—whether to have the wife take over the headship, whether to adopt a son, etc.—one of the principal questions is: Which means best insures the continuity of the family as a corporate group? If a decision is made to adopt an heir, again, the basis of selection of an adoptive son is universalistic: Which candidate can perform the role of the family head and carry on the family occupation best? This universalism is particularly evident in occupations in which highly specialized talent is required. In such occupations, as we noted, a perfectly normal but ungifted son may be judged incompetent and rejected in favor of one of the family head's disciples who is not related but has demonstrated the required talent.

In summarizing, it can be seen that, although the structural rule of succession to the head of the Japanese family has traditionally been and still is to a great extent patrilineal and primogenitural, practical exigencies require solutions deviating from the rule. Certain types of deviations are required to cope with definite situations at the organizational level. The organizational acts of deviation are consequences of the primacy of an instrumental activity, namely, the continuation of the family, its name and its occupation, over the cultural ideology of partilineal and primogenitural succession. The particular deviations resorted to in Japan reveal a universalistic element in the role definition of family headship. It is on the basis of this element that selection of an heir is made when the oldest son is not available for succession.

11. Thus the particular relationship that obtains between ideology and activity here is an example of the second, "non-reciprocal," type of means-end relationship between the cultural system and the activity system (Bennett and Despres, 1960, p. 263).

BIBLIOGRAPHY

ARIGA, KIZAEMON
  1943. *Nihon Kazoku Seido to Kosaku Seido* ("The Family System and the Tenant System in Japan"). Tokyo: Kawade Shobō.
BEARDSLEY, RICHARD K., et al.
  1959. *Village Japan.* Chicago: University of Chicago Press.
BEFU, HARUMI
  1962. "Hamlet in a Nation: The Place of Three Japanese Rural Communities in Their Broader Social Context" (Ph.D. diss., University of Wisconsin).

BEFU, HARUMI, and LEONARD PLOTNICOV
1962. "Types of Corporate Unilineal Descent Groups," *Amer. Anthrop.*, 64:313-27.
BENNETT, JOHN W., and L. A. DESPRES
1960. "Kinship and Instrumental Activities: A Theoretical Inquiry," *Amer. Anthrop.*, 62:254-67.
EMBREE, JOHN F.
1939. *Suye Mura: A Japanese Village.* Chicago: University of Chicago Press.
FIRTH, RAYMOND
1954. "Social Organization and Social Change," *J. Roy. Anthrop. Inst.*, 84:1-20.
FUKUTAKE, TADASHI (ed.)
1961. *Kōza Gendai Nihon no Bunseki* ("Analysis of Modern Japan" Series). Vol. 1: *Nihon no Shakai* ("Japanese Society"). Tokyo: Yūhikaku.
FUKUTAKE, TADASHI, and TETSUNDO TSUKAMOTO
1954. *Nihon Nōmin no Shakaiteki Seikaku* ("Social Character of Japanese Farmers"). Tokyo: Yūhikaku.
KITANO, SEIICHI
1940. "Kōshū Sanson no Dōzoku Soshiki to Oyakata Kokata Kankō" ("*Dōzoku* Organization and Ritual Parent-Child Practices in a Mountain Village in the Kai Province"). *Minzokugaku Nempō*, 2:41-95.
KOYAMA, TAKASHI
1952. "Kachō" ("Family Head"). In: JAPANESE SOCIETY OF ETHNOLOGY (ed.), *Nihon Shakai Minzoku Jiten* ("Social and Ethnographic Dictionary of Japan"), 1:177-79. Tokyo: Seibundō Shinkōsha.
LEVY, MARION J., JR.
1949. *The Family Revolution in Modern China.* Cambridge: Harvard University Press.
NAGAI, MICHIO
1953. "*Dōzoku*: A Preliminary Study of the Japanese 'Extended Family' Group and Its Social and Economic Functions (Based on the Researches of K. Ariga)," *Ohio State University Research Foundation Interim Technical Report*, No. 7.
NOJIRI, SHIGEO
1942. *Nōmin Rison no Jisshōteki Kenkyū* ("Empirical Study of Peasant Emigration"). Tokyo: Iwanami Shoten.
NORBECK, EDWARD
1954. *Takashima: A Japanese Fishing Community.* Salt Lake City: University of Utah Press.
OKADA, YUZURU
1952. "Kinship Organization in Japan," *J. Ed. Soc.*, 26:27-31.
SUZUKI, EITARŌ, and SEIICHI KITANO
1952. *Nōson Shakai Chōsa* ("Rural Social Survey"). Tokyo: Jichōsha.
TAKEUCHI, TOSHIMI
1959. "Yōshi" ("Adoption"), In: JAPANESE SOCIETY OF ETHNOLOGY (ed.), *Nihon Shakai Minzoku Jiten* ("Social and Ethnographic Dictionary of Japan"), 4:1533-41. Tokyo: Seibundō Shinkōsha.
TODA, TEIZO
1944. *Ie to Kazoku Seido* ("Family and Family System"). Tokyo: Haneda Shoten.
YANG, MARTIN C.
1945. *A Chinese Village.* New York: Columbia University Press.

DOZOKU AND IE IN JAPAN: THE MEANING OF FAMILY GENEALOGICAL RELATIONSHIPS

SEIICHI KITANO

It is well known that what is called "*dozoku*" in Japan is composed of the *honke* (main or original family) and its *bunke* (branch family). The *dozoku* is a hierarchical group of *bunke*, with a *honke* at the top of the scale, and its members work together in various fields of endeavor. This group prevails over the country under many names, such as *maki, make, uchiwa, jirui, ikke, itto, ichimyo, kabu, kabuuchi, yauchi, mokka, motto, yoriki*, etc. "*Dozoku*" is a scientific general term for this group. The *dozoku* has been common mainly in rural districts and until quite recently was inseparably related to the social structure of the rural community.

The *dozoku* was originally under the control of the *honke*. The *honke* presided over the ceremonies and festivals of the *dozoku*, including the common worship of the guardian deity. It also made it a rule to give the *bunke* assistance or guidance in the political and economic spheres of its daily life. It is now difficult to find anywhere in Japan a well-ordered ideal *dozoku*, either in structure or in function. For the *dozoku* group has long been disintegrating into subunits, and this trend has become more marked since World War II. The *honke* has been losing its influence over the *bunke*, and its patronage to the *bunke* also has been declining. Consequently, it becomes harder than ever to distinguish the *dozoku* relationship from the other similar ones between kinsmen or master and servant.

Moreover, many complex problems remain unsolved in defining the nature of the *dozoku* bond, and Japanese scholars are divided on this question. Therefore it is necessary to define ideal-typically the nature of the *dozoku* bond before analyzing the present *dozoku*. It is my opinion that the component unit of the *dozoku* is the traditional family called *ie* in Japan and that the family genealogical relationship determines the nature of the *dozoku* bond.

The genealogical relationship of the *dozoku* families is formed only when the *honke* and its *bunke* mutually recognize their family descent status as *honke* or *bunke* in the family genealogy and enter into a definite relationship, under which they are obliged to perform duties or roles ascribed to their respective status. In short, the establishment of the family genealogical relationship means, not the mere divergence of a new family from its original family, but the entrance into a definite social relationship and subordination to a prescribed behavior pattern. Otherwise, they are neither *honke* nor *bunke*. Even though any family member may diverge from his original family by receiving a certain amount of the family property and enrolling himself in the official family record (*koseki*) as an independent household, it does not imply that the genealogical relationship discussed above is formed. He must also recognize his original family as *honke* as well as his family descent status as *bunke* on the family genealogy while accepting a definite social relationship.

This family genealogical relationship is the traditional Japanese family called "*ie*," for the component unit of the *dozoku* is the *ie*, and it is the *ie* that forms the family genealogical relationship and contributes to the chain-like continuance of the relationship. Conversely, a modern family that has no *ie* principle is unable to continue as the same *ie* after the present family members have died. It has no inner *ie*-like bond to connect the *bunke* with their *honke*. It is a universal phenomenon that a family member leaves his original family to form an independent family. The modern family is a typical example of this. Grown-up children leave their parents' home one by one, and the eldest son is by no means an exception. It is almost impossible for him to identify himself with his parent family and to have the responsibility of transmitting the family property to the succeeding generation. Even when he inherits the parent's estate, he has no consciousness as a successor of the *ie*.

On the contrary, the establishment of the *bunke* differs from the mere divergence of a new family. Many of the diverged families, to be sure, are nuclear families in composition, but they diverge from their original family through recognizing themselves as a branch of the *honke* and recognizing a formal connection with the *honke*. Both *honke* and *bunke* recognize that they continue to exist through this genealogical relationship. It is impossible to find this type of bond in the modern family, because both *honke* and *bunke* exist as *ie*. The principle of the *ie* bond forms the link between the stem and the branch.

Now, what is meant by *ie* here is the traditional family of Japan. It is founded on the principle of a large family, into which the component small families are combined and unified by patriarchal authority. Since the Japanese feudal period, the patrilineal family type has been predominant. In rural communities there existed the patriarchal large family that includes some nuclear families of the household head's descent and of non-relatives, and there were some areas where this type of family was relatively well preserved. Even in this large-family system the family headship and the family property were ideally transmitted, as in stem family, to the eldest son. It was the common rule that other family members left in due time, though the length of their remaining inside their parents' home varied. This family type typically embraced the patriarch, his wife, his married sons, their wives, his unmarried children, and his sons' children. Unlike the modern family in which the component family members leave their parents' home, forming an independent nuclear family, these two or three generations lived together under a single roof and identified themselves with the family entirely through the chain-like succession of the family headship, the family property, and the family tradition. Through this process the Japanese family has persisted for generations and is expected to persist unceasingly, independent of the birth and death of its members.

Therefore, the authority of the head within the family is supreme and final, but the family headship and the family property are considered to belong to the family itself in order to unite and maintain the family as a group permanently, though both are under the control of the patriarch. It must be admitted, too, that the patriarch himself is under the control of the family, which demands its continuation, and is obliged to contribute to it through the proper exercise of the *ie* authority entrusted to him. The *ie* is a family that persists supergenerationally. The following are the family traditions symbolizing the *ie:* the family tree, the genealogical table, the family name, any sobriquet of the family head, and the family insignia. The family god, the departed spirits of the forefathers, the graveyard, the cenotaph, the family constitution, the family tradition, the family treasure, etc., are the symbols of the *ie* unity and continuity.

This conception of *ie* is inseparably connected with the formation and structure of the *dozoku*. For the formation of the genealogical relationship between the *honke* and its *bunke* is made possible only through the medium of the *ie*. The *honke* establishes his new branch family as *bunke* and combines with it insofar as the *honke* is *ie*, and, for the same reason that the *bunke* is *ie*, the *bunke* recognizes its original family as *honke* and is subordinate to the *honke*. Accordingly, in establishing the *bunke*, the *honke* gives it a certain amount of the family property, which must be continuously transmitted, and assistance in one form or another to sustain the new branch family. Thus the *bunke* is connected with the *honke* as a branch of the *honke*'s family tree and adopts the family name and family insignia of the *honke*. Furthermore, it participates in such religious ceremonies as that of the guardian god of the *dozoku*, the family god, and the departed spirits of the forefathers of the *honke*, and belongs to the same temple and uses in common the graveyard of the *honke*. These suggest symbolically that the *bunke* is linked with the *honke* through the family genealogy and is the ramified branch of the *honke*. They also tell us clearly that the *bunke* accepts the *honke*'s authority and is subordinate to it. And it must be kept in mind that this *ie* relationship characterizes and sustains the various kinds of social relatedness among the *dozoku* in their daily lives, including the patronage of the *honke* to the *bunke* and the *bunke*'s service to the *honke*.

But now, as the traditional nature of the *ie* is rapidly being lost and the *ie* principle lessens its integrating power over the family life, the concept of *honke* and *bunke* inevitably undergoes changes. Newly ramified families emerge, having no *ie* relationship with the original families. And yet they regard themselves formally as *bunke* and call their original family *honke* only because it is customary usage. We cannot regard them as *bunke* in the true sense of the term. There are also not a few cases where the division of the parent's estate is made according to the equal inheritance provisions of the new Civil Code. It is an entirely different social action from the donation of the family property by the *honke*'s patriarch in establishing the *bunke*. Originally, the donation of a certain amount of the family property was accomplished through the exercise of *ie* authority by the *honke*'s patriarch, and it is in nature identical with the patriarch's duty of supporting family members. The establishment of the *bunke* in itself is the duty of the *honke*, which is closely tied with the maintenance community (*Versorgungsgemeinschaft*) of the patriarchal family. Thus, although the *bunke* makes independent family life a unit of livelihood, it still remains within a maintenance system founded upon the *ie* authority of the *honke*. The relatedness of the *honke* with the *bunke* in their daily economic activities, what is called the patronage of the *honke* to the *bunke* and the *bunke*'s service to the *honke*, is originally sustained by the maintenance system of *honke*.

Along with the transformation of the *ie*, changes have taken place in the *ie* relationship between *dozoku* families and the maintenance system of the *honke*. Especially in the economic sphere of their daily activities, the *dozoku* families co-operate not only with one another in various ways but also with non-*dozoku* families as occasion arises. Thus changes in these relationships also take various forms. Some of them are already modernized, while others are still prescribed by tradition. Even the modernization of these relationships varies in degree, depending upon time and circumstances. Nevertheless, it is undeniable that the traditional character of the *dozoku* relationship is gradually being lost, and a rationalized relationship is taking its place, through which the concept of the *ie* as well as the proper relationship between the *honke* and *bunke* is under the process of change.

Accordingly, it is of great importance to know clearly on what principle the relationship of the *dozoku* families depends, in order to know what change occurs in the proper *dozoku* relationship and what sorts of reorganization are taking place there. For in such situations as described above, where the bonds of the *ie* and *dozoku* are in the process of change, even the phenomena that are the same in form may differ from one another in content. Let us take an example of co-operation in work in the fields. We must make a clear distinction between the aid offered to the *honke* as the *bunke*'s duty and the aid offered in terms of equal exchange of work. They are quite different social actions in terms of social relations. The equal exchange of work tells us that both the weakening of the traditional *ie* relationship between the *dozoku* families and the transformation of the *bunke*'s service to wage labor is now in progress.

The social relatedness of the *honke* with its *bunke* is not confined to farm management. They co-operate with each other in the following: marriage and funeral ceremonies, construction and repair of houses, prevention and repair of damages, and mutual help after childbirth and illness. Besides these, they hold a series of joint religious ceremonies, such as worship of the guardian deity of the *dozoku*, ancestor worship, the Buddhist services for the ancestor spirits, the New Year ceremony, and the lantern festival. Needless to say, these belong to the important functions peculiar to the *dozoku*. The common worship of the guardian deity is a typical example of these. There a great importance is attached to the traditional *ie* relationship and the hierarchical order of the family genealogy; only the *dozoku* families are allowed to participate in the ceremony, and non-*dozoku* families are excluded. This holds true for other ceremonies so long as the *dozoku* relationship plays a significant role. Accordingly, insofar as these ceremonies are held together, the *dozoku* can be said to persist.

However, it becomes difficult to discern the *dozoku* relationship in marriage and funeral ceremonies because non-*dozoku* families participate in them while traditional *dozoku* relationship is expressed officially. This is much more true of the co-operation in the construction and repair of houses. However complicated it may be, it is possible to draw a clear line between the co-operation of the *dozoku* families and other forms of co-operation if the *dozoku* bond is so strong as to solidify the *dozoku* families. In such a well-ordered *dozoku*, the co-operation between *honke* and *bunke* is kept well under the control of the *honke;* they work together in marriage and funeral ceremonies and construction and repair of houses, besides *honke*'s patronage and *bunke*'s service; furthermore, they extend mutual aid after childbirth and illness as their duty. Needless to say, the *honke* bears heavy burdens in most of them, and it is therefore not difficult to distinguish *dozoku* relationships from others. Especially in the well-ordered *dozoku*, the common worship of the guardian deity, ancestor worship, the Buddhist service for the ancestral spirits, and the New Year ceremony are strictly observed and the authoritative control of the *honke* asserts itself.

Nowadays, it can be said generally that remarkable changes take place in the maintenance system of the *dozoku*, while changes in the ceremonies peculiar to *dozoku* are less marked. This not only comes from the individualization of farm management but is accompanied by a change in the nature of *honke* and *bunke* as *ie* under the influence of capitalistic economy. Thus in the marriage and funeral ceremonies and others mentioned above, the co-operation between *dozoku* families weakens its own peculiar features, and therefore it becomes difficult to distinguish it from other forms of co-operation. This complex change now takes various forms, but it will sooner or later have effects on all the ceremonies peculiar to *dozoku*. This also makes it difficult to study how the *dozoku* co-exists or connects with other groupings, including kinsmen and relatives, and with the *oyabun-kobun* relationship.

CHANGING FAMILY STRUCTURE IN JAPAN

TAKASHI KOYAMA

THE Japanese family in the past was an example of the patriarchal extended family system. With this family system, the paramount emphasis was on that group called *"ie."* The patriarch was the governor and delegate of this family group. Since the eldest son alone was, as a rule, entitled to succeed to the patriarch's position, he was, as prospective patriarch, ranked highest next to the present family head both inside and outside the family. In spite of the principle of male dominance, the second and subsequent sons received lukewarm treatment in their daily round of life as *hiyameshi-kui* ("cold-rice eaters," or dependents who deserve to eat leftovers). Rarely did they share the inheritance with the eldest son. Needless to say, with this family system, all women were held in an even more submissive position. Thus, the family traditionally was not an agent to guarantee the equal happiness of the individual members but rather a group that forced them to render service and sacrifice for itself and for the patriarch. Since the *ie* was to perpetuate over generations to come, parents, children, and grandchildren lived together under one roof, and this resulted in various forms of the extended family under different living conditions.

Under the feudal regime, Japanese people lived in discrete local communities isolated from each other politically, economically, and socially, and in many places various forms of the family emerged that one might regard as almost unnatural.

Chart 1 illustrates the historical change of the composition of a Takashima family. The example was taken at Shirakawa-mura in the mountain region of the central districts of Japan, well known for its large extended family system. Chart 1, *a* shows the composition of the family of one hundred and fifty years ago, when it was contented with a life very unequal and unnatural, as one might regard it, of the then closed mountain village under feudal government. Owing to the development of modern industrial society about fifty years ago, this family composition gradually disintegrated, as indicated by 1, *b*, which illustrates the composition of the Takashima family of thirty years ago. The disintegration has proceeded further until it now takes the form of the typical nuclear family, as 1, *c* illustrates. Thus, we learn concretely from Chart 1 how large a change the form of family composition has undergone as the wider society has shifted from a feudal to a modern one.

It is, however, rather a crude generalization if we conclude from the foregoing that the Japanese family in the past was always a large extended family and that

CHART 1
THE CHANGING STRUCTURE OF THE TAKASHIMA FAMILY

a) 1813

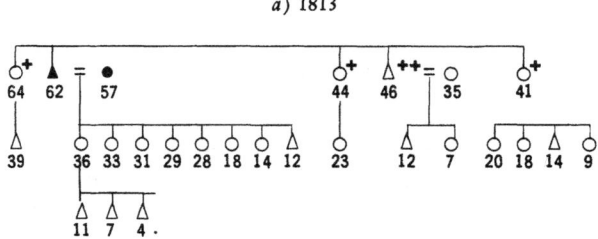

b) 1932

c) 1960

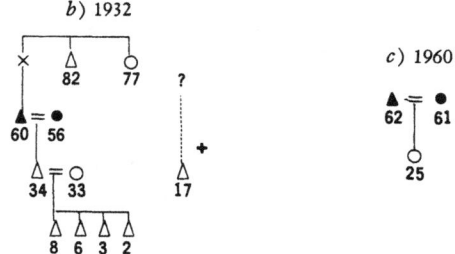

SYMBOLS

+, wife who lives in her own parental home with her children while her husband (not shown) lives with his parents, not being a househead.

++, husband and wife, not househeads but living in husband's parental home, an exceptional case for the period in this area.

▲ , Head of household; ● , his wife; △ , male members of household; ○ , female members of household, ×, deceased.
Each number in the chart shows age.

at present the typical nuclear family prevails. For, whereas the family composition is changed by the social system external to the family, intertwined with this change is one derived from the dynamics of the system internal to the family as such. Even in the case of the Takashima family in the past, the death of family members as a result of epidemics or disasters reduces its size, or the present composition may very likely be transformed into a type of extended family if the son lives with his parents after his marriage.

Here are presented seven typical forms of the family composition in Japan:

I. Single-member household
II. Household of husband and wife
III. Household of husband, wife, and unmarried children
IV. Household of husband, wife, and married children
V. Household of husband, wife, and linear ascendants
VI. Household of husband, wife, linear ascendants, and descendants
VII. Household including collateral kin

These may subsume, in terms of form, all Japanese families both in the past and at present, though the relative frequency of the respective form varies from place to place and from time to time. These seven forms I understand to represent the chains of circular transformation that occur in family composition in the course of family cycles in Japan.

Through tabulation of historical sources found in Yamasaki village, a rural community of Yamanashi Prefecture, I have tried to show in Chart 2, *a* how the circular transformation in feudal days occurred in the composition of thirty family groups for a period of sixty years from 1802 to 1861. The transformation takes place, as the direction of solid arrows in the chart indicates, mainly along the course of VII, VI, III, and IV, in this turn, and back to VII. Once a newly established family enters this main course, transformation is endlessly repeated in a circle, to the perpetuation of the *ie*.

This stands in sharp contrast with the family cycle of the nuclear family as indicated in Chart 2, *b*. Here the family form begins with II, the household of husband and wife, develops into III, adding unmarried children to II. It then goes back to II, ending in I, the single-membered household, which is a step toward the termination of the family. Compared to this, the extended family takes a complex form in the course of the family cycle, and even now many newly established branch families, though they start from a simple form, enter shortly upon the circular course more or less approximate to the one charted. Table 1 shows the distribution of the present Japanese families by the form of the composition.

Comparison by region and occupation indicates that the trend toward the nuclear family is far stronger among urban families in modern industry than among rural families in agriculture. From this we can infer that the relative decline of agriculture and rapid urbanization, such as Japan is now embarked upon, may further reinforce the dominance of the nuclear family. We must bear

CHART 2

a) Main Course of Change in the Form of the Extended Family, 1802–61

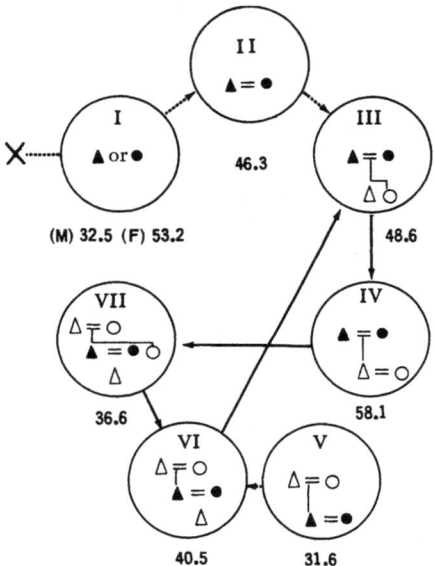

b) Main Course of Change in the Form of the Nuclear Family

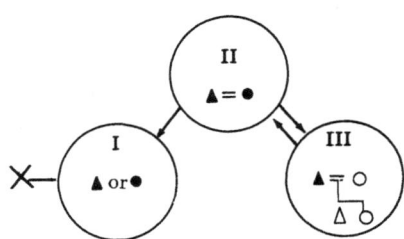

Figures below each circle represent average age of family heads. ▲ , family head; ● , wife of family head; △ , man not family head; ○ , woman not wife of family head; = , marriage; ×, death;⟶, main course of cyclic change of basic family form;⟶, main course of cyclic change of derived family form.

in mind, however, that the complete transformation of the family system throughout all segments of Japanese society cannot be attained in a short time.

As much as fifty years ago, some leaders, seeing the inevitable change in the family system that was to come with the modernization of Japan, insisted on revision of a part of the Civil Code covering the family system. Their efforts were in vain because of countermoves by opponents who regarded the then existing family system as representing time-honored custom essential to Japan's moral and political survival.

The reformist movement, though subdued by traditionalism until the end of World War II, attained its goal almost in an instant, so far as the legislation of its ideal was concerned, when Japan was transformed into a democratic society after the war. The New Constitution, promulgated in 1946, set forth the principle of respect for individual dignity and equality of the sexes upon which to base the new family system. The traditional family system, collectivity oriented and patriarch centered, was thereby deprived of its legal status and gave way before the new family law, which emphasizes the importance of a conjugal-unit-centered married life. In this way, the family system, which had been in a state of "cultural lag" since the emergence of a modernized Japan, now leaped into the leading position of social progress.

This statement is true so far as the principle is concerned, but in practice

TABLE 1*
PERCENTAGE DISTRIBUTION OF JAPANESE FAMILY BY FORM (1960)

Form of the Family		Total	Differences in Region			Differences in Occupation			
			Village and Town	Small and Middle-sized City	Large City	Agriculture	Owner, Manager	Employment	Others
Conjugal family (nuclear family)	I	6.3	4.7	5.2	11.3	0.9	4.0	6.4	14.6
	II	6.4	4.0	7.6	8.5	3.4	6.7	7.7	6.9
	III	50.5	48.0	51.5	53.4	33.3	57.6	59.4	54.5
Linear family (extended family)	IV	12.2	15.1	11.9	7.6	22.3	11.2	6.7	8.4
	V	1.8	1.7	1.6	2.1	1.3	1.3	2.3	2.1
	VI	15.0	18.5	14.3	10.2	29.9	11.8	10.4	10.1
Collateral family (extended)	VII	7.7	7.9	7.9	6.7	8.8	7.2	7.0	3.4
Total		100.0	100.0	100.0	100.0	100.0	100.0	100.0	100.0

* Obtained from Takashige Murai, Statistical Department, Ministry of Health and Welfare.

there is resistance by the farm population, constituting half of the total population, who have been a firm fortress of traditional familism, and old people who have been inculcated with traditionalism while young and who, therefore, are not to be expected to change their attitude very quickly. Very plausibly, alteration of the principle, effected in too short a time, cannot anticipate a uniform attitudinal change throughout the entire population of Japan.

Differences in this regard between urban and rural families, between farm and non-farm families, are shown in Table 2, a finding of the research I and my associates conducted in Tokyo, a fringe area of Tokyo, and a mountain

TABLE 2
PERCENTAGE OF THE RESPONDENTS WHO SUPPORTED EACH ITEM OF THE TRADITIONAL FAMILY PATTERN BY SITE OF RESEARCH IN TOKYO-TO (1956)

	SITE OF RESEARCH			
		Komae		Toyama
ITEM OF TRADITIONAL FAMILY PATTERN	Otaba (Mountain Village)	Farm	Non-Farm	(Apartments in Tokyo)
1. Married children living with parents	72%	71%	28%	19%
2. Retired parents living with married children	87	81	48	36
3. Retired parents supported by children for living expense	72	55	20	15
4. The eldest son held responsible for the support of parents	82	74	37	20
5. The eldest son held responsible for the support of his brothers and sisters	80	64	26	27
6. The eldest son entitled to the succession of the family lineage	63	76	35	28
7. The eldest son privileged to inherit all family properties	74	84	49	40
8. Married-out children not admitted to equal share of inheritance	58	68	40	38
9. Adoption of a child for the perpetuation of family line	93	89	53	36
10. A son-in-law matrilocal to the family lacking male descendants	94	91	46	22
11. Decision-making by parents upon the marriage of the eldest son	21	22	7	5
12. Retention of real estate in the native place	70	37	21	18
Total responses %	100	100	100	100
Total responses N	223	132	120	294

village not far from Tokyo, to study differences of attitude toward the family on the part of persons in different community types and different occupations.

Regarding parent-child relations, in the traditional pattern the eldest son, heir to the family, was to live with parents after his marriage. What is the attitude in this respect at present when the family system is, in principle, based upon the conjugal unit? According to our field study, more than 70 per cent of farmers favor married children living with their parents, as against only 20 per cent of urban-living commuters who answered likewise. All other responses in the urban area give consent to separate living.

As for the support of parents, all children are held equally responsible today, while the eldest son alone was responsible formerly. Even now, however, as many as 70–80 per cent of rural responses insist on the responsibility of the eldest son for the support of parents, whereas commuters in urban areas who answered likewise account for only 20–30 per cent. Another important item in the family pattern is the inheritance, which was based upon the principle of primogeniture in the past but upon equal division among survivors at present. In practice, however, farmers who insist upon primogeniture still account for 80 per cent, whereas only 40 per cent of urban dwellers consent to primogeniture.

It is now evident that rural families more than urban families, and farm population more than non-farm population, support the traditional family pattern based on the former civil code. This may be regarded as a difference of adaptability to the newly established family institutions. It must be noted that this difference not only is not a matter of mere attitudes but is profoundly buttressed

TABLE 3
PERCENTAGE OF THE RESPONDENTS WHO SUPPORT OR DENY WHOLLY THE ITEMS OF THE TRADITIONAL FAMILY PATTERNS, BY DISTRICT, AGE, AND SEX, FOR ALL JAPAN

	Support Wholly	Deny Wholly	Intermediate
All Japan	32	28	40
Six major cities	12	42	46
All minor cities	29	33	38
Rural district	42	18	40
Male			
20–29	18	42	40
30–39	22	32	46
40–49	37	24	39
50–59	44	16	40
60 and up	52	11	37
Female			
20–29	15	45	40
30–39	28	30	42
40–49	44	21	37
50–59	46	13	41
60 and up	50	7	43

by the circumstances of life of the respondents. Therefore, the new family code may be a dead letter if one fails to take into consideration the underlying living conditions.

Besides regional and occupational differences, discrepancies derived from the differences of sex, age, and education are also evidently remarkable. Table 3 shows a part of an opinion survey of the family system conducted by the Japanese government in 1956. It tells how the attitudes vary among different segments of contemporary Japanese society regarding the traditional versus the modern family system. Associated with this variance is the discrepancy of reciprocal role-expectations among family members, for instance between husband and wife or between parents and children. In not a few cases such discrepancies are in fact bringing about family discord.

It must be recognized that, generally speaking, the Japanese family has undergone great change and progress for these fifteen years since the transformation of Japan into a democratic society, though people still leave many problems unsolved, while inertia and nostalgia for the past still linger. A great move toward democratic family relations is in fact in operation. Even to reluctant people, it appears to be an inevitable process. The legal reform, as stated before, has had good effects upon the growth of the younger generation and the improvement of women's social position. What were once regarded as good morals and customs of Japan are now lost, but the contemporary Japanese is going to find a new pleasure in family life, provided that particular solutions are hereafter found for each of the problems, such as insecurity felt by the aged, that may arise in the course of this great reform.

NOTES ON PRIMOGENITURE IN POSTWAR JAPAN

Y. SCOTT MATSUMOTO

INTRODUCTION

TRADITIONALLY, the Japanese family was based on patrilineal descent, patriarchal authority, and patrilocal residence. Great emphasis was placed on the ideal of the biological perpetuation of the patrilineal lineage in order to maintain the unity and continuity of the family. The privilege of masculinity and the custom of primogeniture made the rankings of a son over a daughter and an eldest son over his younger brothers largely unquestioned values. The eldest boy, as heir to the headship, was inculcated early in life with a sense of responsibility to fit him for succession to his father's estate and position. The first-born son remained in his parental home from birth until death. The duty of the eldest son, rather than the younger sons, was to marry, usually according to his parents' selection, and produce a male descendant. The bride moved into the family home of her husband at marriage. Younger sons usually moved out or established "branch" houses. Daughters married out. Upon the death or retirement of the father, the family property was preferentially inherited by the oldest son, who became the new household head. The eldest son inherited not only the family headship and family property but also his aging parents, who continued to live with him and to be supported by him. Succession by eldest son was regarded as right and natural.

The Civil Code of 1948 under the Allied Occupation legally abolished the concept of *ie* ("house") with its system of the family head. It lessened parental powers and provided for equality of the sexes and freedom of marriage. The revised code sought to stress the integrity of the individual, rather than the family, as the primary unit. In matters of inheritance of family property and land, the postwar Civil Code established equal property rights and sought to "reform" the traditional practice whereby the eldest son received the favored position. A fundamental change under the new code stipulated equality in inheritance for *all* children in the family. The critical question to be examined is whether the shift toward equal inheritance is really occurring or whether the traditional principle of primogeniture prevails in spite of the provisions in Japan's revised Civil Code.

One would suppose, since the prerogatives of primogeniture appear significant in any family analysis in Japan, that an abundance of empirical data would be available in the Japanese sociocultural literature. Unfortunately, such material is sparse. This paper primarily presents the findings of the various opinion and attitude studies conducted in postwar Japan that bear on sentiments concerning primogeniture. Results from any single attitude study should, of course, be cautiously treated. However, consistent patterns of replies and recurrent variations among respondents in a variety of opinion surveys can be considered meaningful as indicative of trends.

ATTITUDES TOWARD PRIMOGENITURE

In a survey by the Sōrifu, Kokuritsu Yoron Chōsajo (National Public Opinion Research Institute) in 1952 on a national cross-section of 3,000 respondents between sixteen and fifty-nine years of age, 66 per cent continued to support and approve primogeniture (1953, p. 255). In urban areas 60 per cent and in rural areas 71 per cent of the respondents favored primogeniture. When only agricultural households were considered, the percentage rose to 77. The greater the age of the respondent, the more likely he was to support primogeniture. To the question, "Do you think it better for the eldest son to become the successor of the *ie* ('house') as in the past?" answers were given as shown in Table 1.

TABLE 1

	Yes	No	Don't Know	Total Per Cent
Total	66	31	3	100
By age:				
16–19	55	40	5	100
20–24	59	39	2	100
25–29	63	33	4	100
30 and over	71	27	2	100
By area:				
Urban	60	38	2	100
Rural	71	26	3	100
Agricultural households	77	20	3	100

In 1952, Jiji Press reported that in a national sample of 2,500, 60 per cent favored the parents' residing with the eldest son and his wife, while 21 per cent stated that separate residence was desirable (1952, p. 289). On the question of support of aging parents, 36 per cent designated the eldest son as the responsible person, whereas 54 per cent would have all of the children contribute.

In 1953, Fukutake and Tsukamoto (1954) studied a village in Akita Prefecture as representative of the Tohoku region, with its traditional extended family ties, and contrasted it with another village in Okayama typifying the southwestern section of Japan, where ties of co-operative groups seem to receive greater emphasis than do family and kin ties. This survey of two rural communities indicated a predominant approval of the pattern of primogeniture, but in neither was approval complete. In both villages combined, 71 per cent accepted primogeniture as the natural course of events, whereas approximately 25 per cent expressed dissatisfaction with the traditional system. The survey clearly shows a much stronger approval by the Akita village (81 per cent) as compared with the Okayama group (59 per cent):

	Okayama	Akita
Approve primogeniture	58.6%	80.9%
Disapprove primogeniture	38.8	14.2
Don't know	2.5	4.9
Total	99.9%	100.0%
	N = 273	N = 367

Attitudes of Japanese adolescents and young people toward the family system were studied in 1955 by Baber (1958). Approximately 5,000 students were interviewed in 47 schools, half in high schools and half in universities, from Hokkaido to Kyushu. Responses to the question "Do you think the eldest son should live with his parents after marriage, or should he establish a separate household?" were as shown in Table 2. In high school, 31 per cent of the girls

TABLE 2

Place of Childhood	With Parents		Separate if Possible	
	University	High School	University	High School
Boys:				
Total	20.1	28.3	79.9	71.7
City	16.9	20.5	83.1	79.5
Town	23.8	36.7	76.2	63.3
Village	22.9	36.3	77.1	63.7
Girls:				
Total	7.9	30.7	92.1	69.3
City	6.1	17.6	93.9	82.4
Town	10.1	35.4	89.9	64.6
Village	14.6	41.3	85.4	58.7

N = 4,975

and 28 per cent of the boys thought it best for the eldest son to live with his parents, contrasted to 8 per cent of the girls and 20 per cent of the boys in universities who thought so. The high-school students, especially the girls, were more conservative than were the college and university students, and far more village than city youths expressed preference for the traditional pattern.

Answers to the question, "If aged parents are to be supported by their children, which way is best?" (Table 3) show that only about 1.5 per cent of the total Japanese students thought that the eldest son alone should be responsible for the

TABLE 3

	UNIVERSITY		HIGH SCHOOL	
	Boys	Girls	Boys	Girls
By the eldest son	2.7	0.3	2.3	0.9
By all the sons equally	8.9	0.7	13.3	9.4
By all sons, each contributing according to his ability	59.9	25.7	58.4	37.5
Eldest son should contribute more than any of the others	7.8	2.0	7.3	4.1
By all sons and unmarried daughters	6.0	9.9	5.4	13.1
By all sons and daughters whether married or not	14.7	61.4	13.3	35.0
	100.0%	100.0%	100.0%	100.0%
N = 5,007				

support of the parents. A majority of the boys believed that the proper approach would be for each son to contribute *according to his ability*. Only one-fifth of the university and high-school boys combined thought that the daughters should share the burden. The girls, especially those in universities, would divide the responsibility among *all* sons and daughters, whether married or not. This study indicates that rigid primogeniture is not a deeply embedded tradition among today's young people of Japan.

Opinions on primogeniture were included in the nation-wide poll on Japanese attitudes toward the family system and the new Civil Code reported by the Prime Minister's Secretariat (1957). The sample included 3,000 respondents, both male and female, twenty years and over, from 32 cities and 90 towns and villages throughout Japan with a return of 2,557 (85.2 per cent). When asked "Should one of the children live together with and look after the parents, or do you feel it is unnecessary for any of the children to live with the parents?" the following replies were given:

Better to live together	72%
Not necessary	24
Don't know	4
	100%

Seventy-two per cent of the national sample expressed adherence to the view of co-residency of elderly parents with one of their children. Those favoring co-residency were further asked: "If it is better to live together with the parents, should this be the eldest son or can it be any one of the children?" Replies run as follows:

Eldest son	38%
Any one of the children	32
Don't know	2
	72%

Of those stating that the parents should reside with an offspring, over half (38 per cent of the total sample) designated the eldest son as their candidate. Equally noteworthy, almost an equal percentage expressed the opinion that any one of the children would do rather than specifying the first-born male.

When those stating that parent-child residency was unnecessary were further queried: "In supporting the parents, do you feel that all brothers should contribute according to their capabilities, or do you feel that it should still be the eldest son who makes the major contributions?" their answers were:

Depends upon each individual's income	20%
Eldest son primarily responsible	2
Don't know	2
	24%

The great majority of those who would not burden the children with the parents also felt that support for the parents should come from all the brothers, depending upon the financial circumstances of each. Only 2 per cent would leave aging parents to be supported only by the eldest male.

For respondents preferring that parents and an adult child live together, the opinion that the eldest son should maintain residence with the parents appeared comparatively strong, although almost an equal proportion would shift the responsibility to any of the other children. Those who did not favor sharing a home with the parents likewise felt strongly that economic support should be on an equal basis without placing the main burden on the eldest brother.

Table 4 shows the distribution of opinion by age, sex, education, occupation, and area (urban or rural). Little difference was seen when comparison was made by sex, although the females rather than the males favored slightly more the eldest son's residing with his parents. The difference by age appeared to be more significant. Whereas one-fourth of those in their twenties favored the first-born son's remaining with the parents, over half of those sixty years and over, both male and female, felt this to be imperative.

The higher the educational level, the greater the likelihood of disapproving the necessity of living with parents. Forty-eight per cent of those graduating from grammar school under the prewar school system favored co-residency of parents with the eldest boy, whereas 15 per cent responded "not necessary." However, for those graduating from colleges and universities under the old system, the trend was reversed, with 17 per cent favoring the eldest son and 44 per cent stating "not necessary." Those graduating under the new school system, and hence younger, tended to give less support to the traditional role of primogeniture. It is of interest to note that the percentage of those stating

TABLE 4
Percentage Distribution of Opinions by Age, Sex, Education, Occupation and Area

	No.	Per Cent Total	Better to Live Together			Other
			With Eldest Son	With Any One of Children	Not Necessary	
By age:						
Male						
20	312	100	25	38	30	7
30	260	100	35	34	27	4
40	236	100	39	35	20	6
50	206	100	48	33	16	3
60	158	100	53	27	15	5
Female						
20	396	100	28	32	35	5
30	397	100	32	31	31	6
40	291	100	47	30	16	7
50	192	100	50	29	16	5
60	109	100	59	27	8	6
By education:						
Old system						
Grammar	698	100	48	31	15	6
Higher grammar	932	100	45	30	20	5
Middle	526	100	28	33	33	6
College and univ.	90	100	17	34	44	5
New system						
Middle	142	100	30	28	35	7
Higher	132	100	15	43	35	7
University	37	100	5	49	38	8
By occupation:						
Employed						
Agr. and forestry	846	100	50	31	13	6
Comm. and forestry	389	100	37	32	25	6
Manual workers	273	100	31	35	28	6
Office clerical	238	100	20	39	37	4
Non-employed, by occupation of household head						
Agr. and forestry	156	100	55	26	13	6
Commerce and industry	177	100	36	33	27	4
Manual workers	198	100	33	35	29	3
Office clerical	141	100	25	29	41	5
By area:						
Six largest cities	423	100	21	35	40	4
Other urban areas	1036	100	35	32	27	6
Rural areas	1098	100	49	31	14	6

"not necessary" in the middle school, higher school, and universities under the new school system tended to be similar, at approximately 35 per cent. This was, however, lower than the 44 per cent of the highest educational group under the old system.

A majority of those engaged in occupations in agriculture and forestry favored the eldest son. The category of office clerks expressed a higher percentage of disfavor to co-residency than did any other occupational group. On the basis of the occupation of the household heads of those respondents not employed, the trend was similar to those of the employed respondents.

On a regional basis, a plurality (49 per cent) of the rural persons endorsed the eldest son's co-residency with his parents, whereas only 21 per cent of those residing in the six largest cities of Japan expressed a similar view. Conversely, 14 per cent of those in the rural areas and 40 per cent in the largest cities replied that co-residency was unnecessary.

Concerning inheritance of property upon the death of the parents, the responses in this national survey were as follows:

The eldest son or heir should receive more than the other brothers	59%
Not necessary to do so	36
Don't know	5
	100%

Approximately three-fifths of the total replies favored the practice of giving the eldest son or heir the major portion of the family property. However, use of the words "eldest son *or* heir" in the question blurs the critical point of interest in the study of changing attitudes.

The overlapping relationship of the attitude toward support and the attitude toward inheritance can be clearly noted in that 61 per cent of those who thought that all brothers should help support the aging parents, depending upon their economic ability, also stated that the eldest brother should not receive a larger share of the inheritance. On the other hand, 79 per cent of those responding that the first-born boy should reside with the parents thought that he should simultaneously receive the bulk of the family property.

In this nation-wide survey, among all respondents, twenty years and over, who had any child still living, only 2 per cent lived separately, giving ample evidence that most parents in Japan today live with their children. Furthermore, of those who were eldest sons and married, only 12 per cent did not live with parents.

The most recent empirical documentation on attitudes toward primogeniture is provided by the social survey conducted during November, 1956–December, 1957, by Koyama and his colleagues (1960*a*, 1960*b*; Kazoku kenkyū-bu kai, 1957). Three different types of communities in the Kanto area were intensively studied: (1) Toyama in Shinjuku district of urbanized Tokyo composed of four-story apartment houses whose residents were white-collar wage-earners, young in age, highly educated, with few children or aged parents; (2) a rural community, Komae, in the outskirts of Tokyo with half of the inhabitants engaged exclusively in agriculture and the remaining half consisting of commuters to Tokyo; and (3) a traditional mountain village, Otaba, buried in deep forest with a sound economy based on forestry with some agriculture. The intent was to study and compare attitudes of a group that could be characterized as most urbanized and "Westernized" on the social scale with those of a rural community still deeply traditional and conservative, plus a community that could be designated as in between these two extremes. An attempt was made to observe the sentiments of a traditional, a transitional, and a modern community in Japan. Table 5 shows the response to the question: "Which child do you prefer for continuity of your household?" Over 60 per cent of the mountain villagers specifically acknowledged

TABLE 5

	Mountain Village	Suburban Village, Agric.	Suburban Village, Non-agric.	Urban Apartment
Eldest son	63.2	62.9	32.5	27.9
Younger sons	11.2	10.6	10.0	6.1
Daughters	9.0	9.1	9.2	1.7
Other answers	0.9	3.8	6.7	51.4
No answer	15.7	13.6	41.6	12.9
	100.0% N = 223	100.0% N = 132	100.0% N = 120	100.0% N = 294

preference for the eldest son. The majority of the city apartment dwellers (51 per cent) gave such answers as "any child will do," "never thought about it," or "not necessary." However, one out of four Toyama respondents stated preference for the eldest boy. The attitude of Komae respondents divided sharply as between those engaged and those not engaged in agriculture. The responses of the agricultural population of Komae followed trends similar to those of the traditional village, whereas attitudes of the commuting workers of Komae followed more closely those of Toyama urbanites except for the large number of "no answers."

On the question: "In inheriting property upon the death of the parents, do you think that the eldest son as heir should receive more than his brothers and sisters, or do you think it is unnecessary?" approximately three-fourths of the mountain villagers would pass family property to the eldest son. Forty per cent of the urban apartment residents thought it unnecessary to give such consideration to the eldest son, although an identical percentage (40 per cent) would favor the oldest boy over other children. See Table 6.

Concerning the responsibility of the eldest son in supporting and caring for

TABLE 6

	Mountain Village	Suburban Village, Agric.	Suburban Village Non-agric.	Urban Apartment
Most to eldest son	73.6	84.0	49.1	39.9
Most to eldest son, but depends on circumstances	2.2	3.8	6.7	3.7
Not necessary to give most to eldest son	16.1	11.4	37.6	40.1
Equally, depending on circumstances	0	0	0.8	1.7
Others	2.7	0.8	5.0	10.9
No answer	5.4	0	0.8	3.7
	100.0% N = 223	100.0% N = 132	100.0% N = 120	100.0% N = 294

aged parents: "In cases where the parents have aged, become ill, or have livelihood difficulties, which of the children has the primary responsibility to care for them?" the pattern in Table 7 followed the trend shown for continuity of household and for inheritance. On the matter of maintenance and support of the aging parents, 80 per cent of the mountain villagers emphasized the primary responsibility of the eldest boy; whereas only 20 per cent of the urban respondents so stated. The eldest son was still regarded as old-age insurance by the rural respondents (cf. Sakurai, 1959). The majority of the city respondents stressed the more egalitarian position that all the children should share such responsibilities.

ATTITUDES TOWARD THE YŌSHI SYSTEM

In the traditional society, the strong concept of family maintenance and continuity evolved the system of *yōshi*. Through *yōshi* the house could be

TABLE 7

	Mountain Village	Suburban Village, Agric.	Suburban Village, Non-agric.	Urban Apartment
Eldest son	81.6	74.2	36.7	20.4
Eldest and other sons	4.0	6.1	5.8	8.5
All the children	8.1	12.9	35.0	52.7
Others	4.5	5.3	21.7	16.0
No answer	1.8	1.5	0.8	2.4
	100.0% N = 223	100.0% N = 132	100.0% N = 120	100.0% N = 294

perpetuated even in the absence of a male heir. If a couple had no son, they solved the problem by adopting one. If a couple had a daughter but no son, a man was selected to marry the daughter. Here the procedures were reversed from those of an ordinary marriage. The male moved into the home of his newly acquired wife; he thereafter assumed her family name as his own and his name was deleted from his own family register and added to his wife's family register as son-heir of the household head and husband of the daughter. It was also possible to adopt a son in substitution for a biological son who was incompetent.

Often the adopted male was a younger son of a relative of the household head, but it was equally likely that such a person would be totally unrelated. The continuity of the family household was therefore social as well as biological. Many family lines would have died out had not the *yōshi* adoption system insured the stability of the family as a social institution. Current attitudes toward the system would serve to gauge the persistence of the emphasis on traditional family continuity.

In the 1956 national survey sponsored by the Prime Minister's Secretariat, 69 per cent stated that it was better to adopt a *yōshi* in the absence of any children in the family. The question was asked: "In case there are no children, do you think it is necessary or not necessary to adopt a *yōshi?*" Replies were as follows:

Better to adopt a *yōshi*	69%
Not necessary	18
Don't know	13
	100%
	N = 2,557

Those who stated "Better to adopt a *yōshi*" were then further asked: "Would you feel the same if there was no problem concerning livelihood?" Opinions were:

Better to adopt a *yōshi* even if no problem concerning livelihood	59%
Yōshi not necessary if no problem of livelihood	7
Cannot decide	3
	69%

When the economic factor was introduced, the percentage declined from 69 to 59 per cent, but the majority would still adopt a *yōshi* despite no economic justification. This seems to indicate motivation in terms of perpetuation of the family lineage rather than merely the problem of security in old age.

In Koyama's study, two questions related to attitudes toward *yōshi* adoption: one in event the respondent had only daughters and no son and the other in case the respondent had no children. The first question was: "In case you had only daughters and no sons, would you adopt a *yōshi* husband for your daughter, or would you permit your daughter to marry out into another family?" Table 8 shows in percentages the answers to this question. An overwhelming majority

TABLE 8

	Mountain Village	Suburban Village, Agric.	Suburban Village, Non-agric.	Urban Apartment
Would adopt a *yōshi*	93.7	90.1	46.7	21.8
Would permit daughter to marry out	2.7	6.8	40.0	59.1
Depends on circumstances	1.4	2.3	10.0	14.3
No answer	2.2	0.8	3.3	4.8
	100.0%	100.0%	100.0%	100.0%
	N = 223	N = 132	N = 120	N = 294

(94 per cent) of the respondents in the mountain village of Otaba would adopt a *yōshi* husband for the daughter, whereas the percentage declined to 22 for the urban residents. More than half (59 per cent) of the Toyama apartment dwellers would permit their daughters to marry out of the family, taking the name of the husband. The agricultural portion of Komae followed closely the traditional views of the mountain villagers. The non-agricultural segment of Komae was about equally divided between adoption of an outsider as a family heir and permitting the daughter a normal marriage, showing attitudes somewhat more congenial with the metropolitan respondents.

The second question, "If you had no children of your own, would you adopt a *yōshi*?" elicited the replies shown in Table 9.

TABLE 9

	Mountain Village	Suburban Village, Agric.	Suburban Village, Non-agric.	Urban Apartment
Necessary	92.8	89.4	53.4	35.6
Depends on circumstances	1.8	4.6	10.0	9.2
Not necessary	2.7	3.0	26.6	46.7
No answer	2.7	3.0	10.0	8.5
	100.0%	100.0%	100.0%	100.0%
	N = 223	N = 132	N = 120	N = 294

Almost all the Otaba villagers (93 per cent) would adopt a *yōshi* to perpetuate the family household in case of no children. Nearly half the total (47 per cent) in urban Toyama thought that the *yōshi* was unnecessary, although more than one out of three (36 per cent) did think it was necessary to adopt a *yōshi* when there were no children in the family.

The amount of registration of *yōshi* status into the official family register (*koseki*) constitutes an index to the deeper-lying sentiment toward family continuity. Registration is an overt action, definite and concrete. Yamamuro wrote in the Japanese *Dictionary of Sociology* (Fukutake et al., 1958, p. 914) as follows:

There were over 180,000 cases of *yōshi* adoption registration in Japan in 1952, which is probably the greatest amount of adoption of any nation in the world. Furthermore, of these, approximately 150,000 cases were comprised of adoptions of adults which are rare in other countries.

Examination of the annual reports issued by the Civil Affairs Bureau of the Ministry of Justice (Hōmu-shō, minji-kyoku, 1959–60) revealed the following totals as the number of those officially registering new *yōshi* relationships:

> April, 1956, to March, 1957....149,854
> April, 1957, to March, 1958....155,436
> April, 1958, to March, 1959....148,457
> April, 1959, to March, 1960....145,247

Because of overreporting through duplications where two or more prefectures are involved and because of the known underregistration, since many *yōshi* adoptions fail to become officially documented, these figures must be viewed with caution. The gradual declining trend of the yearly figures, however, is suggestive. Nevertheless, these annual totals serve to indicate the deep feeling of the Japanese today concerning the perpetuation of the family unit even to the extent of adoption.

DISCUSSION

With the termination of war, the traditional Japanese family system underwent a sudden legal alteration based on the principle of individual dignity and equality of the sexes. However, it was legal recognition of a social change that had not yet actually occurred. The impetus of reform was not internal but external and foreign, uninitiated by the Japanese themselves. Equal inheritance by all children has not been enforced and has usually been evaded. The common practice has been for the second and younger sons and the daughters to renounce their claim in order to favor the first-born boy. Traditional importance still seems generally accorded the first male child, and the Japanese family with only daughters is deplored as incomplete. Social realities and behavioral patterns lag behind the new legal codes.

In spite of postwar legislation, the sentiment of the majority of the Japanese concerning primogeniture would still follow the past pattern of succession of the eldest son to his father's position and property. Such an interpretation seems broadly consistent with the fragments of information from the opinion polls and attitude studies. The surveys reviewed showed that the supporters of the traditional pattern of primogeniture tended to be disproportionately older in age, slightly more female than male, less educated, and engaged in agricultural pursuits in rural areas.

A striking impression received from the attitude polls is the greatly widened gap between the city dwellers and their rural relatives. In the agricultural villages the tradition of primogeniture seems to persist as it has previously generation after generation. It possesses a vitality that suggests that the pattern may continue for some time into the future, although the prestige and privilege of the eldest son probably will become weakened (Norbeck, 1961, p. 310). In contrast, for the centers of urbanization and industrialization, the traditional values appear to attenuate, especially among the younger educated groups. The system of primogeniture seems to be undergoing substantial modification in the urban environment.

In spite of the great differences of attitudes and opinions between urban and rural areas, it might be postulated that occupation and education may be of greater importance than residential location in molding attitudes. What may be reflected for the larger Japanese cities are the higher components of industrial employment, greater income, and better education implicit in its way of life. Agricultural occupations, low income, and limited education are characteristics of the level of rural living. If anything, however, the gap between those in urban and those in rural areas has progressively widened in recent years. But the process and degree of change appears uneven in rural sections in different parts of the nation and probably differs within segments of an urban area.

The economic factor remains a relevant aspect in the perpetuation of primogeniture. There is understandable reluctance to break up minor possessions into still smaller segments under a system of equal inheritance. Not only for the farmers with their usually limited land but also for the urbanites with small holdings in retail shops or in household enterprises (Tachi, 1961), greater fragmentation of property can result only in economic disaster. Parents must look toward their children for support and security in old age. Although sympathetic to the plight of the second and younger sons, parents are hesitant about equal divisions among all offspring, for their own security in old age depends on the passage of consolidated family wealth on to the heir. As Professor Fukutake (1961, p. 74) noted, the new civil law seeks social freedom, but it may be compelling the impossible in view of the persistence of economic insecurities.

While the system of primogeniture persists in Japan, the attitude surveys yield clues to the possible direction of future change. The dilemma need not be interpreted as one between single inheritance versus equal inheritance. Obviously, single inheritance is the only sensible course of action when property is too limited to stand further subdivisions. The justification of primogeniture is that an estate remains intact that otherwise would be split into uneconomic units. However, the identical result can be achieved by settling the property on any one child in the family. In Japan today single inheritance predominates, but there may be an increasing trend away from the automatic passage of property to the eldest son toward the selection of any one of the children as an heir, though still usually among the sons. Many eldest sons seek emancipation from the pressures of family responsibilities. The emphasis shifts from the *chōnan* ("eldest son") to the *atotori* ("heir"). Rather than responsibility, obligation, and duty of a Confucian-oriented family, the critical factors involved in the ultimate decision become the personal wishes, capabilities, and happiness of those individuals concerned. Greater weight is placed on the view that responsibility and obligation for the family should be equitably and mutually shared by all the children to the extent possible.

SUMMARY

In the foregoing pages, a series of opinion surveys indicating attitudes toward primogeniture in postwar Japan have been reviewed. The surveys indicated that the majority of older and less educated Japanese generally, and agricultural populations particularly, favored the right of primogeniture. Although it is held with great tenacity in the rural communities, there is no denying that rigid patrilineal succession is weakening in the younger, educated, white-collar groups in the urban and industrial areas of Japan. The tradition of primogeniture definitely persists, but the outlines of the heritage become progressively more diffuse.

The question of the status of primogeniture in the Japan of the future becomes part of the larger question of change in the total Japanese structure. Any movements to restore the legal status of *ie*, or "house," and of its head may be correlated with a strengthening of the role of primogeniture. However, if more heirs to households are based on the choice and decisions of the family members concerned, such a modification would represent a social transformation within the family away from the traditional hierarchical arrangements. The future course of development may be indicative of the progressive weakening of the elements of hierarchy in family relationships and the corresponding strengthening of those more in line with egalitarian values.

BIBLIOGRAPHY

BABER, RAY E.
    1958 "Youth Looks at Marriage and the Family." Tokyo: International Christian University.

FUKUTAKE, TADASHI (ed.)
    1961 *Nihon no shakai* ("Society of Japan"). Tokyo: Yūhikaku.

FUKUTAKE, TADASHI, ROKURŌ HIDAKA, and TŌRU TAKAHASHI (eds.)
    1958 *Shakaigaku jiten* ("Dictionary of Sociology"). Tokyo: Yūhikaku.

FUKUTAKE, TADASHI, and TETSUNDO TSUKAMOTO
1954 *Nihon nōmin no shakaiteki seikaku* ("Social Characteristics of Japanese Peasantry"). Tokyo: Yūhikaku.

HŌMU-SHŌ, MINJI-KYOKU ("Ministry of Justice, Civil Affairs Bureau")
1957 *Koseki jūmin tōroku jiken hyō* ("Tables on Registration Cases concerning Residents and Family Registers"). Tokyo.
1958 *Ibid.*
1959 *Ibid.*
1960 *Ibid.*

JIJI TSŪSHIN-SHA ("Jiji News Agency")
1952 *Jiji nenkan, Shōwa 28-nen* ("Jiji Almanac, 1953"). Tokyo.

KAZOKU KENKYŪ-BU KAI ("Research Circle of the Family")
1957 "Sengo ni okeru kazoku no jittai" ("The Structure and Function of the Family in Postwar Japan"), *Shakaigaku hyōron* ("Japanese Sociological Review"), 7:114–45.

KOYAMA, TAKASHI
1960a *Gendai kazoku no kenkyū* ("Study of the Contemporary Family"). Tokyo: Kōbundō.
1960b *Tōkyō kinkō-son no kazoku* ("Family in a Suburban Village near Tokyo"). In: TADASHI FUKUTAKE (ed.), *Shakaigaku ronshu, chōsa hōkoku-hen* ("Essays on Sociology: Survey Reports"). Tokyo: Kawade Shobō Shin-sha.

NAIKAKU SŌRI DAIJIN KAMBŌ, SHINGI-SHITSU ("Prime Minister Secretariat, Deliberation Room")
1957 *Kazoku seido ni tsuite no yoron chōsa* ("Public Opinion concerning the Family System"). Tokyo.

NORBECK, EDWARD
1961 "Postwar Cultural Change and Continuity in Northeastern Japan." *Amer. Anthrop.*, 63:297–321.

SAKURAI, MARUO
1959 *Shinzoku fuyō ni okeru "ie" no ishiki* ("Consciousness of *house* in the Support of Kin"). ("Kumamoto daigaku kyōiku-gakubu kiyō" ["Memoirs of the Faculty of Education, Kumamoto University"] 7:116–24.)

SŌRIFU, KOKURITSU YORON CHŌSAJO ("Office of the Prime Minister, National Public Opinion Research Institute")
1953 *Shakai kyōiku ni tsuite no yoron chōsa* ("Public Opinion on Social Education"). (Survey No. 51.) Tokyo.

TACHI, ITSUO
1961 "Toshi ni okeru chū-shō kigyō kazoku no jittai" ("A Study on Small–Medium–Enterprise Families in Urban Society"). *Meiji gakuin ronsō* ("Meiji Gakuin Review"), 60:69–113.

III. Village Organization

COMMON-INTEREST ASSOCIATIONS IN RURAL JAPAN*

EDWARD NORBECK

Postwar publications by sociologists and anthropologists have provided us with valuable information and illuminating interpretations concerning social changes in rural Japan. A major point of emphasis in these writings has been kinship, the Japanese family and other kin groups, and ritual kinship modeled after familial relations. Only the briefest examination of demographic data on Japan points clearly to trends of change that must have had strong influence on kin groups and kin relations. Recent population statistics may be cited in illustration. The average size of the family throughout the nation dropped from 4.97 members in 1955 to 4.53 in 1960. During this interval of five years the national population increased 4.6 per cent, but most of the increase occurred in cities and industrial prefectures. Twenty-six of the forty-six prefectures suffered a decline in population (Consulate General of Japan, 1961, pp. 2–4). These statistics represent the continuation and acceleration of trends established long ago, and they suggest extensive changes at both family and community levels.

Published accounts have provided us with some information on the nature of the social changes that these statistics suggest. The principal events reported may be summarized as a decline in the size and functional importance of kin groups, a weakening of the bonds of kin-like personal ties with unrelated community members, and a change in patterns of authority, making kin groups and communities less strongly hierarchical. Principal factors influential in bringing about the changes have usually been cited (e.g., Okada, 1952; Norbeck, 1961) as improved economic conditions of the nation as a whole connected with increased industrialization and world trade, improved technology in farming and fishing, the postwar land reform, and the emergence or increased growth of many impersonal institutions that provide economic and social security.

But social change in rural Japan does not end with the alterations outlined above. An additional and important development that has received far less attention is the growth of associations based upon common interests, the kinds of social groups that we have often called "voluntary associations." Both native and foreign scholars of Japan have generally considered common-interest associations in highly specific or fragmented ways. No systematic attempt has been

---

* Field research upon which this paper is based was supported by the Wenner-Gren Foundation for Anthropological Research and the National Science Foundation. The author wishes to express his gratitude to Robert Anderson, Harumi Befu, Douglas G. Haring, and Robert J. Smith for helpful suggestions.

made to describe and classify them, to present an interpretation of their functional roles, or to compare them cross-culturally. This paper hopes to make a first step in this direction.

As a type of social group, the common-interest association is ancient in Japan (cf. Hoynden, 1958; Konno, 1938; Norbeck, 1953; Segawa, 1947). One of its early forms was undoubtedly age-graded associations, which appear to have been most common in southerly and coastal regions. Japanese scholars have presented historic evidence of the revamping of old age-graded associations into modern groups, such as the Seinendan (Youths' Association), sponsored in modern times by the Japanese government.

It seems reasonable to expect great antiquity for communal associations concerned with irrigation. We know from archeological evidence that wet rice cultivation was established in Japan more than two thousand years ago, and we can assume that its intensive cultivation required the co-operation of many persons to build and maintain substantial systems of irrigation. The necessary co-operation may have come through kin groups, especially when the population of Japan was small. If modern theorizing on this subject (e.g., Cornell, 1956) is sound, however, we may think that common residence was the more important factor in determining the composition of communal work groups associated with agriculture. Formal and informal groups concerned with planting rice, harvesting crops, and other agricultural tasks and community enterprises requiring the combined efforts of many people are also old in Japan (Hoynden, 1958).

Whatever the history of the numerous individual associations found in rural Japan today, it is safe to say that their roots as a class are ancient. In his discussion of the role of agriculture in the Tokugawa era (1600–1868) in the formation of modern Japan, Smith (1959) writes at length of "the decline of cooperative groups." His discussion must be understood as referring to a decrease in the size of the farm family and the decline of co-operative fictive kin groups. Human co-operation by no means declined during Tokugawa times, but it did take other forms.

Hoynden's account of the co-operative movement in Japan, although it concerns chiefly associations connected with credit, production, distribution, and other economic matters, contains information that is relevant here. He discusses the great antiquity of co-operative groups in Japan, and describes the nation as being one of the most highly developed in the world in all types of co-operatives except consumer's co-operatives, which are less well developed than in countries of the West (Hoynden, 1958, Preface and chap. 1). The circumstances of which Smith writes, intensive market agriculture based on techniques that favored cultivation of small holdings by small family groups, very likely encouraged the growth of non-kin associations as well as paved the way for the later industrialization of the nation. Small land holdings may be seen as a factor disfavoring extensive co-operation among kin but favoring co-operation in the form of common-interest associations. Among other social effects, the small size of Japanese farms has made the actively co-operating kin group small and has made loans through banks impossible (Hoynden, 1960, pp. 12–13). Farmers' credit co-operatives first arose in the fourteenth century, before Tokugawa times, and have now had a history in Japan of six centuries (Hoynden, 1958, pp. 7–8). Smith's account of agricultural and social developments that aided the later industrialization of Japan concerns chiefly southwestern Japan, which led the nation in economic change and growth. It is noteworthy that the late Tokugawa and early Meiji eras (the mid-nineteenth century) appear to be the time of emergence of communal associations in small face-to-face living communities (*buraku*) of northeastern Japan, an area that until very recent times lagged behind southwestern Japan in cultural innovations. These were *buraku* associations, concerned with the control and maintenance of local paths and roads, with community forest lands, and with various other matters of communal interest. The name often given to these associations in northeastern Japan, *keiyaku-kō*, is literally translated "contract association." The middle of the nineteenth century is also a period that saw the rapid growth in urban Japan of co-operative associations concerned with finance, production, and marketing. The greatest growth of formal common-interest groups of all kinds has come in the twentieth century. This is a subject to which we will return in considering the functional role of the modern associations.

TYPES OF JAPANESE COMMON-INTEREST ASSOCIATIONS

An examination of reports on modern rural communities of Japan displays marked uniformity in the types of common-interest associations described. Although full data are lacking, it seems fairly certain that rural settlements everywhere follow a common pattern that varies principally in accordance with the occupations that villagers follow (i.e., farming, fishing, dairying, sericulture, forestry, and the like). Local ecological features also exert influence on associations. In communities that offer little employment for young men, for example, the youths' associations are poorly developed by default because the young men migrate to industrial areas.

Customarily, the number of associations to which *buraku* members belong ranges between fifteen and twenty-five. Membership in them depends upon sex, age, occupation, and other special interests. The list appearing below of the associations in a rice-raising *buraku* in Miyagi Prefecture in 1959 may be taken as representative (Norbeck, 1961, pp. 312–13).

Agricultural Co-operative Association (I)
Youths' Division, Agricultural Co-operative Association (I)
Women's Division, Agricultural Co-operative Association (I)
Daruma 4-H Club (young men) (I)
Angel 4-H Club (young women) (I)
Irrigation Association (I)
Parent-Teacher Association (I)
Children's Association (E)
Crime Prevention Association (I)

Fire Prevention Association (I)
Young People's Association (I-E)
*Buraku Association (I)
*Funeral Association (in groups of 10–12 households) (I)
*Neighborhood Association (several small groups) (I)
*Irrigation Association (independent grouping concerned with a small water supply used by a part of the community) (I)
*Tax Association (to remind members of dates payments are due and to facilitate payment of the numerous taxes. Several small groups; all households do not belong) (I)
*Yama-no-kamisama Kō (religious society, brides and young mothers) (E)
*Kobugahara Kō (religious society, men) (E)
*Kōshin Kō (religious society, men) (E)
*Kannon Kō (religious society, women) (E)
*Nembutsu Kō (religious society, women) (E)

(I) = Instrumental; (E) = Expressive; (I-E) = Instrumental-Expressive. See discussion that follows. Classifications (I) and (E), as made here, imply that associations are principally rather than wholly instrumental or expressive. The lone association marked (I-E) seems about equally instrumental and expressive.

Gordon and Babchuk's reformulation (1959) of Arnold Rose's (1954) typology of voluntary associations, although apparently based principally upon data from the United States, lends itself fairly well to the Japanese scene. Based upon an interpretation of their functions, this classification places associations into three categories: *instrumental*, those "designed to maintain or create some normative condition or change" which "focus on activity and goals that are outside the organization itself"; *expressive*, those providing "continuing gratification" to the individual through "activities confined and self-contained within the organization itself"; and *instrumental-expressive*, those combining the goals and functions of the two foregoing types (Gordon and Babchuk, 1959, pp. 25–28). Lack of space prohibits any detailed discussion of the aims and functions of most of the Japanese associations listed above, but these may generally be inferred from the titles.

We would accept the Gordon-Babchuk typology with two reservations. The first, a minor point that Gordon and Babchuk also note, is that instrumental associations probably always have some element of "expression"; that is, they may give personal satisfaction to individuals in varying degrees in ways that are not directly connected with the goals of the associations. The second reservation is more serious. We question the suitability of the word "voluntary," as have others before us in more general discussions of the nature of associations (e.g., Chapple and Coon, 1942; Lowie, 1948). Many of the Japanese associations on the *buraku* level are branches of larger organizations. They were established under pressure from the national government and receive strong encouragement from the prefectural and national governments. During World War II, co-operative associations connected with occupations, and women's and youths' associations, were nationalized, and membership in them was virtually obligatory. No legal provisions today require membership in any *buraku* association, whether

---

* Independent *buraku* associations. All others are segments, usually *buraku* subdivisions, of larger organizations.

instrumental or expressive, but social and economic pressures serve, for most people, to make membership in a large part of the groups obligatory. On the local level, membership in associations is not by ascription. One joins them, but membership often comes close to being ascribed. These circumstances are, of course, not unique to Japan. We wonder, for example, whether participation in such organizations as the Parent-Teacher Association may aptly be called voluntary in the United States or Europe.

FUNCTIONAL ASPECTS

Certain roles of the Japanese associations seem self-evident from their titles: they provide individual satisfaction through recreation, education, and religious acts or they attempt to reach educational, economic, civil, or moral goals. Using the concept of function in another sense, we may say that they are also in considerable measure substitutes for kinship and personal ties. In the Japanese rural community, intra-*buraku* social relations have come increasingly to stress non-kin associations that have ties to neighboring communities and the nation as a whole. It is through them that much of the economic and social life of the *buraku* is conducted, and, increasingly, community solidarity is expressed through identification with the associations. Referring to northeastern Japan and other regions where associations were slower to develop than in southwestern Japan, it is probable that solidarity within the *buraku* and with neighboring communities has increased in postwar years as a result of their growth.

Most important in the respects discussed above are the occupational co-operatives, particularly the farmers' co-operative association, which probably exists in every agricultural community of Japan. This organization is the medium through which machinery, tools, fertilizer, other farm supplies, and education in new techniques of horticulture are obtained; it is the only important agency for obtaining loans of money, the principal repository for cash savings of its members, and the customary agency for the sale of crops. The farmers' co-operative, expectably, has great power. It may be described as a mechanism by which communal action is made to serve effectively for individual or familial ends.

In pointing out the great importance of agricultural co-operatives in Japan, Hoynden goes so far as to state that rural communities in Japan are formed around them (Hoynden, 1958, p. iii). He calls the agricultural co-operatives multipurpose and lists as their major functions: credit, marketing, purchasing, guidance in farming, mutual relief, medical services, and management and finance (Hoynden, 1960; p. v). Under the provisions of the Agricultural Co-operative Law, enacted shortly after the end of World War II, activities in which these co-operatives may engage are:

a) Loaning funds necessary for the business or livelihood of members.
b) Acceptance of deposits from members.
c) Supply of articles necessary for the business or livelihood of the members, or installation of common facilities.

d) Facilities relating to co-operation in agriculture or the promotion of the efficiency of agricultural labor.
e) Reclamation, improvement, or administration of agricultural land or establishment or administration of irrigation facilities.
f) Transportation, processing, storage or sale of articles produced by members.
g) Facilities relating to village industry.
h) Facilities for mutual relief from loss or damage.
i) Facilities for the improvement of village life and culture.
j) Facilities for the education of members to improve their knowledge of agricultural technique and the business of the cooperative, and for the provision of general information to the members.
k) Conclusion of collective bargains for the improvement of the economic position of members.
l) Such business as is incidental to any one of the preceding items [Hoynden, 1960, pp. 18–19].

Since the agricultural co-operatives do in fact engage in all or most of these activities, their importance in community life goes far beyond affairs connected with agricultural technology and economics. Many co-operatives also provide recreation and promote cultural activities by sponsoring or subsidizing movies, concerts, lectures on many subjects, and instruction in dietetics and other matters of domestic life. Some have established public halls for recreation and instruction and provide electric washing machines, barbers, and bathhouses. An especially common facility provided to members is a wire broadcasting system that transmits to the homes of members programs of various kinds, news, weather reports, educational addresses, and entertainment. These broadcasting systems often incorporate telephones. The majority of the agricultural co-operatives have women's divisions. A recent trend toward the formation of young men's divisions is also apparent. These divisions are perhaps better called auxiliaries, since their objectives appear to stress recreation, instruction in non-agricultural spheres, and civil affairs more than they do matters directly connected with agriculture.

It is clear that agricultural and other co-operatives of Japan that are concerned primarily with technological and economic matters have been strongly influenced by Western models (cf. Hoynden, 1958, 1960). Some of the other Japanese associations we have listed (i.e., Parent-Teacher Association, 4-H Club) appear from their names to be foreign-derived and were in fact established by Occupation directives. The whole fabric of Japanese rural associations nevertheless follows a Japanese pattern, historical aspects of which we have already discussed. In even the most backward areas of rural Japan, a tradition of communal action in at least certain spheres of life has long co-existed with hierarchically ordered social groupings based on the model of the family. It is useful to note again circumstances in northeastern Japan, where, until the postwar land reform, most of the land and other property was in the hands of a few individuals. The bulk of the rural population consisted of tenant farmers or people having access to lands through ties of kinship and fictive kinship. Communal associations developed first in connection with religion and such vital community affairs as did not present economic threats to those in power. Once the great landowners were removed from power by the land reform, the way was clear for rapid development of associations. Altered economic and social circumstances in fact gave strong encouragement to their development. The growth of the foreign-derived or foreign-influenced Japanese associations seems thus to follow an indigenous pattern. Policy-makers in the Japanese government, having an established model before them, used native and foreign models of the association to provide an effective and inexpensive channel for reaching and controlling its population during the years that Japan prepared for and actively waged war. Following World War II, additional foreign models reached the Japanese through officials of the American Occupation.

Under the circumstances of modern life in Japan, which discourages elaborate ramifications of kinship and personalized bonds, the nature of common-interest associations offers a number of obvious advantages. Associations are malleable, adjusting to changing conditions with less difficulty than do kin groups. They may be formed, altered, or dissolved to meet changing circumstances, and their presence or absence affects or disrupts family and community membership in no important way. They may be regarded in one sense as a transitional social device, well suited to a rapidly changing society. Their growth has marked a transition from heavy Japanese reliance upon kinship and personal ties, and they themselves have served as one of the instruments of transition. The shift from former conditions that gave greater emphasis to kinship and social relations channeled through a hierarchical ordering of individual community members has not been socially disturbing because it represents a shift of emphasis rather than drastic innovation.

Part of the strength of the modern common-interest associations in rural Japan may arise from the lack of kin. Although still large in comparison with the urban family, the farming family of Japan has shrunk in size and continues to shrink. The rural community, economically based upon tiny farms that cannot support and, during most of the year, do not require a large labor force, generally has no place for any of the mature young males except eldest sons or such younger sons as may substitute for them. It has no place for adult females except those who marry stay-at-home males, and many women marry outside the *buraku* of their birth. It is, then, often difficult to maintain a substantial body of kin within one's own community or even within range close enough so that frequent contact may be maintained.

CROSS-CULTURAL COMPARISON

Research on common-interest associations has rarely been comprehensive or systematic for any nation. We have, however, a number of reports dealing with associations in the United States (see Gordon and Babchuk, 1959) and Great Britain (see Glass, 1954) and a growing number of pertinent writings on other foreign countries. Assuming that the foregoing interpretations of Japanese conditions are sound, let us compare the Japanese rural associations briefly with similar social groups among certain other nations of the world.

In the United States voluntary associations are primarily urban. We have been told in various ways that the lack of widely embracive kin ties, the impersonality of city life, and the waning influence of the church has led the people to turn to these associations to satisfy sociopsychological needs. At one time we were told that the United States was the land of "joiners," but sociological surveys seem to have revealed that membership in associations is confined mostly to the middle class and, although common enough, is not so prevalent as once thought. The American lower class is said to rely more heavily for these "needs" upon the family and kinship (Dotson, 1951; Freeman, Novak, and Reeder, 1957; Wright and Hyman, 1958).

Circumstances reported for England resemble those in the United States. Reports on France, however, differ somewhat, and differ from one another. Rose (1954, pp. 74–75) states that associations, especially those seeking to exert "social influence," are relatively rare, and he points to functional equivalents: the French family, trade unions, and the extensive use of parks and cafés for social interaction. Gallagher (1957) holds that associations are not rare in France and describes them as being mostly urban, connected with occupations, and found among the "rootless bourgeoisie *radicale*." He states further that the French government has repressed various kinds of associations. A study of rural Ukrainian immigrants to France (Anderson and Anderson, in press) describes a luxuriant growth of voluntary associations of all types and states that the social life of these people centers on them. We may note that this group of Ukrainian Frenchmen might also be called rootless, since its core is composed of nuclear families migrating from the Ukraine from 1921 to 1939, which, in their new environment, lack any substantial number of kin. Again the associations here may be classed as urban, since the community is composed of industrial workers living on the outskirts of Paris.

An account (Anderson and Anderson, 1959) of a suburb of Copenhagen reports the development of an abundance of voluntary associations since the end of the nineteenth century in connection with urbanization. In Italy, development of voluntary associations is described as poor, especially in southern Italy, where an ethos of "amoral familism" is said to inhibit them (Sillo, 1959, p. 19).

Writings on Negro Africa (e.g., Banton, 1957; Little, 1957) report the recent growth of voluntary associations among former tribesmen in various of the new industrial cities. Many, but not all, of these associations follow European models, and their growth is characteristically interpreted as resulting from urbanization. Little (1957, p. 594) states that two conditions are required for their growth in Africa: a socially heterogeneous, unstable urban population composed largely of immigrants and "adaptability of native institutions to urban conditions." (At least some development of comparable social groups is found in many of the tribal societies from which the modern Negro urban residents come.)

A brief account of voluntary associations in Guadalajara, Mexico, states that associations are poorly represented among the working class, where kin ties perform the functions filled in various other places by associations (Dotson, 1953). A similarly brief account on Korea discusses the past and present abundance of associations closely resembling those of pre-industrial Japan (Knez, 1961). I am aware of no other substantial accounts useful for comparison. (Considerable has been written, of course, on common-interest associations in primitive society and on commercial co-operatives in Europe and various former colonies of European nations.)

If we examine these various writings to see what they hold in common, two ideas appear prominently. One is that the associations serve as a substitute for or functional equivalent of kinship and other personalized ties under conditions that make social relations based upon these latter considerations inefficient, difficult, or impossible. The second commonly recurrent idea outlines the conditions; that is, the associations are said to be a phenomenon connected with urbanization.

Now let us examine the Japanese associations from these standpoints. An interpretation of the role of the Japanese groups as a partial substitute for kinship seems reasonable, and it is one that I have previously offered (Norbeck, 1961). This statement does not seem to imply that common-interest associations are everywhere necessarily or inevitably correlated with the weakening of kin ties. It seems, however, to be a pattern that many societies can and do easily take when the maintenance of close or ramified kin ties becomes difficult. Perhaps there is merit in the idea, expressed by myself and others (Norbeck, 1961; Anderson and Anderson, 1959; Little, 1957), that the blossoming of the associations has been greatest and fastest in industrialized societies that provide long-established models, such as age-graded groups, co-operative work groups associated with irrigation, and the like.

The theory that associations are products of urbanization and find their greatest development in the socially heterogeneous and depersonalized city does not seem at first glance to fit the Japanese scene. Unfortunately, quantitative data on the cities of Japan are not available, but it is my strong impression that common-interest associations find far greater development in its rural areas. This statement does not, however, necessarily indicate a lack of correlation between urbanization and common-interest associations in Japan. The question hinges on the definition of urbanization. Japan is certainly urbanized in at least the sense that it has become heavily industrialized and more and more of its population is concentrated in large cities. Japan's cities may also be described as socially heterogeneous and impersonal. In the rural world, a continuing process of amalgamation of formerly independent small communities into towns and cities has left only a relatively few politically independent small villages in all Japan. The rural *buraku*, although still physically isolated from neighboring communities, small and large, is in increasing contact with them. Many farming communities are now in fact administratively parts of cities, and their members participate more and more in urban affairs. The growth of the industrial city has had far-reaching effects. With each succeeding year, as techniques of agriculture, animal husbandry, and fishing have grown more efficient, the work of the farmer and fisherman has accordingly become more specialized. As a specialist, the rural resident may be regarded as a highly integrated part of a complex, co-operative national economic and political scheme. The term "peasant," with its connotations of emotional attachment to a fixed way of life, self-sufficiency, subsistence economy, and sharp segregation from other segments of the total society, no longer seems suitable for the Japanese farmer. It does not seem inappropriate to think that most of Japan has become urbanized.

We may note various other characteristics of the common-interest associations of rural Japan. Unlike circumstances in the United States and various countries of Europe, membership in Japan in the associations under discussion is, of course, linked almost entirely with what must be called the working class. Various reports on the United States and Europe hold that ties of kinship are the most intimate among members of the working class, those who least frequently join associations. Kinship surely remains important to the rural resident of Japan, more important than either "true" or ritual kinship in Japanese cities. As we have noted, however, common-interest associations appear to have their greatest development in the country, where the bonds of kinship are also the more pervasive. Japan, then, differs in this respect not only from Europe but also from Africa, where membership in associations is strong among urban workmen as a surrogate for kinship.

I wish to call attention again to the farmers' co-operative associations of Japan. No close counterpart appears to exist in other countries. As we have noted, the roles in community life of this association cover a very broad range and are extremely important to the welfare of the people. It is not surprising that this association shows a tendency to engulf other, sometimes much older, associations as auxiliaries. I noted this trend in several communities of Miyagi Prefecture in 1959 (Norbeck, 1961), and I have the impression that it is a national tendency wherever the farmers' co-operative is economically powerful (i.e., where farm lands are highly productive).

We may note also that there is virtually no development in rural Japan of associations attempting to exert "social influence" except those encouraged by the government. (The farmers' co-operatives may form something of an exception. Although such activities fall outside their stated and primary objectives, these powerful associations seem well suited for use in influencing opinion in political matters. The extent to which they actually engage in political activities is unclear and needs investigation.) Governmental control over associations during the third and fourth decades of this century and until the end of World War II was very strict. With the exception of suppression of Communist activities, however, present-day governmental policies do not appear actively to discourage the formation of associations aiming toward social change. Perhaps the shadow of the past continues to inhibit the independent emergence of associations with goals of social reform.

The study of common-interest associations in Japan has bearing upon another subject that has concerned social theorists. Since the seventeenth century, Western social philosophers have linked associations and the growth of democracy, holding that associations serve the important function of encouraging greater involvement of their members in the affairs of the general society. We have no convenient yardstick for judging quantitatively the democratization of rural Japan, but many observers in addition to myself have stated more or less impressionistically that familial and other social relations have become more democratic since World War II. It is certain that through the medium of the common-interest association participation in local community affairs is greater than in former times. Moreover, since many associations are subdivisions of national networks and are therefore linked to outside communities and the nation as a whole, the association has also brought about greater participation in the affairs of the total society. We may note also that members of the Japanese associations, as representatives of their households, ideally have equal voices in determining policy and deciding issues. But these circumstances do not necessarily imply democracy. Common-interest associations were well developed in Japan before and during its war years, a period that can hardly be looked upon as democratic. Certain of them at this time served in fact as important media for strict governmental control of the people, a function that they seem not to have served in most other nations. Perhaps in some measure they continue to serve in this capacity today in a less rigid fashion. Such diverse governmentally sponsored activities as instruction in contraception, education in the metrical system of weights and measures (adopted in 1959), and a movement to shorten the length of traditional festival seasons continue to flow from the government through various of the nationalized associations. The actual role in Japan of the common-interest associations as a democratizing force remains unclear, and thus far it has hardly received scholarly mention.

As these remarks indicate, much remains to be done before we can offer an assured interpretation or even an adequate description of common-interest associations in Japan. We need in particular information on circumstances in Japan's cities and, for both rural and urban areas, information on the internal organization of the associations, motives for participation in them, trends of change, and knowledge of their relationships to governmental bureaus, kin groups, fictive kin groups, and other segments of society, and to the society as a whole.

BIBLIOGRAPHY

ANDERSON, ROBERT T., and GALLATIN ANDERSON
1959 "Voluntary Associations and Urbanization, a Diachronic Analysis," *Amer. J. Soc.*, 65:265–73.
n.d. "Associations and Ukrainian Peasant-Urban Change." (In press.)

BANTON, MICHAEL
1957 *West African City*. London: Oxford University Press.

BARBER, BERNARD
1950 "Participation and Mass Apathy in Associations." In: ALVIN GOULDNER (ed.), *Studies in Leadership*. New York: Harper & Bros.

CHAPPLE, E. D., and C. S. COON
1942 *Principles of Anthropology*. New York: Henry Holt & Co.

CONSULATE GENERAL OF JAPAN
1961 *Japan Report*, 7:2–4. New York.

CORNELL, JOHN B.
1956 "Matsunagi, a Japanese Mountain Community." In: CORNELL, JOHN B., and ROBERT J. SMITH, *Two Japanese Villages*. (Center for Japanese Studies, University of Michigan, Occasional Papers, No. 5.) Ann Arbor, Mich.

DOTSON, FLOYD
1951 "Patterns of Voluntary Association among Urban Working Class Families," *Am. Soc. Rev.*, 16:687–93.
1953 "A Note on Participation in Voluntary Associations in a Mexican City," *ibid.*, 18:380–86.

FREEMAN, HOWARD, EDWIN NOVAK, and LEO G. REEDER
1957 "Correlates of Membership in Voluntary Associations," *Amer. Soc. Rev.*, 22: 528–33.

GALLAGHER, ORVOELL R.
1957 "Voluntary Associations in France," *Social Forces*, 35:153–60.

GLASS, D. V. (ed.)
1954 *Social Mobility in Britain*. Glencoe, Ill.: Free Press.

GORDON, C. W., and N. BABCHUK
1959 "A Typology of Voluntary Associations," *Amer. Soc. Rev.*, 24:22–29.

HOYNDEN, YOSHIO
1958 *Cooperative Movement in Japan*, Vol. I, ed. ASIA KYOKAI. Tokyo: Maruzen Co.
1960 *Agricultural and Fishery Cooperative in Japan* (*Cooperative Movement in Japan*, Vol. II). Tokyo: Azuma Shobo Co.

KNEZ, EUGENE I.
1961 "Ke Mutual Aid Groups: Persistence and Change," *Korean Report*, 1:17–20.

KONNO, MARUSUKE
1939 "Wakamono-gumi, Musume-gumi" (Youth Associations, Girls' Associations). In: KUNIO YANAGITA (ed.), *Kaison seikatsu no kenkyū* (Studies of Life in Fishing Villages). Tokyo: Nihon Minzokugakkai.

LITTLE, KENNETH
1957 "The Role of Voluntary Associations in West African Urbanization," *Amer. Anthrop.*, 59:579–96.

LOWIE, ROBERT H.
1948 *Social Organization*. New York: Rinehart & Co.
NORBECK, EDWARD
1953 "Age-Grading in Japan," *Amer. Anthrop.*, 55:373–84.
1961 "Postwar Cultural Change and Continuity in Northeastern Japan," *ibid.*, 63:297–321.
OKADA, YUZURU
1952 "Kinship Organization in Japan," *J. Ed. Psych.*, 26:27–31.
ROSE, ARNOLD M.
1954 *Theory and Method in the Social Sciences*. Minneapolis: University of Minnesota Press.
SEGAWA, KIYOKO
1947 "Dōrei Shūzoku ni tsuite," *Minzokugaku Kenkyū* (Japanese J. Ethnol.), 12:46–51.
SILLS, DAVID L.
1959 "Voluntary Associations: Instruments and Objects of Change," *Human Organization*, 18:17–21.
SMITH, THOMAS C.
1959 *The Agrarian Origins of Modern Japan*. Stanford: Stanford University Press.
WRIGHT, C. R., and H. H. HYMAN
1958 "Voluntary Association Membership of American Adults: Evidence from National Sample Surveys," *Amer. Soc. Rev.*, 23:284–94.

VILLAGE COMMUNITY (*BURAKU*) IN JAPAN AND ITS DEMOCRATIZATION

TADASHI FUKUTAKE

I

THE small village community commonly called "*buraku*" still remains the most important community for Japanese peasants. And we may say that the pattern or norm of life in the *buraku* lies at the root of Japanese social structure.

Most *buraku* at present are no longer purely agricultural—many households are only part-time cultivators and a considerable number are non-agricultural.

Owing to this growing heterogeneity, mechanisms for self-government in the *buraku* are changing gradually. For example, methods of rationalizing the imposition of *buraku*-tax are developing. In a considerable number of *buraku*, the levy for field and water management has been separated from the *buraku*-tax itself, and is imposed upon the beneficiaries according to acreage by the agricultural co-operative group. In view of the growing difficulty of enforcing communal labor, money collected on an acreage basis has been used for entertainment, to reward communal participants for their services, and a growing number of *buraku* actually pay a stipulated per diem allotment to participants in communal work. In many villages on the urban fringe, immigration is contributing to heterogeneity, and the differentiation of peasants from newcomers has become so sharp in some villages that the agricultural co-operative group has split away from the administrative system of the *buraku* as a local community.

Notwithstanding that growing heterogeneity and divergence of class interests have sharpened the conflict among villagers, the *buraku* still continues to exist as a self-governing body and performs a variety of undifferentiated functions. As functionally specific and presumably voluntary groups have appeared within the *buraku*, every resident has usually been pressed into participating willy-nilly in each group. In this respect part-time peasants and non-agricultural villagers are no more emancipated from community control than are the purely agricultural peasants. The villagers have not yet mastered democratic principles and are still unable to weigh their particular duties and rights and to respect each other as equally independent individuals. Nor does it mend matters when the *buraku* is delegated tasks but no authority from the local administrative entity (the *chō* or *son*) above it, on account of the financial poverty of this entity. The *buraku* can expect no financial aid from the local administrative office (*chō-yakuba* or *son-yakuba*), unless it acts as the proxy of that office.

A vicious circle makes the link between the *buraku* and the local administrative entity unhealthy. *Buraku* life is likely to be hampered unless its interests are strongly and unanimously voiced. Petitions, thus, are used in the normal course of local politics in the same pattern as that seen in national politics. Consequently, the *buraku* selects persons well experienced in petitioning as its representatives, and they become the rulers of the *buraku* as local *yūryokusha*. A pertinent consequence of amalgamation of villages and town recently enforced by the central government and the prefectural government was to make the administration of the newly established local entity more bureaucratic and to increase the social distance between it and the villagers. Petitions supported by strong pressure became indispensable in getting grants of financial aid. Thus it has become vital for the *buraku* to act politically as a whole, since, as a rule, no alternative groups exist.

This leads to stronger *buraku* esprit in voting to elect assemblymen (*chōkai-giin* or *sonkai-giin*). The elected assemblymen acquire boss-like influence as spokesmen for the *buraku*'s interests, on the one hand, and personal connections with prefectural assemblymen and Dietmen, on the other hand. In every election, therefore, the interest of the *buraku* overrides other interests. For example, even in electing Diet members, villagers support a particular candidate in terms of advantages to their village. The undemocratic character of Japanese politics is linked to that of *buraku*—or, each depends on the other.

II

Thus, it is clear that the *buraku* is not yet a democratic local community formed by voluntary relationships among free inhabitants. The rights of villagers are not satisfactorily protected, nor are their opinions fully respected. The interest of the *buraku* as an undifferentiated entity is given the highest value of all. If anyone opposes the interest of the *buraku* (which usually means the interest of the more well-off peasants), he is censured and viewed as a heretic upsetting the unity of the *buraku*. This notion of the "peace and unity of the *buraku*" overrides every conflict of interest among different classes or occupational groups and deters the open play of such conflicts.

Accordingly, to democratize the *buraku*, measures are needed to nullify the slogan of "peace and unity of the *buraku*." In other words, it is necessary to transform the *buraku* from a traditional folk community into a functional local unit and to differentiate the accumulated functions of the *buraku*, assigning them to appropriate functionally specific groups. Of course, there are various kinds of functional groups inside the *buraku* that certainly have gained a degree of independence, but many are still adjuncts of the *buraku* and subordinated to it. Under the present situation, it is difficult to form such genuinely functional groups because they are contradictory to the character of the traditional "village community" and cannot persist even when formed. But these are circumstances that must be changed.

Such functional groups include the agricultural co-operative (*nojijikkō-kumiai*), the irrigation co-operative (*suiri-kumiai*), the fire brigade (*keibō-dan*), the women's association (*fujin-kai*), and the youth association (*seinen-dan*). When they come to be organized as genuinely voluntary groups, the *buraku* itself will become merely a social unit serving certain indispensable functions for the locality and, at the same time, be a territorial subunit established for administrative convenience. In such circumstances, its officials should be elected by the vote of all qualified adults of the *buraku* and should be appropriately paid for their services. The present allowance given to the *buraku* head for his work is likely not to be enough to buy a pack of cigarettes, and his election is sometimes considered a misfortune by other members of his family. On the other hand, the villagers hesitate to criticize him because he sacrifices his own affairs to work for the village. This is indeed far from democracy. However, this problem can be cured by stripping away duties that are not inherent to the *buraku*. The resultant shrinkage of *buraku* affairs will permit fair compensation of the officers. Moreover, *buraku*-tax will be collected at a lower rate and imposed for clear purposes. Villagers will become aware of functions delegated to the *buraku* by the local administrative office, consider these functions and the double burden of tax a problem, and question this problem.

Functional groups, instead of including every member of the village, irrespective of his interests, should exist as the will of villagers, who participate in them expressly to realize the group purpose, once they are dissociated and made independent from the *buraku* mechanism. Members should select as leader a person who democratically represents the members. These groups can be democratized by simplifying them down to their pure functions and severing all hints of *buraku* control. Moreover, their expenses can be shared rationally by participants because their purpose is clear. Thus will be avoided the vagueness now characterizing the *en bloc* imposition of village expenses and the unfair burden created by collecting them equally from all residents.

When functionally specific groups are thus differentiated, the mechanism by which *buraku yūryokusha* have spread their control over villagers and forced them into subordination to the *buraku* will not be warranted. For the villagers will not be totally absorbed within the *buraku*. They will require scope to assert and realize their interests independently through their functional groups. Response to local administrative organs will shift away from unanimous petition, presented by village units, and toward rational demands made by functional groups in co-operation with parallel groups elsewhere without regard to *buraku* boundaries. This step will naturally dissolve the *buraku* mechanism, which not only had hidden conflicts of interest within it but has preserved irrationality of policies and administration on the part of local self-government. Since the several interests of the villagers will be differentiated from those of the *buraku* as a whole and class and occupational interests will emerge into the open, local policy and administration will have to be executed rationally by balancing the new demands of the diverse functional groups.

Thus, *buraku* parochialism (*buraku-konjō*) will wither and healthier relations will link the *buraku* to its local administrative entity. Villagers heretofore interested in local government's fiscal problems only to the extent of getting grants for public works in their own *buraku* will lift their sights and give over-all scrutiny to local government finances. The assemblymen of local governmental entities also will tend to be the representatives of class, occupation, or generation interests rather than of the parochial and narrow interest of their respective *buraku*. They will no longer be able to fall back on the vague phrase "in the *buraku* interest," as a slogan, and they will lose the opportunity to become bosses through granting their *buraku* special privileges and favors at the expense of another. Villagers will be liberated from traditional community control and able to select their representatives democratically in the light of their unfettered individual interests. This is democratization within the *buraku*, which in turn will lead to reform in the corrupt election of Diet members.

Such transformation seems, indeed, to be difficult but not impossible. In *buraku* that include many non-agricultural households, certain functional groups, such as a salaried man's league or an agricultural study group, are beginning to be differentiated from the general *buraku* structure. Moreover, in recently amalgamated towns and villages candidates for the assembly can rarely win elections if supported by votes from only one *buraku*. These developments open the possibility of replacing the *buraku* interests with supra-*buraku* occupational and class interests. The contrary possibility, previously discussed, that *buraku* localism will merely be reinforced in newly amalgamated communities is a real and present danger. Its solution must be sought within the *buraku* and will come about if and when villagers find avenues for democratizing it.

III

These avenues favor non-agricultural residents, who, until now, have been slighted in favor of peasant interests, especially those of the upper-class peasants. Lower-class peasants, also, will be freed of the unreasonable burden they have been carrying for small benefit. Moreover, these trends will bring advantage even to upper-class peasants who are now hampered in any free and progressive co-operative relation because they, too, are now bound to the communal group that must embrace all villagers alike.

Japanese agriculture in the future will require new forms of co-operation. This co-operation will not cover the full-time peasants, or the large-scale to petty peasants. The new modes must come into being rationally and voluntarily on the basis of common interest. This is forestalled by the principle of communal grouping in the *buraku*. Petty peasants must have their burden lightened to a fair share. Upper-class peasants should promote co-operation among peasants sufficiently near their own status to co-operate without difficulty. Petty peasants who have supplemental jobs should foster co-operation among themselves, meanwhile pressing for rationalization in the rates of local tax and *buraku*-tax. To be sure, as such rational groups form, the accent will fall on class differentiation according to acreage. Better to have this brought into the open, however, than—as now—to submerge conflicts of interest by throwing upper and lower together into one mass. This does not mean that petty peasants, the forgotten men of national agricultural policy, can be cast aside; it means that petty peasants may better be shifted to other industries by rationalizing agricultural enterprises, while, at the same time, a demand for social security is aroused by making clear the inequities among economic classes.

While this liberation from bondage to traditional communalism is in progress, villagers will sense that they are more than just members of a mere locality. Becoming more sensitive to the interest of their own class and occupation, they will not regard *buraku* solidarity as a paramount principle. They will feel it undemocratic to suppress their personal interests under the call for "peace and unity within the *buraku*." When villagers realize that voluntary co-operation among free individuals is the only way to liberate themselves, they will learn to democratize their own local meetings and affairs. Villagers have been masquerading, swayed by a sense of duty and by overly tender regard for each other's feelings. For, at the same time, they have been jealous and competitive; there has been self-seeking under the guise of *buraku* harmony. However, this egoism should be transformed into individualism in its true sense, and rational co-operation must commence in order to develop individualism. Out of such co-operation a new type of man will be born who will cherish his own right and value his own opinion but, at the same time, observe the rights and respect the opinions of others.

It might be noted that the problems discussed above are also found in the centers of cities, since the *buraku* as a social phenomenon exists not only in the countryside but also in the cities. Liberation from communalism is the problem not only of rural society but of all Japan. Hence, it is important to analyze the social character of the *buraku*, the prototype of Japanese society, and then to consider how to achieve liberation from it.

THE EMERGENCE OF A SELF-CONSCIOUS ENTREPRENEURIAL CLASS IN RURAL JAPAN*

ERWIN H. JOHNSON

A SUBSTANTIAL part of the literature in the social sciences dealing with individual motivation and social change has concentrated on the functional relationship between ethical systems and economic change. The directions indicated in the major works of Max Weber (1930, 1951, 1952) have been built upon and developed by others, primarily under the stimulation of Talcott Parsons, to a point where they present a formidable body of theoretical and substantive material. The positive stimulus of a new ethical system in encouraging economic rationalization in the face of traditional values is featured in these works. Robert Bellah has adopted this framework and applied it to Japan, showing in the Shingaku movement in Buddhism a functional equivalent to Protestantism in western Europe (Bellah, 1957). Both Parsons and Bellah, following Weber, appear to view the change in ethics as a prior requisite and as a positive motivation to economic change. In reading these analyses, one cannot escape the feeling that a new spirit spreading among the people of a nation jars them from their traditional ways and moves them to take an active role in the newly developing economic system.

The analysis that follows will take a new tack. Assuming that economic change is a continuing process that needs an adjustment in its sanction system more or less continuously, it will attempt to show that, in the case of Japan, personnel capable of occupying newly developing status positions are regularly available, not for specific slots requiring specific orientations, but for any new positions, so long as these do not conflict with specific cultural taboos.

Specifically, we will deal with the stem-family as the primary structure that transmits cultural values and the way in which it produces first sons thoroughly committed to traditional values as well as second and succeeding sons who may remain flexible in their commitment to at least some of these values. Material on differential socialization in the Japanese family is extensive. Unfortunately, the effect of this differential treatment on the younger sons is not well described. The eldest son is singled out as the heir to the headship of the house. He is re-

---

* Field work on which this paper is partially based was carried out from 1956 to 1958, with the support of the Social Science Research Council. The National Institute of Mental Health has also provided financial support for this project. The views here are those of the author, however, and neither supporting agency is in any way responsible for them.

ferred to as the *chōnan* (principal son) and distinguished from the succeeding ones, the *jisannan* (literally second and third sons, but actually referring to the category "all but the eldest son"). As the heir apparent, the *chōnan* receives special treatment because he is the one who will remain in the household and also simply because he is the eldest of the brothers. The succeeding sons are distinguished by birth order, and their respective ages will affect the way in which they are treated, but the distinction among them is much less than that between the eldest and the rest. There is, then, in the structure of the family itself, a mechanism for producing heterogeneous attitudes in each generation. This heterogeneity may involve only the immediacy of the values learned—for example, the eldest son knows he must fit into the same community as his father; he knows his future peers in the present and can apply any learning to a real, not merely a possible, situation, whereas the younger sons, not knowing their future, cannot. For as long as the special position of the *chōnan* existed, we assume there was some regular heterogeneity in family socialization.[1]

We are not suggesting that this family structure is the source of cultural or social change but only that it provides the source material for this change. This important element, however, should not be overlooked. In the specific matter dealt with here there is a closer relationship between the family structure and the change analyzed. We suggest that the socialization of the *jisannan* in rural Japan today produces, in a number of individuals, an orientation toward achievement and self-sufficiency that can be and is quickly converted into an entrepreneurial attitude, which, if local conditions permit, finds roots in the local community and provides a locally derived entrepreneurial class.

The essence of the term "entrepreneur," we believe, lies in the use of risk capital, in producing, buying, selling, or moving products in order to maximize income. A self-motivated entrepreneurial class is said to be missing in many societies presently classified as underdeveloped, and it is such a class that looks to the stability and economic prosperity of the nation for a better future for itself. The entrepreneur, or enterpriser, is almost by definition an ambitious man. It is this ambition which generally distinguishes him from his agricultural counterpart in a traditional society. This distinction between traditional and conservative, on the one hand, and enterpriser and progressive, on the other, seems to correspond generally with such sociological dichotomies as *gemeinschaft* and *gesellschaft*, sacred and secular, folk and urban, etc. Our material on Japan suggests that both the conservative agricultural elements and the rural entrepreneurial elements derive from a common base. If this is true, it is unnecessary to rely completely on a dichotomy concept and the influence of an urban subculture on a rural one to explain the origin of a rural entrepreneurial class.

---

1. James Abegglen (1957) has also suggested this flexibility or "psychological preparedness" of the *jisannan* to account for the less traditional orientation of these younger sons from rural backgrounds employed in the city, when compared with urban-reared fellow workers. Norman Jacobs (1958, p. 155) recognizes the differential inheritance implicit in primogeniture and a feature undermining the orderly operation of feudalism.

We are at a disadvantage as far as the Japanese material is concerned, since most of the studies on rural Japan have been studies of *buraku* or *sonraku* or *shūraku* units, that is, of hamlets. These studies have focused on older, self-sufficient communities. The community of the past has clearly expanded in scope beyond the hamlet as the money economy has penetrated the rural areas (Johnson, 1961). Nowadays, few hamlets provide the full round of goods and services for their constituent households, or even approach it, unless they themselves are shopping centers for a larger area. If the latter is the case, then the shopping hamlet lacks the primary production area of the full community (see Arensberg, 1954). One community study that did use the modern *mura* as a unit was Embree's study of Suye (1939).

Embree noted different attitudes for the shopkeeper *buraku* and the regular farming *buraku* of Suye. He noted the extra-*mura* origins of most of the merchants and artisans in the shopkeeper *buraku* and, at least by implication, saw two patterns of behavior. The first, of which he approved, was the local, conservative, agricultural pattern. The second, of which he spoke less favorably, was that of the townsmen—frivolous, argumentative, free spending, and generally originating outside the local setting. The shopkeeper *buraku*, to Embree, was not the real Suye *mura*.

A case quite contrary to that of Suye, however, is Nagura *mura* in Aichi Prefecture. Nagura is situated in a mountain basin with a single road connecting it to towns on either side. This gives a certain degree of self-containment to the village and allows us to see features of social structure in a more concise microcosm than would be possible in a plains village. It is doubtful, however, that the general origin of Nagura's entrepreneurial group differs in kind from that of any other relatively closed rural area in Japan.

The growth of this group in Nagura seems important enough in this discussion to warrant presentation in some detail. At the beginning of the Meiji period, Nagura was producing no notable cash surplus. Horse-breeding supplemented the grain produce of the village, but the lack of adequate transport for the mountain paths made commercial lumber production unfeasible. Records of this period are not complete, but those which are available indicate that, while a few specialists were present, agriculture was the dominant industry in all the fifteen *buraku* in the basin. These were small *buraku* ranging in size from 7 to 46 houses and from 49 to 199 persons. In the census of 1874, 10 numbered less than 100 persons and only one *buraku* numbered more than 20 houses (Miyamoto, 1957, pp. 18–19).

One *buraku*, Ōdaira, was later to develop into a specialized shopkeeper area, but in 1874 it had only 17 houses and 100 persons. Several of the older houses in this *buraku* have *yago* ("house names") indicating that they were in trade then: Kyūzakaya ("sake brewer"), Kōya ("dyer"), etc. The settlement pattern for this *buraku* in early Meiji was typical of the region. Paddy fields were in the level area of the basin, houses were on foundations leveled out in the side of the lower reaches of the mountains, and dry fields surrounded the houses on relatively steep slopes. Each house had a bamboo grove nearby. The land above the houses was devoted to forests, which provided the raw building materials for the village and the grass for agriculture and horse breeding. In the course of nearly one hundred years, this pattern has changed substantially, while most of the other *buraku* have retained the general pattern of the earlier period.

Ōdaira has shown a regular and spectacular growth from this early time to the present. In the 1880's a prefectural road was built through the level farmlands of the basin, replacing an earlier path that had gone along the mountain above the houses. As new houses were built, they were located along this road, and even some of the older houses were moved down to the road. With the gradual development of supplementary money products made possible by the good road, retail establishments were begun in the village. These new establishments were located along this road convenient to transportation.

From 18 houses in early Meiji, Ōdaira had grown to where, in 1956, it contained 88 houses. During this time other *buraku* showed only modest gains in population. Only a small fraction of these houses are primarily agricultural. Shops and businesses dominate the *buraku*.

While one could hardly call Ōdaira a thriving town center, it does have many attributes of a *machi* ("town"). Its residents show characteristics attributed to *chōnin* ("townsmen," but also merchants and artisans in a town of the Edo period) or the *shōbainin* ("tradesmen") of the present. Another feature emphasizing the town-like nature of Ōdaira is the presence of virtually all the *mura* administrative and service organizations. Here are found the village office, the agricultural co-operative, the lower and middle schools, the town meeting hall, with its telephone switchboard, and the single policeman assigned to Nagura.

Ōdaira does not contain all the entrepreneurial activities of Nagura. It exemplifies, however, the total development of the twentieth-century village. Only Ōdaira exhibits a predominance of non-agricultural families. The sense, the feeling, of Ōdaira differs from other *buraku*. The adults are not shy with strangers. They feel free to speak of money in the presence of others. They make money, and they spend it freely. Being in business, they are willing, actually anxious, to expand their income base through new work, new products, and new techniques.

They are not, however, interested in living in a fashion that would notably distinguish them from the rest of the village. They dress in a manner similar to that of the farmers, their children play with the farm children, their shops are neither better looking nor poorer looking than the farm houses, and their living quarters are virtually identical with those of their farming neighbors. We find, in effect, an interesting blend of traditional and non-traditional features. Attitudes break with tradition on matters concerning business, but this change does not appear to flow into other aspects of life.

Nagura differs from many other communities in that it has both the primary production in agriculture and forestry and the basic services and processing activities in a single *mura*. The geography of the region, the fact that Nagura is situated in a mountain basin, contributes to this self-contained character. This only means, however, that we can see the primary aspects of the economy as well as the secondary and tertiary ones clearly. In a region where there is a functional division between completely agricultural *buraku* and completely industrial *machi* ("town"), researchers have not, in general, gone to the trouble of identifying the origins of the families involved in non-agricultural activities. We doubt that the situation in the plains differs, in kind, from the situation in this mountain village. The plains geography has simply led to a more dispersed settlement pattern for what probably should be identified as a large regional community.

In Nagura similarities between the specialists and the shopkeepers, on the one hand, and the traditional agriculturalists, on the other, are great. We find a reason for this similarity merely by examining the genealogies. The residents of Ōdaira are, on the whole, branch families of houses both from Ōdaira and from the other *buraku* in the village. Their origins lie in the fact that only one child may succeed to the family land. The basic family unit in Japan is the *ie*, the stem-family plus persons born into the family who may reside elsewhere but who have an emotional tie with the homestead and who frequently retain financial ties with it. This stem-family has, for centuries, given a stability and continuity to the rural *buraku* of Japan. A single heir in each generation assured that land would not be subdivided through succession to a point where, even if population remained relatively stable, the plots of land would become increasingly numerous and correspondingly small. The Japanese inheritance rule has also guarded the country from excessive concentration of persons on each holding. It has done this by assuring that children, in excess of a single heir, must leave the homestead and take care of themselves when family resources are inadequate for land subdivision. Thus, the Japanese have avoided the pitfalls of the Chinese extended family system, in which the inheritance of property made no such provision.

While the stem-family provides for a basic agricultural stability, a stability on which the development of a modern industrial nation depended, it also supplied a certain number of individuals, the second and third sons, who were available for new occupations.

The support between those members of the *ie* who left home and those who remained was reciprocal. The absent worker received financial support from the farm family while he made his way in the city. He could also receive aid in the form of food. If he was out of work, he was welcomed, or at least accepted, back in his home in the village until he could find work again. If he was able, the absent worker contributed money to the homestead. A major category of Japanese workers—in the past—worked for room and board away from home and wages were paid to their family. This system of labor is called *"dekasegi"* and has been extensively commented on as an important aspect of the Japanese industrial system (e.g., Abegglen, 1958; Nakamura, 1957). This system aided capital formation in industry and served as a money source for the rural areas. This money was converted, as purchasing power, into agricultural improvement as well as into consumer goods. One result of this gradual capital accumulation was the development of an entrepreneurial and service group exemplified in Ōdaira *buraku*.

It must be emphasized that the entrepreneurial and merchant group in Ōdaira is not an export from a nearby urban center. The Nagura businessmen are Nagura born and raised. Nevertheless, they show a basic business orientation quite similar to their urban counterparts. Entrepreneurship on the local level, however, presents an interesting pattern. Agricultural work is primarily a family affair, and when additional labor is necessary it is drawn from among the kindred or from among *buraku* neighbors. If possible, labor reciprocity is the preferred form. The house requiring labor is expected to return this labor sometime in the future. Some large farms cannot reciprocate and thus pay for their labor. This is acceptable in the village, but it is not looked upon as desirable. An egalitarian theme permeates the agricultural side of the village, and reciprocity in kind is the normal pattern. Even when outside labor is hired, the farm owner and his family are expected to work side by side with the other hands.

In contrast, in the lumber industry, which now rivals agriculture in economic value, the saw mill operators hire non-kin as well as kin and hire from the entire basin without thought to *buraku* membership. If they tend to hire from certain *buraku*, this reflects only the presence in these *buraku* of many available mill hands. This same break with the traditional agricultural pattern of work and labor is followed in all aspects of the lumber industry.

The group of entrepreneurs, mill owners, truckers, brokers, etc., form what might be called an incipient class within the village. While their land holdings are usually not as large as those of the richer farmers and mountain landowners, their income, on an annual basis, ranges higher than that of the landowners. In Nagura reforestation is old, and most land is in its optimum use as timber land. Thus, the potential for a landowner to increase his land base is severely limited. Farmland, too, is at about maximum acreage. Per acre productivity may be increased, but there is little land that can now be converted from mountain use to dry fields or from dry fields to paddy land.

Thus, it is relatively impossible to increase the income base of the village through investment in land holdings, and it is virtually impossible for an individual family to increase his land holdings, except through some relatively rare misfortune to a present-day farmer. The only possible increase in income base is in the expansion of business. This expansion has not led in any way to serious breakdown of traditional forms of organization in traditional activities.

The prominent businessmen still show maximum deference, in agricultural activities, to local custom. They have, however, through their business activities outside agriculture, moved into an area of national life, which is unusual for the village. They may aspire to political office in something other than their home town or region. Generally, this will be no more than prefectural office, but this is a giant step from what they might have aspired to in earlier periods when, because of their peasant background, their opportunities outside the village were limited. Their business activities bring them into contact with persons outside the village. They are not usually in a position economically subservient to these outsiders, since even the small-scale businessmen are generally able to complete their local end of the work without paying until they themselves are paid. Thus, they have economic connections with the city market and, at the same time, both economic and social connections with the local *buraku*.

Since the future of the business group depends on the increase of the village's money base, the group tends to support local measures favorable to the lumber industry even if they are not immediately involved. This puts them in some conflict with the traditional farmers who are less favorable to political measures that aid forestry at the expense of agriculture. This conflict is clearest in the activities of the village in requesting and planning new roadways. The farmers wish to see their field roads improved so that power equipment can be used more conveniently. The businessmen wish to see more timber roads cut back into the mountains. The business group can convince the prefectural office that the latter alternative is more advantageous to the prefecture since it increases the industrial potential and the tax base for the area.

Since there is a real gain possible in controlling local institutions, the activities of the business group have shifted into the local political as well as economic arenas. A large mill owner, by Nagura's standards, is the chairman of the town council (*sonkaigiinchō*) and numbers among his close friends the office manager of the town office and several other influential villagers. A broker who owes much to this man was recently elected to the town council, and several others of comparable persuasion are on this council. Before his untimely death, the recent mayor of the village was also a member of this group.

Regardless of a man's power in or through his business, his activities on the *buraku* level are cautious. His position in non-traditional aspects of life in the village is not allowed, in this egalitarian hamlet structure, to carry over into *buraku* affairs.

Unlike the urban elite, these men must participate in the local social groupings. While they themselves are surviving on a money income, they must still participate in the *kyodōtai* co-operative groups of their own *buraku*. To isolate themselves from their neighbors would be economic suicide. Not only would they cut off their income source, but they would run the risk of at least partial ostracism. Since the local communities have not shifted to a cash and tax set of relationships in such important aspects as fire fighting and since cemeteries are community, not commercial, property, they would lose these services —or could—if they ignored these local traditions. There are other important mutual-aid services provided by the *buraku* such that even the successful businessman would be in difficulty were he denied them.

These businessmen, born of local families, seem quite capable of acting as intermediaries between modern business practices and traditional social organization. It is doubtful that someone raised outside the area could fit as neatly into the village, as it is now constituted, as these second and third sons.

Since one of the important roles of the conference for which this paper was prepared is to suggest important areas for future research, I should like to take this opportunity to offer a hypothesis that is verified in the Nagura material and that I believe will be substantially verified in other and later studies. In the Japanese stem-family system the eldest son is selected to replace the father in the local society. Second and subsequent sons know, from early childhood, that they will not be in a position to carry on in their father's footsteps. The fashion in which these locally born second and third sons carry on their entrepreneurial activities with rather amazing efficiency, without being raised in an urban subculture that emphasizes these new values, indicates that something in the socialization process of the Japanese stem-family is favorable to at least a flexible attitude on the part of second and third sons. In a number of cases second sons have returned to the village after the premature death of an older son. In a surprisingly large portion of the cases, these second sons have not contented themselves with simply carrying on in their fathers' footsteps. They have, rather, attempted to expand the family income base to include some sort of enterprise in addition to the farm. This suggests that it may not be necessary to look to some sort of subcultural variation, urban or secular or *gesellschaftlich*, to explain the values that are exemplified in this rural business but rather to see them as at least potentially present as a result of differential socialization within the same family.

In summary then, certain tentative conclusions can be drawn. The first is that a middle-class or entrepreneurial orientation seems possible in a village that is still predominantly traditional and conservative. This orientation does not require immigration from towns or cities. The stem-family seems admirably suited to provide flexibility in attitudes among second and third sons. Second, when the land resources of the community have been fully utilized and other use of time and capital developed, these new orientations seem to emerge *in situ* so long as the local social structure is not actually prohibitive. Finally, since both ways of life seem to exist compatibly, side by side, there would seem to be no need for the traditional subculture to disappear. The values of this subculture can be respected even by the businessman who does not basically conform to them in the business areas of village life. Thus, the local businessman, born and bred in the village, is still a villager, even though he has expanded the scope of his interests well beyond traditional village life.

BIBLIOGRAPHY

ABEGGLEN, JAMES C.
1957 "Subordination and Autonomy Attitudes of Japanese Workers," *Amer. J. Soc.*, 63:181–89.
1958 *The Japanese Factory: Aspects of Its Social Organization.* Glencoe, Ill.: Free Press.

ARENSBERG, CONRAD
1954 "The Community Study Method," *Amer. J. Soc.*, 60:109–24.
BELLAH, ROBERT N.
1957 *Tokugawa Religion: The Values of Pre-industrial Japan.* Glencoe, Ill.: Free Press.
EMBREE, JOHN F.
1939 *Suye Mura: A Japanese Village.* Chicago: University of Chicago Press.
JACOBS, NORMAN
1958 *The Origin of Modern Capitalism in Eastern Asia.* Hong Kong: Hong Kong University Press.
JOHNSON, ERWIN H.
1961 *Nagura Mura: An Historical Analysis of Persistence and Change in Community Structure.* Ann Arbor: University of Michigan Microfilms.
MIYAMOTO TSUNEICHI
1957 "Ringyō kinyū kōsō chōsa hōkoku" ("Report on Research in Monetary Planning in Forestry"). Tokyo. (Mimeographed.)
NAKAMURA KICHIJI
1957 *Nihon shakai-shi* ("Social History of Japan"). Tokyo: Yūhikaku.
WEBER, MAX
1930 *The Protestant Ethic and the Spirit of Capitalism.* Trans. TALCOTT PARSONS. London: Allen & Unwin.
1951 *The Religion of China.* Trans. and ed. H. H. GERTH. Glencoe, Ill.: Free Press.
1952 *Ancient Judaism.* Trans. and ed. H. H. GERTH and D. MARTINDALE. Glencoe, Ill.: Free Press.

SOCIAL AND TECHNOLOGICAL CHANGE IN RURAL JAPAN: CONTINUITIES AND DISCONTINUITIES*

IWAO ISHINO

IN WRITING this paper, I found most difficult the matter of establishing the proper frame of reference for evaluating the change that has taken place in the Japanese farming communities. Writing in 1959, Thomas C. Smith (1959, p. lx) states that there has been very little change in Japanese agriculture:

> In the course of its long history, Japanese agriculture has in some respects changed remarkably little. Farming is scarcely less a family enterprise now than it was a thousand years ago; holdings are still tiny and fragmented, tools simple, and rice the main crop. Although a Heian peasant would no doubt be perplexed by many things about contemporary farming . . . the main operations of planting, tilling, and harvesting he would understand.

Somewhat the same general point has been made by a geographer, Peter Gosling, who is a specialist on rice cultivation in Southeast Asia. He maintains that contemporary Japanese agriculture is basically no different from that found in China two thousand years ago. The machines, chemical fertilizers, and metal tools used today are mere extensions of the farming principles established centuries ago and involve no departure from the fundamental pattern of rice cultivation found throughout Southeast Asia.

On the other hand, most sociologists and anthropologists doing research in contemporary rural Japan have emphasized the progress and change that have taken place, especially in the postwar years. Changes in tenancy patterns, in mechanization, in farm technology, in family relationships, in neighborhood co-operative efforts, and in living standards are only a few of the aspects of the contemporary rural scene that have been researched and duly described.

Obviously, then, the writers who claim that little or no basic change has taken place and those who claim that much change has taken place hold different frames of reference for evaluating change. One way to resolve this is to obtain agreement on the appropriate base line from which to measure change. I wish to return to this discussion of selecting the base line for change after a brief summary of the investigation that John Donoghue and I conducted in 1958 and 1959.

---

* The author gratefully acknowledges the critical reading given his paper and the improvements made in it by Robert J. Smith. He also wishes to acknowledge the partial support provided by a grant from the Office of International Programs, Michigan State University.

When we began this field investigation, we were not concerned with the question of establishing a proper base line for studying change. We assumed a more or less common-sense basis. There was available the rather detailed body of data collected by the members of the Public Opinion and Sociological Research Division ten years earlier during the Occupation of Japan. Our aim was to revisit the same villages and to cover the same general topics investigated by them. The general objective of the original survey was to measure the human consequences of the land-reform program that was in the process of being completed. While Donoghue and I did not conduct an attitude survey, as was done in the first study, we interviewed many of the same village leaders who participated in the first survey. We also discussed our findings with some of the Japanese ethnologists who participated in the first research operation.

We had to schedule our visits to the villages as they conformed to the vacation periods in the academic year. This meant that we could not spend any extensive period in the field—our visits to each of the original twelve communities varied from two days to four days. But most of the ethnographic details that we required had been obtained by the first survey. Our task was made easier in that we concentrated on the change features.

To get some depth in our research materials, we selected three communities for more intensive study. Fifteen students in cultural anthropology at the University of Tokyo assisted in this phase. They were divided into three teams and spent two weeks during the spring vacation in three different communities selected for more intensive investigation. I took a team to Yoshida-mura, a mountain community in Shimane Prefecture, Professor Seiichi Izumi led a team to Nikaido-mura in Nara prefecture, and Donoghue a team to Aioi-mura in Kagawa Prefecture on the island of Shikoku. Following these more intensive investigations, the combined teams held a week-long seminar, where notes were compared.

To fill gaps in our data, letters were written to co-operating people in the various villages, and five of the villages were revisited for supplementary data. The thirteenth community, Ebetsu in Hokkaido, was covered later by Donoghue.

Unknown to us until we were well into the research was a series of studies conducted in 1954 by David E. Lindstrom, a rural sociologist at the International Christian University's Rural Welfare Research Institute. He and his colleagues there had surveyed five of the communities in our sample. These were Ebetsu, Yokogoshi, Karako, Obie, and Honami. Because his data relied heavily on opinion questionnaires, they supplemented our material rather well. While we had to rely on the statements of a more limited sample of informants for attitudinal material on change, he provided a more gross public-opinion type of data.

Our findings were not as neat and as consistent as we hoped they would be. The various measures of change that we established for this study did not move in the same direction or to the same extent for the ten-year period covered by the survey period. Some communities increased in a given index, while other villages remained the same or even decreased in this same index. Thus, to take a simple example, we found in one village that the number of dairy cows increased from 2 in 1948 to 130 in 1959, while in another it decreased from 3 to 2 in the same period. Similarly, with respect to the number of power cultivators, much variation from village to village was found. The village of Aioi had a most spectacular increase from 43 units to 322; while Obie, a few miles across the Inland Sea from Aioi, showed a modest rate of increase, from 278 to 358 units. A third village, Yokogoshi, which started with 18 units in 1948, did not show any gain during the decade.

These differential rates of change present a special problem for the researcher who includes a dozen or more representative communities in his sample. In the case of a researcher who puts all his research eggs into one village basket, any change he finds in his village can be interpreted as a modification of the previous stage of development. But when a researcher adds more villages to his sample, the interpretation of changes and trends becomes more complex, because the particular circumstances of each village intervene to make a given change index very different from those of other villages.

Nevertheless, I think the data indicate that some very significant and widespread changes are taking place in our sample of Japanese villages. While the details differ somewhat from village to village, at the highest level of generalization we found a consistent trend toward change and this was the trend toward reducing the uncertainties and insecurities related to the occupation of farming.

In every village we asked the standard questions of what were the primary problems concerned with farming in their village and what solutions had been attempted in the last ten years. The answers we received touched most frequently on problems of land, water, crop yields, climate, markets, and transportation. On the problem of land, there was nearly unanimous agreement that the land reform has done much to encourage the proper care and use of land, especially for those who were former tenants. More than ever before, the pride of ownership that has resulted from the land reform has encouraged a more rational approach to land usage. At the same time, every village emphasized the shortage of land and those which had many repatriates from Manchuria and other former overseas areas were especially concerned with the shortage of land. On the other hand, some progress had been made toward a more efficient utilization of the available land. Where possible, land was being reclaimed, and experiments were being tried with new crops, such as tobacco and tomato, in regions where they had never been grown before. Though the new Japanese Constitution nullified the primogeniture system, the pressure on the land was too great to make practical the further fractionization of the land implied in the new law.

After land, water was designated as the most important problem facing the villagers in the past decade. Here again, thanks to government subsidies, considerable progress has been made in a majority of the villages. Dams were constructed and irrigation canals straightened in areas where water was needed, and tile drainage pipes were laid in areas where too much water was the problem. Such man-made controls over the water supply not only made possible some of the reclamation projects just alluded to but also ended long-standing feuds between hamlets over water rights. Also, as the result of the so-called amalgamation program, in which several independent villages were annexed into a single administration unit, a more equitable distribution of water supply was possible. Where formerly several villages fought with one another for the water from the same river, they now were able to handle the allocation of water through a single administrative agency. The same kind of co-operative spirit was possible for handling flood conditions where too much water could be equally damaging to the crops. Thus, in most villages we found that some basic improvement had been made to insure a better supply or control of water in the ten-year period.

In addition to these age-old problems of farming, there was the concern about ways of improving the yield of specific crops. Here we found a veritable chemical and biological revolution taking place. While not every farmer was taking advantage of them, practically all farmers were aware of the contributions of chemical and biological sciences to farming. In chemicals, the new commercial fertilizers were replacing human manure because it was more reliable and yielded greater results. Weed-killers, insecticides, and soil conditioners of a wide variety were being used not only to reduce possible crop damage but also to reduce the labor required in farming. Knowledge of plant and animal biology was being rapidly diffused. While the farmers did not understand the intricacies of recent biochemistry and genetics, the majority appreciated the advantages to be gained from the new strains of seeds and livestock. For example, in rice, strains with early or late maturation, with resistance to cold weather and to special kinds of disease, were being utilized. With poultry and livestock, care in diet, inoculations, and sanitary measures was being exercised. Incidentally, there was a noticeable increase in milk cows for most villages. The number of draft animals declined, however, probably in response to the increase of small cultivators and single-axle tractors. Thus there was general agreement in the villages not only that the quality of the crops had improved over the past ten years but also that the yield per acre had increased.

The problems associated with crop production are only one side of the coin. The other side of the coin deals with marketing and obtaining a fair price. The villagers were concerned with the marketing of their produce and livestock. They were not only production oriented; they were also becoming market oriented. The national government had established a compulsory crop-insurance system, improved dissemination of marketing news, and a compulsory delivery-quota system for rice. A wide variety of marketing co-operatives, often for such specific products as milk, oranges, or tea, has been organized to provide the individual with a greater control than formerly over the price of their commodities. Transportation to the markets has also been a recent theme in our investigations. A particular case is that of the Shimane village, which has been lobbying for the construction of a national highway that would traverse a mountain range separating the Japan Sea coast and Hiroshima Prefecture. If such a highway were built, this Shimane village could send its produce to the Hiroshima markets, where prices are better than the village's present markets for produce. In every village in our sample, roads have been widened and truck and bus transportation has been improved.

To summarize briefly, our investigations suggest that a good deal of the more obvious changes taking place in the villages can be viewed as contributing toward a reduction of some of the basic sources of insecurity that face every Japanese farmer. In a word, these modifications in land tenureship, farm technology, and marketing were intended to reduce the uncertainties inherent in the occupation of farming. As an occupation, it is in this regard little different from urban trades, where union and other labor associations attempt to seek immunity from certain risks inherent in their employment.

There is, of course, more to a Japanese village than its agricultural production. There is the complex aspect concerned with human relationships and cultural transmission. In this latter aspect, too, some innovations have been noted. But here again we need to discuss these changes at the most general level, for each was unique because of its particular historical and situational circumstances.

One of the most obvious changes was the general proliferation of partly functional, partly social, organizations, such as the women's clubs, the P. T.A., the 4-H youth clubs, and the like. In most villages we visited we found such organizations active in purely social activities as well as serving as channels of communication for new ideas concerning home improvement, health and sanitation, self-improvement, local history, and to a lesser extent political and economic ideology. These organizations also sponsored lectures often given by specialists from the government farm-extension service, sight-seeing tours, and even work projects that would "uplift" and raise the social horizon of the members. They also served informally for discussion and helped to establish social norms concerning issues in their changing world. For example, in several villages it was claimed that young married women used such meetings to plot strategies to educate their mothers-in-law to the changing times. Mothers-in-law, in turn, were saying that it was becoming impossible to control and discipline their sons' wives because young mothers wanted more freedom and greater independence with regard to raising their own children and with regard to division of labor in the farm household.

Other changes were less obvious. One concerned the slight tendency noted toward a decline in the strength of the larger kinship group and extended family. Many have commented that young people, in particular, were becoming more self-centered, independent, and individualistic. The elders claimed that the young were in need of learning and observing the traditional ethics (obligation system). Exchange labor for agricultural functions as well as for ceremonial occasions was frequently said to be on the decline, though communal service for road repairs, cleaning of streets, and the like was still maintained. When extra help was needed, most informants stated that they would prefer to hire someone rather than be obligated under an exchange labor system.

There was no question that the standard of living had increased in the past decade, as indicated by a number of indices. Most villages had five or six television sets. Sewing machines, washing machines, electric rice cookers, and other appliances were on the increase. Certain basic house improvements, such as tile baths (in place of wooden baths), piped-in water systems, improved cooking stoves, and wide glass windows in the kitchens are examples of this. The diet has been generally improved, and fish and meat are increasingly consumed. Taxi and bus service to nearby towns was generally available, and youths in particular availed themselves of the movies in town. Motorcycles were purchased by some of the wealthier farmers' sons. Clothes, even the farmer's work clothes, were no longer made at home but were purchased readymade. The village stores carried a varied stock of canned foods, appliances, sporting goods, and other so-called luxury items. In short, the gap in living standards between the villagers and the urbanites was being reduced even though the urban population in the postwar years was enjoying an unprecedented prosperity.

So far, I have described the more obvious and directly observable aspects of change in the thirteen rural communities of our sample. Much more detail could be given, but I would like to shift to a discussion of whether or not the rural communities are undergoing a more fundamental reorientation and to raise the question whether the improvements in farm technology, the rising standards of living, and the modifications in social relationship mean a significant change in rural life from the past. I would like to ask whether the attitude toward the future is changing in some significant way and whether the younger generation of farmers is being socialized in the same attitudes toward life and farming held by the older villagers.

My answer to these questions is that "it depends." It depends upon one's frame of reference and what one takes as the base line for measuring these changes. If we compare the contemporary village situation with conditions found in the years between the two world wars, especially in the 1930's, then I would say the change is considerable. On the other hand, if our base line is the Meiji period and the beginning of Japan's modernization, then, paradoxically as it might seem, I would say that the present trends are a continuation of the traditions of the past and that they constitute no significant departure from the past. From this perspective the years between the two world wars seem to be a brief deviation from the trends established earlier.

To explain this, a brief review of the history of modern agriculture is necessary. For convience, this history can be divided into two periods. The first, covering the years from the Meiji Restoration to 1917 at the beginning of World War I, was the period of initial industrialization for Japan. The other period covers the years in between the two world wars, and it represents a "coming-to-term" period of economic development.

The First Period. In their concern for modernization of their society, the Meiji leaders rightly saw the necessity for increasing agricultural production. As a consequence of their efforts and the response given by the farm villages to these efforts, agriculture played a key role in the early phase of Japan's march toward industrialization and urbanization. The agricultural village provided the essential manpower and population resource for the growing urban areas and industries, it developed the food surplus necessary to sustain the growing cities, and it created the initial capital resources for Japan to begin her industrialization.

During this fifty-year period of early industrialization, Japan's population nearly doubled. It expanded from an estimated 30 million to about 58 million in 1918. The Japanese farmer, in spite of such rapid growth, was able to produce sufficient agricultural surplus to keep the demand and the supply for food in balance. Though land had been cultivated intensively for many centuries before, the arable land was increased some 35 per cent in the Meiji period, from 4½ million to 6 million hectares. The productivity of land also expanded, so that by 1918 it had increased 80 per cent over its base period. Each year during this initial phase of modernization, the food supply was increased at an average rate of 2 per cent. Moreover, the contribution of agriculture to the expansion of foreign trade was not insignificant. "Export surpluses" in silk were produced to enable Japan to purchase necessary foreign goods.

During this period, also, agriculture constituted the main source of saving and capital formation. One necessarily crude index of this can be gleaned from tax revenues collected by the central government. The land tax, most of which came from farm lands, constituted more than 85 per cent of total revenues in 1882–92. Other forms of tax revenue, such as income tax and customs duty, did not substantially increase until the end of the Meiji period. As late as 1913–17, the land tax amounted to nearly 38 per cent of the total government revenues.

Obviously, in order for agriculture to play such a key role in the initial industrialization phase and to increase its productivity, some changes in agricultural technology was necessary. Ronald Dore (1959, 1960) describes how the Meiji government and the progressive farmers, particularly the landlords, cooperated to achieve this significant increase in agricultural yields. He describes experimentation with European seeds and tools, how successful innovations in one farm region would be diffused to other regions of the country, how experimental stations were established, how agricultural bulletins were published and disseminated, and how local agricultural associations and study groups were encouraged. Farm exhibitions were held, new seed strains were exchanged, model villages were described, and a general enthusiasm for improvement in agricultural technology was established.

The most important innovators during this period were the large landlords, many of whom were ex-samurai and literate men, who actively promoted experimentation in new seeds, new fertilizers, and new weeding methods. They appreciated the fact that such innovations served their own economic interests, but they also encouraged among their tenants and fellow villagers a positive attitude toward novelty, science, and progress. The establishment of the public school system during this period reinforced the same attitudes. In short, the landlords during this period were production oriented and actively engaged in the business of farming. Very few absentee landlords were present at this time, but they were to appear later.

While the improvements in fertilizer, seed, tools, and techniques of farming were the most important factors in expanding agricultural productivity, improvements in land use were also made. These required capital and were therefore generally beyond the means of small farmers and tenants. The Meiji government, with the assistance of some private landowners, reclaimed additional land, constructed irrigation works, and improved drainage facilities.

It is difficult to convey the spirit of the times in such impersonal terms. Perhaps some biographical data will help. Ronald Dore (1960, p. 82) characterizes the accomplishment of Karasawa Annin in this manner:

A samurai of Aizu, a fief scholar and official, he was imprisoned for anti-Imperialist activity at the time of the Restoration. Released, he set off, in 1873, to start a ranch in the northern tip of Honshu. He was given a government subsidy, employed two Englishmen for five years as advisors, and by 1876 was able to show the Emperor on a visit 180 head of cattle of mixed Western and indigenous breeds, and 24 horses. He also experimented with various new crops and carried out afforestation schemes. By 1889 he had created a village as an appendage to his ranch which he then left to his son. He himself moved to Tokyo to establish selling outlets for the ranch's products. He became founder of the Japan Livestock Association before he died a few years later.

The innovations and the spirit of the Meiji times just alluded to reminds one of the conditions that we found in our village survey. We found progressive farmers like Karasawa Annin, we found a healthy respect for scientific methods in agriculture, and we found ample evidence for the successful diffusion of new agricultural practices and tolls. These are the reasons for my suggestion that, if we take the Meiji period as the benchmark for measuring change, the intensified activity in the contemporary farm villages represents no basic change in patterns. If anything, there were only style changes. The Meiji farmers did not use electric pumps and gasoline-powered cultivators, of course, but these are mere "stylistic" changes and not changes in "basic" patterns—to use Kroeber's designations. These machines have not changed the sequence or the nature of operations in the agricultural cycle. They and other improvements of the 1950's were refinements built upon the Meiji base.

Both the Meiji period and post–World War II farmers carried out their occupation within the traditional framework. Farming is still a small family operation, each household averaging about one hectare. The work still requires an inordinate amount of human labor. Primogeniture is still the rule of succession, and other sons leave the farm for other occupations. Rice is still the sacred crop, and paddy fields are the most desirable. Kinship relations and community solidarity are still vital to the daily operation of village affairs.

The Inter-War Period. Now let us look for a moment at the next period, the years covering 1918 to the beginning of World War II. World War I saw a spurt in the industrial development of Japan and a steady increase during the rest of this period. Agricultural production, while it increased also, did not develop at the same rate. If we divide the economic factors into the usual primary, secondary, and tertiary industrial sectors, the primary or agricultural sector increased in net output from an index of 119 to 156. The index for the secondary or manufacturing sector increased from 123 to 477; for the tertiary, from 138 to 397. Thus, in relative terms agricultural output declined vis-à-vis the other sectors of the economy.

Another indication of the relative decline of agriculture is the statistics on real income for the three sectors of the economy. By 1939–42, the real income per gainfully occupied person in primary industry (agriculture) rose to ¥220. In secondary industry it climbed to ¥928, and in tertiary industry to ¥838. The farmer's share of the national income declined sharply in this period between the two world wars.

Ohkawa and Rosovsky (1960, pp. 56–57), who provided these statistics, comment that such figures represent a "shift from the period of agricultural 'balanced growth' to the period of agriculture as a retarded or depressed sector."

Throughout the entire period, the number of farm households did not change and the farm labor force remained constant, between 14 and 16 million. The acreage under cultivation did not change to any appreciable extent. Meanwhile, the birth rates were high and the nation was producing during this period a population almost equivalent to the entire population in Tokugawa times. It was clear that the agricultural sector of the economy was producing a surplus population that was not being absorbed in the non-farm sectors. Increasingly, the villages were being characterized by low productivity and overemployment. Food production also lagged behind population growth. To feed the population, vast quantities of rice and other products were imported from Korea and Taiwan. Such imports drove downward the price levels of farm products.

The principal change of the period was in the landlords' role. With the depression of the 1930's and the declining price of farm products, many owner-cultivators lost their lands and absentee landlordism increased. Tenants had a difficult time feeding and clothing their families. The landlords as a class shifted in their orientation from production to the market. No longer were they the innovators and progressive elements in rural development.

Symptomatic of the changing orientations of the landlords and the general poverty prevailing in the villages, the so-called rice riots set the tone for the countryside. Numerous farmers' movements developed, sectionalism between the city and the countryside was expressed in slogans, and a general regressive attitude toward farm problems was expressed by the Ministry of Agriculture and echoed by the landlord. For instance, in 1934 one bureau chief in the Ministry addressed a national conference in these terms:

"What the village needs is not so much people skilled in agricultural techniques or the theory of management, as a peasant who can wield a mattock and experience a sense of joy in doing so. In the depth of distress which our villages have reached the creation of 'peasants of the soil' in the true sense of those words offers the only possible road to rehabilitation" [Dore, 1959, p. 101].

In line with the rise of nationalism, the conservative position in agriculture was fostered by the famous *nōhon shūgi* movement. This movement spread with religious zeal that contradicted many of the progressive gains made in the Meiji period. The *nōhon shūgi* movement promoted the ideology that agriculture was the principal base of nationhood; that the farmers were therefore serving both a sacred and a patriotic duty; that poverty and other economic problems of the farm could be solved by diligence, thrift, and personal sacrifice; that the farmers were to eschew the life of the urban culture and to center their own social and cultural life within the framework of a self-sufficient village community. *Nōhon shūgi*'s answer to the farmer's question, "Why am I so poor?" was, "You don't work hard enough; you don't have the proper spiritual attitude; and you forget that agriculture is a way of life, not a business."

Perhaps the real problem in this phase of Japan's economic growth and urbanization process was that the non-agricultural sectors were not able to absorb more of the surplus farm-labor force than they did. The world-wide depression, the rise of nationalism, and the traditional methods of agricultural production also contributed to the problems. In any event, where agriculture played a dominant role in the previous history, it now played a passive and limiting role. Where it had contributed substantially to the flow of investment capital, it now exerted a drag.

Given these conditions as a benchmark by which to measure postwar changes, we can see that the present farm situation can be considered as both a change and a departure. Instead of a moralistic or religious orientation toward solving the economic and technical problems of farming, the present trends clearly suggest a strong scientific, rational, and empirical approach toward their solution. In place of Confucian moral principles, the contemporary ideology recommends closer attention to the latest genetic and biochemical facts obtained from the government experimental stations. Instead of subscribing to a belief that agriculture is the sacred base of the society, the present outlook is to treat it as an occupation and enterprise, albeit honorable, but not one charged with nationalistic overtones. Instead of encouraging a tightly knit and self-sufficient community social structure, the mid-twentieth century trend is to bring the village in closer contact and a sense of interdependence with the larger region and especially with the urban society. The industrial culture of the urban community has all but shattered the isolationism of the villages.

In conclusion I would like to present one more benchmark for evaluating the current changes we have observed in the village. If we stake out a benchmark that is oriented to the future, we may be able to see to what extent the present developments can be considered as basic and significant trends for the future.

In spite of the rosy picture that seems to prevail in the current agricultural situation, the future does not look bright for the average Japanese farmer. His morale may be good and his enthusiasm for technological innovations may be high, but the fact remains that his income is not keeping pace with the increased incomes of other sectors of the economy. An awareness of this was indicated in our interviews when we asked about income. The majority we interviewed stated that their relative income was the highest during the few years following the end of the war. Since that time, they said, they have been feeling the pressure of the high price of goods. With the pressures for them to buy materials for home improvements and for mechanized farm tools, the farmers are feeling the "price squeeze." The price of agricultural products is being reduced relative to the inflated cost of manufactured foods upon which they have come to be so dependent.

One way to increase his income would be to obtain more land, but under the present laws this is virtually impossible for the average farmer. The prospects are poor for the farmers to continue receiving the large government subsidies for improving agricultural lands, irrigation works, and the like. From the standpoint of the nation, it seems that the economic rewards would be greater if the government invested in sectors of the economy other than agriculture. While the farmer might, as is done in the United States, form a strong political organization and lobby for greater benefits from the government, this in the long run would seem to be uneconomical and merely a stopgap measure. He might also attempt to exert through improved organizational means a better position in the marketing of his products. But the fact that many of the domestic crops can be purchased on the international market at lower prices than he can produce them suggests some sort of limitation on this score. Co-operatives and government price support have no doubt helped in this regard, but the village leaders we interviewed were pessimistic about it.

The relative decline in the farmer's income is being accentuated by a number of features in the contemporary rural scene. One is the effect of various mass media, such as radio, newspapers, and TV, which entice the rural folk into trying to keep up with their city cousins. Both adults and children are aware of the latest fads in diet, clothes, hair styles, and other costly items. The schools play a role in the farmers' aspirations for a higher standard of living. As part of the indoctrination program of the schools to train children to be forward-looking, progressive, and more hospitable to change, they encourage more expensive tastes in entertainment, recreational activities, and hobbies like photography.

The Japanese farmer, like the American farmer, is caught up in this dilemma:

> On the one hand the farmer participates in the larger society in which he must compete with people who have ready access to specialized knowledge, who are highly organized, and who enjoy the material benefits and leisure time of a highly developed economy. On the other hand, he is bound by the limitations of a relatively inflexible land-based enterprise, subject to the uncertainties of natural forces, of a lack of organization for effective market bargaining, of a lack of leisure pursuits, and of the carryover

of values and a social structure more appropriate for the model T Ford than for the fin-tail car [Wilkening, 1958, p. 36].

In light of these facts, it would seem that the only assured way of increasing the farmers' share of the national income—about 40 per cent of the labor force are farmers, and their proportion of the national income is about 17 per cent—would be to increase the farm holdings of each farm household. This in turn means that the number of farm households needs to be sharply decreased. Large-scale farming would make possible a greater mechanization of the farms. The number of farmers with little managerial ability will be reduced (even with present conditions of rapid spread of farm technology, these are a problem), and the more efficient farmers will remain.

A not unrelated development would be the greater encouragement of livestock and dairying. Experts from the World Bank have suggested both the latter and expansion of landholding size.

Thus if we view them from the standpoint just suggested, the attempts at change over the ten-year period seem feeble indeed. The so-called changes seem merely to be refinements of past tendencies and traditions. The land-reform program and the government subsidies have done much to raise the standard of living and to rationalize the farm economy, but the basic problem remains unsolved. The farmer is receiving a *decreasing* share of the national income and to continue to do so would be to keep some 30–40 percent of the population in a depressed condition.

The solution to increasing the farmer's share of national income is to reduce the number of farm households and to increase the size of farm acreage per farming unit. It is the solution toward which American farmers are moving. Some suggestions in this direction were made by our informants in Japan. One agricultural consultant in Iwate Prefecture suggested the move toward farm corporations. Another even suggested "vertical integration." Whatever the special directions taken toward solving this problem, the principal decision involves something more than economics. It involves a question of values, and as such it has implications for Japanese politics, economy, and society. It also means that the Japanese farm family system will have to socialize its children for urban types of occupation. The idea that the Japanese farm is an ideal "seedbed" for tomorrow's generation needs to be given up because such an idea is simply not true. Japanese urban families are providing a more alert and realistic approach than are farm families to problems the next generation will face as adults.

In conclusion, let me return to the theoretical issue with which I began this paper. It was a question of the frame of reference for evaluating culture change taking place in the Japanese farm villages. We have seen that if the Meiji period is taken as the base line, then the present conditions seem to be a logical development of the trends foreshadowed in that period. If, on the other hand, we use the regressive period between the two world wars, then the present village situation can be viewed as a renaissance and therefore a distinct change. Or, if we look to the future development of the total Japanese society, we find that the Japanese villages are still conservative, tradition-bound social structures, and therefore unchanging.

BIBLIOGRAPHY

DORE, RONALD P.
1959 *Land Reform in Japan.* London: Oxford University Press.
1960 "Agricultural Improvement in Japan: 1870–1900," *Economic Development and Cultural Change,* 9, No. 1, Pt. 2: 69–92.

OHKAWA, KAZUSHI, and HENRY ROSOVSKY
1960 "The Role of Agriculture in Modern Japanese Economic Development," *Economic Development and Cultural Change,* 9, No. 1, Pt. 2: 43–68.

SMITH, THOMAS C.
1959 *The Agrarian Origins of Modern Japan.* Stanford, Calif.: Stanford University Press.

WILKENING, E. A.
1958 "Trends in the Farm Family." In: "Rural Sociology in a Changing Economy: Report of the North-Central Regional Rural Sociology Committee." Urbana: University of Illinois. (Mimeographed.)

IV. Culture and Personality

PATTERNS OF EMOTION IN MODERN JAPAN*

WILLIAM CAUDILL

THE data on patterns of emotion presented here were gathered in 1959 as part of one of several studies carried out in order to provide a general cultural perspective that would be helpful in evaluating the symptoms of Japanese psychiatric patients and the nature of relationships between patients and staff in Japanese psychiatric hospitals (Caudill, 1961; Caudill and Doi, 1963). It seemed to me that behavior and methods of treatment in the hospital should be related to broader patterns of values and emotions in Japanese culture, and I made a beginning attempt specifically to explore these latter topics.

The data on value orientations have been published elsewhere (Caudill and Scarr, 1962) and need be referred to here only as background for the study of emotional patterns. Using a theory and method derived from the work of Florence Kluckhohn (Kluckhohn and Strodtbeck, 1961), a schedule of twenty-three items designed to test four areas of value orientations was administered in 1954 to two samples of Japanese persons (respectively, of 464 and 619 subjects) each of which was fairly equally divided by sex and generation and by residence in a rural village, a medium-sized city, and a ward area of metropolitan Tokyo. From the results of this study, I wish to point out only that on those schedule items which measured value orientations in the area of the relations among men, and particularly in the sphere of family life, there was a strong emphasis on "collaterality." Collaterality stresses the welfare of the group, and consensus among its members, as primary goals. As such, in terms of the theory behind the schedule, collaterality is distinct from lineality or individualism—the former emphasizing superior and subordinate relationships, the latter focusing on the relative autonomy of persons. In the Japanese data, surprisingly, the younger generation had a greater preference for collaterality as a value than did the older generation, although this value was strongly represented in both generations. This result was further highlighted when the responses of parents and their children were matched: a substantial gain occurred in the preference for first-rank collateral orientations in the movement from parents to children in all three communities. This trend was particularly true on those items in the schedule referring to family and occupational life but was reversed in the sphere of political life, where the young were more individualistic than the old.

* The gathering of the data for this paper was aided by a grant from the Foundations' Fund for Research in Psychiatry. The analysis of the data and the writing of the present paper were carried out after the author had joined the staff of the National Institute of Mental Health.

Values can be linked to preferred channels of impulse gratification or restraint. Given the fondness of the Japanese for the value of collaterality in family life, I wished to try to find out what sort of emotional patterns formed an underlying part of this value emphasis. But how is one to go about studying impulses or emotional patterns? The psychiatrist would tell us that this might be done through psychotherapy, and particularly through the study of the fantasy life of people. Anthropologists, however, do not have easy access to such data. And yet in Japan, on an observational level, these cultural differences in the expression of impulses are impressed upon one every day. They can be seen in such simple things as the headlines of the daily papers. For example: "Diet Plunged into Utter Chaos: Fists Furniture Fly in Battle of the Diet," or "Kyoto Homeowner Plagued by Flying Motorcycles: On the Night of June 14, No Less than Seven Motorcycles Fell Off the Highway into His Backyard in a Single Hour," or, in another area of life, a popular sports magazine features a new wrestling (*sumō*) champion showing his collection of whiskey to his wife. It is hard to imagine the occurrence of this last example as publicity for an American baseball champion.

It would be possible to do a systematic content analysis of such everyday literature, but I chose to develop a series of pictures of everyday-life events (concerning eating, drinking, sleeping, bathing, sex, sickness, and so on) in Japan and to use these as "visual questions" (on this technique see Caudill, 1958, pp. 133–34; Goldschmidt and Edgerton, 1961) in an interview designed to elicit feelings about impulses and emotions in the situations covered by the pictures. I had a Japanese artist make simple drawings of the desired scenes and then had these photographed. Eight pictures were used in the final series. My wife, who is Japanese, and I usually conducted the interview with the pictures together—she in her fluent, and I in my less adequate, Japanese. All the interviews were tape recorded. In this way, seventy-two interviews were carried out in three small psychiatric hospitals in the Tokyo area during 1959. The sample was fairly equally divided among doctors, nurses, *tsukisoi*, and patients.[1]

In this article, the responses to three of the pictures are analyzed from sixty-eight of the interviews (there are problems of translation still to be worked out on the four remaining interviews). The three pictures used here may be seen in Figure 1 and are respectively concerned with minor illness (Picture 5), adult heterosexual interaction (Picture 6), and bathing (Picture 7).

In constructing these three pictures, as well as the others in the series, I had, naturally, certain ideas in mind. As a result of previous work in Japan, it was my impression that minor illnesses were handled very indulgently both by the person having the illness and those who took care of him. I also felt that sexual behavior was approached in a rather matter-of-fact manner, frequently leavened with rather earthy humor. Finally, so far as the three pictures here are concerned,

---

1. *Tsukisoi* are subprofessional nurses who, in many private psychiatric hospitals in Japan, are assigned on a one-to-one basis to patients. The *tsukisoi* cares for the patient continuously throughout his hospitalization. She sleeps in the same room as the patient and serves as housekeeper and companion (see Caudill, 1961).

FIGURE 1

Picture 5

Picture 6

Picture 7

I believed that bathing was an enjoyable, and in a minor way even sensuously luxurious, daily event in the lives of most Japanese. As will be seen, these expectations about emotions in the particular areas of life under consideration were confirmed in some ways and negated in others. Obviously, I do not believe that the emotional patterns presented here from sixty-eight individuals divided into four groups constitute a representative sample of Japanese (although on a priori grounds I do have a hunch that these samples at least represent fairly well the role groups from which they are drawn). Nevertheless, it is interesting, and useful, to deal with such delimited samples in a systematic way as a control on general impressions.

Following the collection of the interviews, the material was gone over in order to clarify, and state specifically, the content categories to be used in the analysis. After these categories had been listed for each picture, two raters[2] independently scored the interviews. There was an inter-rater agreement over the categories of 85 per cent on Picture 5, 93 per cent on Picture 6, and 87 per cent on Picture 7 (see Tables 1-3). The results of the analysis will first be presented for each picture in turn, followed by a discussion of interrelations among the responses to the pictures. These interrelations will then be grouped by the frequency of appearance of various emotional patterns.

Turning to the content categories for Picture 5, as may be seen in Table 1, most of the subjects saw the picture as a husband and wife, and it was next most frequently seen as a mother and son. In general, the picture was seen as one of mild illness. Although the numbers are not large, it is interesting that a greater proportion of the *tsukisoi* saw the picture as serious illness, and this may be related to the backgrounds of the *tsukisoi*, many of whom have had long periods of chronic illness (Caudill, 1961).

Emotionally, the picture was interpreted predominately as showing sympathetic concern and care on the part of the woman for the sick man. Among the four role groups, the *tsukisoi* have the greatest proportion of persons seeing sympathetic care, which, again, may tie in with their specific job in the hospital. The nurses have the next largest proportion of sympathetic care, while the doctors are about equally divided. The patients are the only role group having a majority of persons who do not see sympathetic care. This might be due to the feelings of the patients about life in the hospital, or, as I think more likely, it may have to do with their personality dynamics, which do not permit them to express easily this type of emotion—that is, they have more difficulty than other people in either giving or receiving sympathy and care.

A further step along this dimension is the use of sickness itself as a form of communication. This seems to me to be quite characteristic behavior in Japan and to fit in with the great amount of attention given to minor aches and pains. People in Japan "like to" go to bed with mild illnesses, and sickness in this regard

---

2. I wish to thank Mr. Steven Schreiber and Miss Gertrude Jackson for doing the rating of the interviews.

TABLE 1
Picture 5: Sick Man Cared for by a Woman

Content and Emotional Theme	Tsukisoi (N = 12)	Nurses (N = 17)	Doctors (N = 20)	Patients (N = 19)	Total (N = 68)
Interacting roles:					
Husband and wife	9	9	15	13	46
Mother and son	2	4	2	4	12
Father and daughter	1	1	—	—	2
Unrelated persons	—	3	3	2	8
Condition of man:					
Serious illness	4	1	2	1	8
Mild illness	8	16	18	18	60
Sympathetic concern and care by woman:					
Yes	11	11	11	8	41
No	1	6	9	11	27
Use of sickness as a form of communication:					
Yes	4	2	3	1	10
No	8	15	17	18	58

(Inter-rater agreement, 85 per cent.)

is a very ego-syntonic condition. In general, it is my impression that emotion is not so much verbally expressed in Japan as it is "lived out." I use this term purposely and in distinction to the psychoanalytic term "acted out" with its more pathological connotations. It is this quality of "living out" emotions that was being expressed by the ten people (see Table 1) who saw sickness used as a form of communication in the interview on Picture 5. For example, one nurse said:[3]

[Miss S, HN] It could be one month after the previous picture of the mother, the baby, and the children. This has the same sort of feeling. One month later, and the husband got sick. The mother is taking care of the husband, so it has the same sort of peaceful feeling. (Tell me a bit about that feeling.) They understand each other quite deeply. Even though a couple may have enough money, they may not get a certain kind of life and peacefulness. . . . Japanese won't express their feelings such as "I love you" or "I like you" or "I dislike you" or that sort of thing in words. Rather than using words, they often show their feelings in their behavior, and sick time is a very good time for

---

3. In giving examples, the material in brackets at the beginning is a code used to facilitate reference to the complete interview. A fictitious initial is assigned to the person, followed by the first letter of the name of the hospital, and the first letter of the role group to which the person belongs. The names of the hospitals were Seiwa, Koseiin, and Hiyoshi. The role groups are doctors, nurses, *tsukisoi*, and patients. Thus, in the first example cited, Miss S, HN, refers to my interview with Miss "Sumi," Hiyoshi hospital, nurse.

this. It is the one time you can show in action how much you love the other. Often with young couples just after getting married, the wife will feel very lonely, since the husband comes home late all the time, and she feels that he does not love her anymore, and then he happens to become sick and she would take care of him nicely, and that's her way of saying that she is in love with him. Then he will understand what she is doing, and what sort of feeling she has toward him. That is a good chance, for both of them, to communicate not with words, but in another way. In this case the wife is taking care of him nicely. . . .

The next two examples are from *tsukisoi*. The first is, for me, rather "saccharine" in its sentiment, although this is probably a Western way of putting it that misses the point in terms of Japanese culture. The second shows sympathetic concern coupled with a level-headed ability to be objective.

[Mrs. M, ST] The wife is worried about him. This is the beautiful feature. The wife is worried about the fast recovery and the husband is grateful to her. . . . (What sort of feeling in this regard do you have for your patients?) When the patient is very dejected during the day, and when I look at her at night, she is restfully sleeping. And earlier I told her that she is a little girl and naughty during the day, and to have a good night's sleep. And once in a while I have tears in my eyes. . . .

[Mrs. N, ST] Husband is sick with a cold and wife is taking care of him. . . . It has a very peaceful feeling. (How about this sort of situation with your patients?) It is better to have a family kind of feeling toward the patient, but you have to have a little distance between the patient and yourself. If you are too involved, things wouldn't go well for the patient; so in a way, while I am attached to him, in a way, I am not attached to him. . . . Also, often the families of the patients are quite unmanageable, and if you are involved emotionally with the patient, you will become just like the family. . . . (Where do you learn these things?) The old *tsukisoi* tell us about their experiences and we learn naturally.

Then there is a nice story that illustrates the relation of mother and son, along with the conflict with the potential daughter-in-law. The nurse, in telling of this experience, used the Japanese verb *amaeru*, which is translated as "to coax" here. Dr. Doi, in his paper in this symposium and elsewhere (see Doi, 1960), has made a concept of this word.

[Miss H, SN] . . . The doctor has just gone and the mother is very much worried, and the son has a temperature and is "coaxing." Why I say this is that recently my fiancé became sick and I went to see him. His mother was there, so there wasn't any such "coaxing" thing. To tell you the truth, I wanted to have him "coax," and to talk with him. The day he got sick his mother called and said that he was sick. She didn't tell me that I should come or that he wanted anything. . . . When I talked with him at the house he said he had a person who would take care of him, and so he didn't need anybody, and didn't want to make me worry. . . .

Finally, and in contrast to the feelings expressed by the majority of hospital staff, somewhat over half of the patients did not see sympathetic concern and care in this picture. For example, one patient said:

[Mr. S, SP] Sickness and taking care of others, and I don't understand the connection between sickness and care. (Why do you say that?) Human beings . . . cannot trust each other, and not being able to trust each other they just have to be patient when they get married. (Might they come to trust each other more after a while?) They were toiling at their tasks, not being able to trust each other. (How do you think this man feels here?) Perhaps his feelings are distrust. He might be sick, and I myself don't think I could handle the situation. (Tell me a little more about the wife.) It might be a good aspect, but I still feel the minus aspect is greater. (What might the woman be thinking about?) Before this [sickness] the man supported the family. She is hoping he can get back to work. . . .

Picture 6 was used in the attempt to get at feelings and impulses concerning young adult heterosexual interaction. It was hard to get people to talk, even indirectly, about the possibility that sexual feelings occurred in the situation shown in this picture. Since over half of the interviews were conducted with women (the nurses, *tsukisoi*, and half of the patients), it is true that my presence as a male, and a foreigner to boot, may have played a part in such reticence, and this must be taken into consideration. On the other hand, my wife was present as an active participant in the interviews; and beyond this, as will be seen, certain interrelations showed up across the three pictures that probably would not have occurred if my presence had been the crucial factor. As shown in Table 2, some

TABLE 2
Picture 6: Man and Woman in Room—Bed in Background

Content and Emotional Theme	Tsukisoi (N = 12)	Nurses (N = 17)	Doctors (N = 20)	Patients (N = 19)	Total (N = 68)
Interacting roles:					
Husband and wife	8	14	18	15	55
Unrelated man and woman	4	3	2	4	13
Location of interaction:					
Couple is "at home"	9	13	19	17	58
Couple on trip or honeymoon	3	4	1	2	10
Expression of sexual interest by couple:					
Yes	1	3	11	6	21
No	11	14	9	13	47

(Inter-rater agreement, 93 per cent.)

persons in each of the role groups did speak of sexual interest in this picture, and among the six patients who did so four were women.

Perhaps it might have been easier for people to talk about sex in this picture if the bedding had been somewhat messed up. Be that as it may, most people spoke of the picture in terms of a peaceful couple at home in a quite non-sexual situation. Comments were often made about the rising standard of living of this couple, since they had a television set, and so on. Along these general lines, and typical of this sort of story, a patient said:

[Mr. M, SP] This is a married couple, and he came back from his work and had finished dinner, and he had been reading, and pretty soon they will go to bed because the bed is ready. Looking at this man, he has a good manner and taste because of the tea cups and the books. And the wife might be saying, "Well, are you tired?" And having television, I can say that this family is a middle class family. And the wife is being nice to him. This couple is very Japanese, and this room too. . . . It's a very peaceful couple.

In those interviews which did indicate sexual interest on the part of the couple, it was done either quite directly or else indirectly through reference to the expression in the eyes of the couple or to the condition of the bedding (*futon*). It is interesting that the *tsukisoi* and nurses saw the least amount of sexual interest, and this might go along with the demands of their job, which would be jeopardized if sexual impulses were to be acted out. The patients were also on the side of not speaking of sexual interest, although this was less extreme than for the *tsukisoi* or nurses. A majority of the doctors, however, saw the couple as having a sexual interest in each other. There are, perhaps, several reasons for this. The medical background of the doctor might lead him to be somewhat more open in the discussion of sexual interest, and also he belongs, by virtue of his professional training, to the most Westernized of the four groups. *Tsukisoi,* nurses, and patients tend to be more traditionally Japanese in comparison with doctors. It was also among doctors that sexual interest was seen most positively, albeit rather clinically. For example:

[Dr. U, SD] This is getting close to the sexual point, so I would say that this is the honeymoon and they are just out of the bath, and she is making him wear the *haori* [a Japanese coat]. (What sort of problems do young couples have in adjusting to each other?) . . . They haven't had a sexual experience before, they might want to do that. (How does it turn out, what adjustment do they reach?) It is beyond me if they will do it in the Japanese inn, or maybe they will do it at home, I don't know this. Is this what you are asking, that I should tell about the newly-married couple's feelings? (So, so.) They have known each other before, and they have experienced some sexual playing. If the girl or wife has not had sexual experience, she will be worried the first time. And also they have a certain expectation of getting satisfaction. In modern times both sexes have sexual knowledge. And they are expecting to get a certain enjoyment out of it, out of sexual intercourse, and at the same time they have curiosity about sex, too. . . .

Neither the *tsukisoi* nor the nurses were very willing to talk openly about sexual interest. Indeed, I was impressed during the interviews with the probability that they did not even think about sex to themselves, or, if so, only veiledly and with discomfort. Such discomfort is indicated in the considerable amount of attention given to the *futon* ("bedding") laid out in the room just beyond the two people in the picture. In general, in Japanese sleeping habits, people lie down next to each other in separate *futon*. This is true in the Kantō area around Tokyo, but in the Kansai area around Kyoto there is a greater use made of double *futon*. Since this picture was used in Tokyo, people often seemingly focused on the *futon* as an indirect means of expressing certain uncomfortable feelings aroused by their interpretation of the picture. This is the case, for example, in the following two stories, the first from a nurse and the second from a *tsukisoi*:

[Miss K, SN] Disgusting eyes. (Tell me about the eyes.) They give a "lascivious" look. Let's not talk about this picture. (Oh, come on.) It may be a *machiai* [literally, "awaiting and fitting together" house, performing one of the functions of the motel in the United States]. The girl is seeing the man, and he has come again. (Why is it a *machiai*?) If they had a family they wouldn't keep the *futon* in the room, they would put it away....

[Miss I, ST] This may be inside of the home ... but what I felt strongly about when I saw this is where the *futon* is placed. In Tokyo everybody sleeps alone, but when I went to Kansai, then two people, young, or even older couples, sleep together. When I stayed at my friend's house and saw it, I was terribly shocked. ... I had heard from my childhood that to sleep together makes one tired, so when I went to my friend's house in Nagoya and saw a big *futon* I was really surprised. ... (In your own family how did you sleep?) When I was small we slept in a big room together, but with separate *futon*. Well, since my father did not have many daughters, he was particularly giving me affection in my childhood. Until I was just about to go to elementary school he tried to make me sleep with him, but I disliked to sleep with my father. My older brother said to me, "I will buy something for you tomorrow, so you should come and sleep with father, since he is asking for it." ...

These two stories seem to be concerned with sex by indirection, and this was often true of those stories by patients which gave evidence of sexual interest on the part of the couple. Thus, one patient said:

[Mr. K, KP] I don't think this is an ordinary family because of the woman's expression and the man's expression, and these expressions give me an unpleasant feeling. ... I would say they have a very sloppy kind of life.

Finally, among the role groups other than the doctors, one of the few directly sexual responses to the picture, in this case by a *tsukisoi*, was:

[Mrs. Y, ST] The husband is playing, he is not in the family. (Tell me about his playing.) He is at his mistress's house, or just having a physical association. I should say that he is at his mistress's house. Their eyes are caught. And he is satisfied. ... Some will go home afterwards, and some will stay all night. (And in his case?) After all, he is young, and it would be better for him to go home....

Picture 7 shows a scene of a boy and girl in a Japanese bathroom. The Japanese artist made something of a mistake in drawing a fancier than average bathroom, so the picture was sometimes interpreted as at a hot spring or public bath rather than in a private home. Often those persons who saw the scene as in a private home would comment along the lines of wishing that they had such a splendid *furo* ("bath") in their own house.

The majority of people spoke of this picture as showing a younger brother (*otōto-san*) and older sister (*o-nēsan*) or, more frequently, used the term "*kyōdai*," which is an everyday word in Japanese but can be translated only by the more technical English term "siblings." The spoken Japanese term *kyōdai* is used loosely to refer to various combinations of sibs and tends to blur sex distinctions (you do not know except by context whether the speaker is referring

TABLE 3
Picture 7: Boy and Girl in Japanese Bathroom

Content and Emotional Theme	Tsukisoi (N = 12)	Nurses (N = 17)	Doctors (N = 20)	Patients (N = 19)	Total (N = 68)
Interacting roles:					
Brother and sister (or siblings, i.e., *kyōdai*)	7	9	17	7	40
Boy and girl (or children)	5	8	3	12	28
Bathroom seen as:					
In a private home	9	14	11	16	50
At a hot spring	2	1	4	—	7
A public bath	1	2	5	3	11
Concern about modesty (e.g., mention of use of towel by girl to cover genital area):					
Concern	3	2	9	2	16
No concern	9	15	11	17	52
Expression of special pleasure in bathing:					
Yes (sensuous and enjoyable)	7	6	11	5	29
No (just a bath, or dislike)	5	11	9	14	39

(Inter-rater agreement, 87 per cent.)

to several brothers, to several sisters, to a mixture of brothers and sisters, or even to a single sib).[4] It is close, in a sense, to the English word "children," but this lacks the kinship reference of the Japanese word. In English, "our children" conveys the meaning of the Japanese word, but *kyōdai* emphasizes the related children themselves, whereas "our children" refers to the parents as much as to the children. It is interesting that the patients were the only group having a majority of persons who used the vaguer terms of boy (*otoko no ko*) and girl (*onna no ko*) or children (*kodomo-san tachi*), and in so doing they would seem to be putting more distance between themselves and the subject matter of the picture.

There was relatively little concern about modesty in the picture, and among those persons who did place some emphasis on the towel (*tenugui*) covering the girl's genital area, this was mentioned in a manner that indicated really little

---

4. There is a more formal Japanese term to refer to a combination of male and female sibs, *kyōdai-shimai*, but this term is used mainly in writing and is seldom heard in spoken Japanese.

concern over "modesty" in the American implications of that term. For example, a *tsukisoi* and a doctor had the following to say:

[Mrs. K, ST] In the bathroom, and the older sister and younger brother are playing with soap. They are a nice family because the girl puts the towel on her lap. . . . I bathed often with my mother, and it was the greatest thing for me. . . .

[Dr. I, SD] Brother and sister [*kyōdai*] taking a bath, and the mother said to the older sister that she should wash the younger brother, so she brought him to the bathroom. The older sister is old enough to sit nicely [i.e., cover her genital area with a towel], but the little boy doesn't know, and he doesn't have any particular feeling that he is in the bath, and it is a continuation of playing. The older sister is joining him in play and making him happy. The older sister will wash his body and then let him go out of the bath, and then she will get out too. (What memories do you have of your own childhood bathing?) I was told to put my body inside the tub and count, 1, 2, 3, 4, and so on. My mother washed my hair, and I had the soap all over my hair, and put my hair way up and looked in the mirror. That sort of thing I remember. (Those seem like nice memories; what was the counting?) . . . Children always jump around, so that parents often say, "Well, you count from 1 to 10, and while counting you just sit in the bathtub."

For purposes of this paper, the most important aspect of the interviews on Picture 7 is whether the bath was seen as pleasurable or merely used for cleanliness and, beyond this, even actively disliked. Two of the role groups, the *tsukisoi* and the doctors, had a majority of persons who expressed special pleasure in bathing. On the other hand, the nurses and particularly the patients both had a majority of persons who were neutral about or actively disliked bathing. It is interesting that once again the patients are the group least able to express emotional gratification—most of them did not speak of sympathetic care, or of sex, or of pleasure in bathing.

Among the twenty-nine persons who did see the bath as pleasurable, they spoke of this not only in terms of the children in the picture but also in terms of themselves. For example:

[Mrs. Y, ST] . . . The time we are allowed to take a bath is the happiest time in the day. I like to take a bath for cleanliness. Also, at the same time I am away from the strain, and psychologically I feel I am expanding myself in the tub.

[Mrs. K, KN] . . . When we go into the *furo* we are out of attention, so you can talk more freely. . . . It is not only the steam, but you are free from clothes. To touch some warmness, not only being naked, the bathroom is the place. To touch warm things, and to be in the hot water.

[Dr. M, SD] . . . This is sister and brother, and they are playing, passing the soap to each other. This is the family bath, and it is a very large, splendid, wonderful bath. I hope sometimes to have such a bath. (So do I.) In the United States the boys and girls, brother and sister, both about the same age, should not take a bath together? (They don't usually.) In Japan that situation is not so extraordinary. . . .

In contrast to these stories, the following examples show the types of feelings expressed by those persons who were neutral toward or had a dislike of bathing. Note that the feeling of dislike in these stories usually refers to remembered "events" in the person's childhood bathing experiences with adults in his family.

The analysis of these stories, coupled with further interview material, would open up the fascinating, but complex, problem of the formation in childhood of psychological defenses and character traits. I intend to take up this problem in another paper (see also Caudill, 1962). For now, the examples are given as illustrations of feelings about bathing:

[Miss H, SN] It might be a public bath or a family bath, and I haven't had this sort of experience . . . and I don't have any other feelings. . . . (Tell me about your own experiences in bathing as a child.) I can only recall that my father washed the back of my feet and I despised that intensely. I always ran away at the time for the bath, and the maid called me to come back. I always took a bath with him, but the only thing I remember was that he wiped the back of my feet. (How about nowadays?) Well, a bath is necessary.

[Miss I, SN] Two kids are playing in the bath. About this age, maybe they like the bath. When I was very little, mother almost drowned me and washed my hair, and I didn't like it. Later I was with my sisters and brothers in the bath and I was scolded by mother and other people who were waiting. (How about the bath nowadays?) There is so little time in which to take a bath.

[Mr. S, SP] . . . (Do you enjoy the bath?) In my childhood I didn't like it. Sometimes my family would go to the hot spring and I disliked being naked in front of others. . . . At home I bathed with my grandmother, and she washed my face and I disliked it. (Why?) It wasn't the getting clean, I felt I was going to suffocate. (In what way?) Because of the way she used the towel. . . .

The next step in the analysis of the emotional responses was to see how they were interrelated among the three pictures. My hypothesis was that if a person spoke openly, and particularly with distaste, of sexual interest in discussing Picture 6, then he would not express sympathy for the sick man in Picture 5, and also he would not indicate pleasure in bathing when talking about Picture 7. On the other hand, I felt that if a person did express sympathy on seeing Picture 5 and did speak of pleasure in bathing on looking at Picture 7, then he would not see sexual interest in Picture 6.

The results of comparing the interrelations of emotional themes on pairs of pictures combined in several ways can be seen in Table 4. Among those persons who did not see sympathy in Picture 5, the great majority of them (21 of 27 persons) also did not express pleasure in bathing on being shown Picture 7. On the other hand, those who did see sympathy were about equally divided (23 to 18 persons) as to whether they expressed pleasure or not in bathing. One way of interpreting this result would be to say that if a person showed sympathy for sickness, then he would be about equally likely either to find pleasure in bathing or not to do so. But, if a person did not express sympathy for sickness, then he would also not be likely to get pleasure in bathing.

A similar result can be seen in the interrelations of themes on Pictures 6 and 7. If a person saw sexual interest in Picture 6, he was likely not to indicate pleasure in bathing on seeing Picture 7 (17 of 21 persons). But, if he did not show sexual interest, then there was about an equal chance of his responding with pleasure to bathing (25 to 22 persons).

Finally, if a person showed sympathy on looking at Picture 5, then he was likely not to see sexual interest in Picture 6 (32 of 41 persons). But, if he did not show sympathy, then there was about an equal chance that he would see sexual interest (12 to 15 persons). These comparisons of pairs of pictures tend to give support to the hypothesis concerning emotional patterning that was stated earlier.

As a final step in the analysis for this paper, the responses to all three pictures will be considered together in terms of the frequency of emotional patterns. The three sets of alternatives (that is, for each picture a certain emotional response was given or was not given) used in scoring the responses can be arranged in eight logical patterns. These patterns are listed in Table 5 in order of the fre-

TABLE 4
INTERRELATONS OF EMOTIONAL THEMES ON THE THREE PICTURES
FROM RESPONSES OF TOTAL SAMPLE OF 68 SUBJECTS

		Picture 5: Sick Man	
		Sympathy	No Sympathy
Picture 7: Bathing	Pleasure	23	6
	No Pleasure	18	21

$\chi^2 = 7.60$, 1 df, $p < .01$

		Picture 6: Couple	
		Sexual Interest	No Sexual Interest
Picture 7: Bathing	Pleasure	4	25
	No Pleasure	17	22

$\chi^2 = 7.04$, 1 df, $p < .01$

		Picture 5: Sick Man	
		Sympathy	No Sympathy
Picture 6: Couple	Sexual Interest	9	12
	No Sexual Interest	32	15

$\chi^2 = 3.94$, 1 df, $p < .05$

quency of their actual occurrence in the sample. Thus, the most frequent pattern, represented by 20 persons, is No (sexual interest), Yes (pleasure in bathing), Yes (sympathetic concern). This is one of the two reciprocal patterns anticipated by the hypothesis already presented, and it is the pattern I would most expect to find, on general cultural grounds, among Japanese.

TABLE 5
DISTRIBUTION OF PATTERNS OF EMOTIONAL THEMES OVER THE THREE PICTURES,
WITH PICTURES ARRANGED ACCORDING TO SITUATIONS OF GREATEST TO LEAST INTIMACY

THEME EXPRESSED AS:							
Sexual Interest (Picture 6)	Pleasure in Bathing (Picture 7)	Sympathetic Concern (Picture 5)	Tsukisoi (N = 12)	Nurses (N = 17)	Doctors (N = 20)	Patients (N = 19)	Total (N = 68)
No	Yes	Yes	6	5	6	3	20
No	No	Yes	4	4	1	3	12
Yes	No	No	—	1	6	4	11
No	No	No	—	4	1	5	10
Yes	No	Yes	1	2	1	2	6
No	Yes	No	1	1	1	2	5
Yes	Yes	Yes	—	—	3	—	3
Yes	Yes	No	—	—	1	—	1

In my own mind, I link the second most frequent pattern (No, No, Yes), represented by 12 persons, with the first pattern. My reason for this is related to the arrangement of the pictures on Table 5 according to situations of greatest to least physical intimacy in interpersonal relations (from sexual relations, to taking a bath together, to caring and being cared for in sickness). Thus, the 12 persons in the second pattern were able to express sympathetic concern in the least physically intimate situation, but in the more intimate situation of bathing they apparently did not feel free enough to indicate pleasure. And, as noted, in both these patterns there was no expression of sexual interest, but rather the situation in the picture was structured in a very non-sexual way (for example, as a "peaceful couple"), thereby avoiding the question of physical intimacy.

The third most frequent pattern (Yes, No, No), represented by 11 persons, is the other of the reciprocal patterns anticipated by the hypothesis. That is, those persons expressing sexual interest, usually with distaste, do not indicate sympathetic concern or pleasure in bathing. These persons seem to be struggling with problems of emotional expression and to have reached the "decision" that there is no satisfaction or pleasure to be had in such expression. The denial of satisfaction or pleasure can be carried one step further to include the denial of emotional expression altogether—whether pleasurable or unpleasurable. This more drastic "solution" seems to be the one followed by those 10 persons in the next most frequent pattern (No, No, No). I would link this pattern with the preceding one, since the responses are largely characterized by the absence of emotion and hence were scored as no sexual interest, no pleasure in bathing, and no sympathetic concern.

If the foregoing line of thought is followed out, then the two most frequent patterns are represented by 32 persons who have a positive emotional response to one or the other, or both, of the situations of sickness and bathing and who handle the situation of the man and woman in the room in a rather emotionally warm but very non-sexual manner. On the other hand, the two next most frequent patterns are represented by 21 persons who do not have a positive emotional response to situations of sickness and bathing and who handle the situation of the man and the woman either by indicating with distaste the existence of sexual interest or by a flat response lacking emotional feeling.

The first of these general patterns might be thought of as "an emphasis upon non-sexual satisfactions" to be found in a variety of situations extending even to those situations in which sexual interest ordinarily would be expected. The second general pattern might be characterized as "a denial of pleasure and emotion" in an equally wide variety of situations, including specifically sexual ones. Although a sample of 53 persons (32 in the first general pattern and 21 in the second) is not really large enough, it is intriguing to look at the distribution of these two general patterns among the four role groups. The rank order of relative concentration on "non-sexual satisfactions" is: (1) *tsukisoi*, (2) nurses, (3) doctors, and (4) patients. Obviously, the reverse rank order occurs in "denial of pleasure and emotion," with the patients having the greatest concentration in this general pattern. These results can be seen in Table 6 (which is constructed from the four most frequent patterns in Table 5).

TABLE 6
DISTRIBUTION OF THE TWO MOST FREQUENT GENERAL
PATTERNS OF EMOTIONS OVER THE THREE PICTURES

General Emotional Pattern	Tsukisoi (N = 10)	Nurses (N = 14)	Doctors (N = 14)	Patients (N = 15)	Total (N = 53)
An emphasis on non-sexual satisfactions	10	9	7	6	32
A denial of pleasure and emotion	0	5	7	9	21

$\chi^2 = 9.9$, 3 df, $p < .02$

I believe that these two general patterns of handling situations in which emotional impulses may easily be aroused are very common ones among Japanese. Why should this be so? In brief, many everyday-life events in Japan, whether for children or adults, offer greater opportunities than is true in the West for the gratification of simple physical pleasures in situations of close contact with other persons—as in bathing, sleeping arrangements, nursing care, child rearing, and so on (see Dore, 1958; Caudill, 1961; Caudill and Doi, 1963). If sexual feelings were allowed to intrude into these events, then this would complicate matters, and the simple pleasures to be derived from these situations would be reduced. Japanese value such simple physical pleasures very highly, and one way of assuring their continued existence is to ignore, to exclude, or in some way to isolate (as by joking) any sexual feelings that might arise. This mode of operation (or, for adults, one might even say, this character structure) results in the general emotional pattern that is tagged here as "an emphasis upon non-sexual satisfactions." The "price" paid for adherence to such a pattern is the tendency to emphasize the non-sexual satisfactions to be gained from situations in which an interest in directly sexual matters might well be not only biologically but also socially appropriate. And I use the term "socially appropriate" here in a rather strict sense, meaning appropriate to the social structure, though not necessarily appropriate to the culture, of the situation. Thus, both biologically and socially, one would expect a man and wife, under reasonable conditions, to have a sexual interest in each other, but culturally this is not necessarily so.

So much for the first general pattern, which I believe is a major one in Japanese life. What about the second general pattern of "a denial of pleasure and emotion," which I think is a strong minor theme? Again starting from the frequency of occurrence in Japanese life of events that offer opportunity for the gratification of physical pleasures in situations of close contact with others, it seems likely that a significant number of persons (possibly for various combinations of genetic, social, and cultural reasons) have not been able to meet the emotional impact of such events by "an emphasis upon non-sexual satisfactions." For these persons, their sexual feelings do tend to intrude, insistently and uncomfortably, into such situations. Thus the "answer" is a general restriction of impulse gratification and a distaste for all too consciously recognized sexual matters. In the extreme this may result in an over-all denial of emotional feeling, whether positive or negative. These persons would fall, then, into the second general pattern of "a denial of pleasure and emotion."

There are, of course, alternatives to the two general patterns that have been discussed. One alternative is the Yes, Yes, Yes pattern represented in Table 5 by three doctors. These persons, from their responses, seem to be able to separate life events into fairly sharply differentiated spheres and to deal with each in terms of its own requirements: thus sexual situations are seen with positive sexual interest, bathing is enjoyed, and sickness is viewed with sympathetic concern. But such persons, probably in any society, are rare.

At present I have no general theory to encompass the residual patterns in Table 5. The persons who are represented in the remaining patterns can, I think, be "explained" on individual grounds, but this paper is not the place for that sort of explanation. Much more work needs to be done, of course, with all the interviews, including the analysis of the responses to the five pictures that have not been considered. What I hope I have been able to communicate in this paper is the essence of several common emotional patterns among Japanese people and a sense of variation in emotional patterning that has, nevertheless, its major and minor themes.

In summary and conclusion, then, of the material that has been presented, what can be said about the relation of patterns of values and emotions in Japan? I think that the dominant value orientation of collaterality, particularly prominent in the sphere of family life, is in line with the major emotional pattern of an emphasis on the non-sexual satisfactions to be derived from everyday events, specifically discussed here in terms of sympathetic concern and care for those who are sick, pleasure in bathing in the company of others, and a rather peaceful and unexcited married life. The theoretical connections between these patterns of values and emotions remain to be worked out in future publication.

BIBLIOGRAPHY

CAUDILL, WILLIAM
1958 *The Psychiatric Hospital as a Small Society*. Cambridge: Harvard University Press.
1961 "Around the Clock Patient Care in Japanese Psychiatric Hospitals: The Role of the *tsukisoi*," *Amer. Soc. Rev.*, 26:204–14.
1962 "Anthropology and Psychoanalysis: Some Theoretical Issues." In: W. C. STURTEVANT and T. GLADWIN (eds.), *Anthropology and Human Behavior*. Washington: Anthropological Society of Washington.

CAUDILL, WILLIAM, and HARRY A. SCARR
1962 "Japanese Value Orientations and Culture Change," *Ethnology*, 1:53–91.

CAUDILL, WILLIAM, and L. TAKEO DOI
1963 "Interrelations of Psychiatry, Culture and Emotion in Japan." In: IAGO GALDSTON (ed.), *Medicine and Anthropology*. New York: International Universities Press.

DOI, L. TAKEO
1960 "Psychopathology of *jibun* and *amae*," *Psychiatria et Neurologia Japonica*, 62: 149–62.

DORE, R. P.
1958 *City Life in Japan*. London: Routledge & Kegan Paul.

GOLDSCHMIDT, WALTER, and ROBERT B. EDGERTON
1961 "A Picture Technique for the Study of Values," *Amer. Anthropol.*, 63:26–47.

KLUCKHOHN, FLORENCE ROCKWOOD, and FRED L. STRODTBECK
1961 *Variations in Value Orientations*. Evanston: Row, Peterson & Co.

AMAE: A KEY CONCEPT FOR UNDERSTANDING JAPANESE PERSONALITY STRUCTURE

L. TAKEO DOI

I AM particularly interested in the problem of personality and culture in modern Japan for two reasons. First, even though I was born and raised in Japan and had my basic medical training there, I have had further training in psychiatry and psychoanalysis in the United States, thus exposing myself for some time to a different culture from that of Japan. Second, I have had many opportunities of treating both Japanese and non-Japanese (mostly American) patients with psychotherapy. These experiences have led me to inquire into differences between Japanese and non-Japanese patients and also into the question of what is basic in Japanese character structure. In this paper I shall describe what I have found to be most characteristic in Japanese patients and then discuss its meaning in the context of Japanese culture.

The essence of what I am going to talk about is contained in one common Japanese word, *"amae."* Let me therefore, first of all, explain the meaning of this word. *Amae* is the noun form of *"amaeru,"* an intransitive verb that means "to depend and presume upon another's benevolence" (Doi, 1956). This word has the same root as *amai*, an adjective that means "sweet." Thus *amaeru* has a distinct feeling of sweetness and is generally used to describe a child's attitude or behavior toward his parents, particularly his mother. But it can also be used to describe the relationship between two adults, such as the relationship between a husband and a wife or a master and a subordinate. I believe that there is no single word in English equivalent to *amaeru*, though this does not mean that the psychology of *amae* is totally alien to the people of English-speaking countries. I shall come back to this problem after describing some of the clinical material through which I came to recognize the importance of what this word *amae* signifies.

It was in my attempt to understand what goes on between the therapist and patient that I first came across the all-powerful drive of the patient's *amae*. There is a diagnostic term in Japanese psychiatry, *shinkeishitsu*, which includes neurasthenia, anxiety neurosis, and obsessive neurosis. Morita, who first used *shinkeishitsu* as a diagnostic term, thought that these three types of neuroses had a basic symptom in common, *toraware*, which means "to be bound or caught," as by some intense preoccupation. He considered *toraware* to be closely related to hypochondriacal fear and thought that this fear sets in motion a reciprocal intensification of attention and sensation. In psychoanalytic work with neurotic patients of the *shinkeishitsu* type I have also found *toraware* to be a basic symptom, but I have evolved a different formulation of its significance (see Doi, 1958). I have observed that during the course of psychotherapy the patient's *toraware* can easily turn into hypersensitivity in his relationship with the therapist. This hypersensitivity is best described by the Japanese word *kodawari*. *Kodawari* is the noun form of *kodawaru*, an intransitive verb meaning "to be sensitive to minor things," "to be inwardly disturbed over one's personal relationships." In the state of *kodawari* one feels that he is not accepted by others, which suggests that *kodawari* results from the unsatisfied desire to *amaeru*. Thus *toraware* can be traced back through *kodawari* to *amae*. In my observations the patient's *toraware* usually receded when he became aware of his *amae* toward the therapist, which he had been warding off consciously and unconsciously up to then.

At first I felt that if the patient became fully aware of his *amae*, he would thereupon be able to get rid of his neurosis. But I was wrong in this assumption and came to observe another set of clinical phenomena following the patient's recognition of his *amae* (see Doi, 1960). Many patients confessed that they were then awakened to the fact that they had not "possessed their self," had not previously appreciated the importance of their existence, and had been really nothing apart from their all-important desire to *amaeru*. I took this as a step toward the emergence of a new consciousness of self, inasmuch as the patient could then at least realize his previous state of "no self."

There is another observation that I should like to mention here. It is about the nature of guilt feelings of Japanese patients (see Doi, 1961). The word *sumanai* is generally used to express guilt feelings, and this word is the negative form of *sumu*, which means "to end." *Sumanai* literally means that one has not done as he was supposed to do, thereby causing the other person trouble or harm. Thus, it expresses more a sense of unfulfilled obligation than a confession of guilt, though it is generally taken as an indication that one feels guilty. When neurotic patients say *sumanai*, I have observed that there lies, behind their use of the word, much hidden aggression engendered by frustration of their wish to *amaeru*. So it seems that in saying *sumanai* they are in fact expressing their hidden concern lest they fall from the grace of *amae* because of their aggression. I think that this analysis of *sumanai* would also apply in essence to the use of this word by the ordinary Japanese in everyday life, but in the case of the neurotic patient *sumanai* is said with greater ambivalence. In other words, more than showing his feeling of being obligated, he tends to create a sense of obligation in the person to whom he makes his apology, thus "forcing" that person eventually to cater to his wish.

I have explained three clinical observations all of which point to the importance of *amae* as a basic desire. As I said before, the state of *amae* originally refers to what a small child feels toward his mother. It is therefore not surprising that the desire to *amaeru* still influences one's adult years and that it becomes manifest in the therapeutic situation. Here we have a perfect example of transference in the psychoanalytic sense. But then is it not strange that *amaeru* is a unique Japanese word? Indeed, the Japanese find it hard to believe that there is no word for *amaeru* in European languages; a colleague once told me that he could not believe that the equivalent for such a seemingly universal phenomenon as *amae* did not exist in English or German, since, as he put it, "Even puppies do it, you know." Let me therefore illustrate the "Japaneseness" of the concept of *amaeru* by one striking incident. The mother of a Eurasian patient, a British woman who had been a long-term resident of Japan, was discussing her daughter with me. She spoke to me in English, but she suddenly switched to Japanese, in order to tell me that her daughter did not *amaeru* much as a child. I asked her why she had suddenly switched to Japanese. She replied, after a pause, that there was no way to say *amaeru* in English.

I have mentioned two Japanese words that are closely related to the psychology of *amae*: *kodawaru*, which means "to be inwardly disturbed over one's personal relationships," and *sumanai*, which means "to feel guilty or obligated." Now I should like to mention a few more words that are also related to the psychology of *amae*. First, *amai*, which originally means "sweet," can be used figuratively to describe a person who is overly soft and benevolent toward others or, conversely, one who always expects to *amaeru* in his relationships with others. Second, *amanzuru*, which is derived from *amaeru*, describes the state of mind in which one acquiesces to whatever circumstances one happens to be in. Third, *tori-iru*, which means "to take in," describes the behavior of a person who skillfully maneuvers another into permitting him to *amaeru*. Fourth, *suneru* describes the behavior of a child or an adult who pouts and sulks because he feels he is not allowed to *amaeru* as much as he wants to, thus harboring in himself mental pain of a masochistic nature. Fifth, *higamu* describes the behavior of a child or an adult who feels himself unfairly treated compared to others who are more favored, often suggesting the presence of a paranoid feeling. Sixth, *tereru* describes the behavior of a child or an adult who is ashamed of showing his intimate wish to *amaeru*. Seventh, *hinekureru* describes the behavior of a child or an adult who takes devious ways in his efforts to deny the wish to *amaeru*.

One could readily say that the behaviors or emotions described by all these Japanese words are not unknown to Westerners and that they appear quite frequently in the therapeutic situation with Western patients. But there remains the question I raised before: Why is there no word in English or in other European languages that is equivalent to *amaeru*, the most central element in all these emotions? To this, one might answer that the absence of a word like *amaeru* is no inconveniency, since it can easily be represented by a combination of words such as the "wish to be loved" or "dependency needs." That may be so, but does not this linguistic difference point to something deeper? Perhaps it reflects a basic psychological difference between Japan and the Western World. Before discussing this problem further, however, I would like to mention a theory of Michael Balint, a British psychoanalyst, which has much bearing on what I am talking about now.

In his psychoanalytic practice Balint observed that "in the final phase of the treatment patients begin to give expression to long-forgotten, infantile, instinctual wishes, and to demand their gratification from their environment" (Balint, 1952a). He called this infantile desire "passive object love," since its primal aim is to be loved; he also called it "primary love," since it is the foundation upon which later forms of love are built. I imagine that he must have wondered why such an important desire is not represented by one common word, for he points out the fact that "all European languages are so poor that they cannot distinguish between the two kinds of object-love, active and passive" (Balint, 1952b).

By now it must be clear that the "primary love" or "passive object-love" described by Balint is none other than the desire to *amaeru*. But then we have to draw the curious conclusion that the emotion of primary love is readily accessible to Japanese patients by way of the word *amaeru*, while to Western patients, according to Balint, it can become accessible only after a painstaking analysis. In my observations I have also noticed that the recognition of *amae* by Japanese patients does not signify the final phase of treatment, as it did in Balint's patients. I think that we have to try to solve this apparent contradiction very carefully, because therein lies, in my opinion, an important key to understanding the psychological differences between Japan and Western countries.

The reasoning behind Balint's observation that primary love appears in its pure form only in the final phase of treatment is as follows: The primary love of an infant is bound to be frustrated, leading to the formation of narcissism; as though he said to himself, "If the world does not love me enough, I have to love and gratify myself." Since such narcissism is part of the earliest and most primitive layer of the mind, it can be modified only in the last stage of treatment, at which time the long-repressed urge to be loved can re-emerge in its pure state. Then what shall we say about the Japanese, to whom this primary desire to be loved is always accessible? Does it mean that the Japanese have less narcissism? I think not. Rather I would say that the Japanese somehow continue to cherish the wish to be loved even after the formation of narcissism. It is as though the Japanese did not want to see the reality of their basic frustration. In other words, the Japanese, as does everybody else, do experience frustration of their primary love, as is well attested to by the existence of the rich vocabulary we have already encountered relating to the frustration of *amae*. But it seems that the Japanese never give up their basic desire to *amaeru*, thus mitigating the extent of violent emotions caused by its frustration.

In this connection I want to mention an interesting feature of the word *amaeru*. We do not say that an infant does *amaeru* until he is about one year old, thereby indicating that he is then conscious of his wish to *amaeru*, which in turn suggests the presence of a budding realization that his wish cannot always be gratified. Thus, from its inception, the wish to *amaeru* is accompanied by a secret fear that it may be frustrated.

If what I have been saying is true, then it must indicate that there is a social sanction in Japanese society for expressing the wish to *amaeru*. And it must be this social sanction that has encouraged in the Japanese language the development of the large vocabulary relating to *amaeru*. In other words, in Japanese society parental dependency is fostered, and this behavior pattern is even institutionalized into its social structure, whereas perhaps the opposite tendency prevails in Western societies. This seems to be confirmed by recent anthropological studies of Japanese society, notably that of Ruth Benedict, who said: "The arc of life in Japan is plotted in opposite fashion to that in the United States. It is a great U-curve with maximum freedom and indulgence allowed to babies and to the old. Restrictions are slowly increased after babyhood till having one's own way reaches a low just before and after marriage" (Benedict, 1961). It is true that the restrictions Benedict spoke of do exist for adults in Japanese society, but it should be understood that these restrictions are never meant to be drastic so far as the basic desire to *amaeru* is concerned. Rather, these restrictions are but channels through which that desire is to be duly gratified. That is why we can speak of parental dependency as being institutionalized in Japanese society. For instance, in marriage a husband does *amaeru* toward his wife, and vice versa. It is strongly present in all formal relationships, including those between teacher and student and between doctor and patient. Thus William Caudill (1961), in his observations on Japanese psychiatric hospitals, spoke of the mutual dependency he encountered in all relationships.

In this connection I cannot resist mentioning an episode that happened when I gave a talk on some characteristic Japanese words to a professional group in the United States. *Amaeru* was one of those words. After my talk one distinguished scholar asked me whether or not the feeling of *amaeru* is something like what Catholics feel toward their Holy Mother. Apparently he could not recognize the existence of such a feeling in the ordinary mother-child relationship. And if his response is representative of Americans, it would mean that in American society the feeling of *amaeru* can be indulged in perhaps only in the religious life, but here also very sparingly.

I would now like to mention a study by a Japanese scholar, Hajime Nakamura, professor of Indian philosophy at the University of Tokyo and an authority on comparative philosophy. In his major work, *Ways of Thinking of Eastern Peoples* (1960), he presents a penetrating analysis of thought patterns of Indians, Chinese, Japanese, and Tibetans on the basis of linguistic studies and observations on variations in Buddhist doctrine and practice in these four countries. What he says about the Japanese pattern of thought is parallel to what I have been saying here, though he reaches his conclusions from an entirely different source. He says that the Japanese way of thinking is greatly influenced by an emphasis on immediate personal relations and also that the

Japanese have always been eager to adopt foreign cultural influences, but always within the framework of this emphasis on personal relations. To state this in psychoanalytic terms: the Japanese are always prepared to identify themselves with, or introject, an outside force, to the exclusion of other ways of coping with it. This character trait of the Japanese was touched upon by Benedict, too, when she said that "the Japanese have an ethic of alternatives" and "Japan's motivations are situational," referring particularly to the sudden complete turnabout of Japan following the defeat of the last war.

This leads, however, to the very interesting and important question of whether or not Japanese character structure has changed at all since the war. I think that Benedict was quite right in assuming that Japan as a whole willingly submitted to unconditional surrender because it was the Emperor's order, that Japan wanted only to please the Emperor, even in her defeat. But it cannot be denied that things have been changing since then. For instance, the Emperor had to declare that he no longer wished to be considered sacred. Also the Japanese have been disillusioned to find that the paramount virtue of *chū*, that is, loyalty to the emperor, was taken advantage of by the ultra-nationalists, who completely failed them. With the decline of *chū* there was also a decline of *kō*, that is, of filial piety. In other words, the tradition of repaying one's *on*, that is, one's spiritual debts to an emperor and to one's parents, was greatly undermined. Thus there developed the moral chaos of present-day Japan.

I think, however, that the nature of this chaos has a distinctly Japanese character and can best be understood by taking into account the psychology of *amae*. It seems that heretofore the stress upon the duty of repaying one's *on* to the emperor and to one's parents served the purpose of regulating the all too powerful desire of *amae*. Since the Japanese were deprived of this regulating force after the war, it was inevitable that their desire to *amaeru* was let loose, with its narcissistic element becoming more manifest. That perhaps explains why we now find in Japan so many examples of lack of social restraint. I wonder whether this recent tendency has also helped to increase the number of neurotics. I think it has, though we have no reliable statistics to confirm it. But I am quite certain that an analysis of the psychology of *amae* such as I am attempting here would not have been possible in prewar days, because *amae* was concealed behind the duty of repaying one's *on*. It certainly was not visible to the outside observer, even to one as acute as Ruth Benedict. I would like to give you one clinical example to illustrate this point.

One of my recent patients, who was a student of law, revealed to me one day his secret thoughts, saying, "I wish I had some person who would take the responsibility of assisting me." The remarkable thing about this confession was that the Japanese word that he used for "assist" was a special legal term *hohitsu*, which was formerly used only for the act of assisting the emperor with his task of governing the nation. In saying this, as the patient himself explained, he wanted, like the emperor, to appear to be responsible for his acts but to depend completely on his assistant, who would really carry the burden. He said this, not jokingly but, rather, with complete seriousness. It is obvious that this confession revealed his secret desire to *amaeru*, about which he spoke more clearly on another occasion. But what I would like to point out here is that in prewar days the patient could hardly have made such a confession, using a special term reserved only for the emperor. Of course, this is a special case, and the fact that the patient was a law student accounted for his use of such a technical term. Yet I think that this case illustrates the point that I want to make, that is, the more emphasis placed upon repaying one's *on*, the less clearly seen is one's desire to *amaeru*.

In this connection, let me say a few words about the nature of so-called "emperor worship," which served as the Japanese state religion in prewar days. It is true that the emperor was held sacred, but the element of taboo was greater than that of divinity. It is really tempting to apply what Freud said about taboo to the Japanese emperor worship. As a matter of fact, he did mention the Japanese emperor in his book on *Totem and Taboo*, but not from the viewpoint of what is being discussed here. I will not go into this subject any further now, except to add one more comment concerning the effect of elimination of the emperor taboo and its related system, apart from the already discussed release of the desire to *amaeru*. Some Japanese critics voiced the opinion that the tight thought control deriving from the emperor and the family system in prewar days stifled development of healthy selfhood, that one could assert himself in those days only by way of *suneru* and *higamu*, which are interestingly enough the very same Japanese words that I have described before as indicating frustration of *amae* (Maruyama, 1960; Isono, 1960). I agree that this opinion is generally true, but I do not believe that elimination of the emperor and family system alone can lead to development of healthy selfhood or personality. This is shown by many patients, who confess that they are awakened to the fact that they have "not had self" apart from the all powerful desire to *amaeru*. Then what or who can help them to obtain their "self"? This touches upon a very important problem of identity, which I will not attempt to discuss in detail. I can say only that the Japanese as a whole are still searching for something, something with which they can safely identify themselves, so that they can become whole, independent beings.

In closing I should like to make two additional remarks. First, it may seem that I am possibly idealizing the West in a way, since I have looked at the problem of personality and culture in modern Japan from the Western point of view. I do not deny that I have. In fact I could not help doing so, because Japanese culture did not produce any yardstick to judge itself critically. I really think that it is a fine thing for the West to have developed such a yardstick for critical analysis. And it seems inevitable that it involves a kind of idealization when the non-Westerners attempt to apply such a yardstick to themselves. I know, however, that in the psychoanalytic circles of Western countries idealization has a special meaning and is not something commendable.

So they would certainly not call their use of the analytical method idealization. But I wonder whether they are entirely right in assuming that their use of the analytical method stands on its own without involving any idealization on their part.

Second, though I have stated that there is no exact equivalent to the word *amaeru* in all European languages, I do not say that *amaeru* is unique to the Japanese language. I have some information that the language of Korea and that of Ainu have a word of the same meaning. There seems to be some question about whether or not the Chinese language has such a word. I am now most curious to know whether or not the Polynesian languages have a similar word. I have a feeling that they may have. If they do, how would their psychology compare with that of the Japanese? It is my earnest hope that these questions will be answered by anthropological and psychological studies in the not too distant future.

BIBLIOGRAPHY

BALINT, MICHAEL
1952a "The Final Goal of Psychoanalytic Treatment." In *Primary Love and Psychoanalytic Technique*. London: Hogarth Press.
1952b "Critical Notes on the Theory of the Pregenital Organizations of the Libido." In: *Ibid*.

BENEDICT, RUTH
1961 *The Chrysanthemum and the Sword*. Boston, Houghton Mifflin Co.

CAUDILL, WILLIAM
1961 "Around the Clock Patient Care in Japanese Psychiatric Hospitals: The Role of the *tsukisoi*," *Amer. Soc. Rev.*, 26:204–14.

DOI, L. TAKEO
1956 "Japanese Language as an Expression of Japanese Psychology," *Western Speech*, 20:90–96.
1958 "Shinkeishitsu no seishinbyori" ("Psychopathology of *shinkeishitsu*"), *Psychiatria et Neurologia Japonica*, 60: 733–44.
1960 "Jibun to amae no seishinbyori" ("Psychopathology of *jibun* and *amae*), *ibid*., 61: 149–62.
1961 "Sumanai to Ikenai ('*Sumanai* and *Ikenai*')—Some Thoughts on Super-Ego," *Jap. J. Psychoanal.*, 8:4–7.

ISONO, FUJIKO
1960 "Ie to Jigaishiki" ("Family and Self-consciousness"). In: *Kindai Nippon Shisoshi Kōza* ("History of Thought in Modern Japan"), Vol. 6. Tokyo: Chikuma Shobo.

MARUYAMA, MASAO
1960 *Chūsei to Hangyaku* ("Loyalty and Rebellion"). In: *ibid*.

NAKAMURA, HAJIME
1960 *Ways of Thinking of Eastern peoples*. JAPANESE NATIONAL COMMISSION FOR UNESCO (comp.). Tokyo: Japanese Government Printing Bureau.

ENTRANCE EXAMINATIONS AND EMOTIONAL DISTURBANCES IN JAPAN'S "NEW MIDDLE CLASS"*

EZRA F. VOGEL

As YET there is neither a sufficiently precise nosology nor an adequate supply of scholars properly trained in psychiatry and the behavioral science to even attempt a definitive comparison of rates of mental disorders in different countries. Data is available for hospitalization rates, but there is no indication that this accurately reflects incidence rates because hospitalization policies vary so greatly from country to country. There have been a few studies of prevalence, but, since care and treatment has an effect on mental condition, even studies of prevalence may not accurately reflect incidence rates. The few incidence studies that have been attempted have been insufficiently standardized between countries and have relied on brief interviews done by partially trained interviewers (or else on very small samples). Where reliability checks have been made on diagnostic classification, the reliability has been extremely low.[1]

In the absence of precise statistical data, one way to estimate the frequency of disturbances in various countries is to rely on local opinions about relative rates and to see whether they accord with what we know of general social and cultural features of the society. One problem judged very common by a large number of Japanese psychiatrists (and less common by psychiatrists in America) fits precisely with other things we know of Japanese society: the high frequency of disturbance connected with gaining admission to academic institutions. While we cannot say precisely how much more common this problem is in Japan than in other countries, the fact that there is such wide agreement among expert in-

---

* The field work for this paper was financed by a research training grant from the Foundations' Fund for Research in Psychiatry. The research was carried out with the co-operation of the Japanese National Institute of Mental Health. The analysis of the data was facilitated by the financial support of the American National Institute of Mental Health.

1. Dr. Morton Kramer, consultant to WHO on mental-health statistics has suggested to WHO that careful cross-cultural comparisons would require the development of reliability procedures, involving joint rating by psychiatrists in different countries. Such a project would be of enormous magnitude and would require solutions to difficult technical and organizational problems. To the present author's knowledge, no such project is as yet even being seriously considered. Cf. Morton Kramer, "The Implications of Some Observations on Epidemeological Studies of the Mental Disorders and on the Collection and Utilization of Statistics on the Treatment and Rehabilitation of the Mentally Ill in Japan, Formosa, Australia and the Philippines." Mimeographed.

formants about its relative importance suggests that examining some of the cultural features underlying it may be useful.

The problem of gaining admission to good academic institutions is not peculiar to Japan. Those who fail to make the grade are probably disappointed in any land, and the tension surrounding admission is probably found in every society in which admission to academies of higher training is not determined solely on ascriptive bases. What is peculiar to Japan is the severity and intensity of this problem. Even those Japanese who say they do not worry about examinations spend, by American standards, a great deal of time preparing for them. Because the difference in intensity is so crucial to the present argument, it will be necessary to give extended discussion of the process of gaining admission, from the point of view of the applicant and his family.

1. PREPARATION FOR EXAMINATIONS

In many "new middle class"[2] families, the child first takes an entrance examination at the junior high school level. But whether he takes his first examination then, at nursery school entrance, or at college entrance, examination season is a climax of months and even years of long preparation and planning. Even if short of funds, the family will have struggled to provide their children with desks and other facilities conducive to long hours of study. Most of the children will have done more than the required school assignments for several years before the examination. Most "new middle class" families can now afford to hire a tutor for perhaps a year or two to work regularly with the child in preparation for the examination. (A large number of college students work as part-time tutors for students preparing for examination.) If a family has expanded its home facilities in recent years by adding another room or two, the extra room will probably be a separate study room for the children.

Since the first grade, the parents, and especially the mother, will have gone over the children's homework carefully to make sure the children understand the assignments, and they will have made themselves available to answer questions whenever a tutor is not around. The parents will have read carefully the newspaper and magazine articles advising how to select the school and will have followed very closely the stories of success of their friends' children. They will know what proportion of students from a given junior high school advance to the best high schools and what proportion of students from a given high school enter the best colleges. In many cases the expense of tutors and study supplies will force them to tap their moderate savings, leaving inadequate amounts to provide for their own old age. Their hope is that, if necessary, the child will

---

2. The "new midde class" consists of white-collar workers in the large bureaucracies of government or business. Since the author's field work in Japan in 1958–60 was with the "new middle class," it is difficult to say how generally the comments in this paper apply to other groups in Japan, but it is his impression that, while these trends are strongest in the "new middle class," they are widespread throughout Japanese society.

then be able to support the parents or contribute to their income in their old age. Since many applicants to the best universities are admitted only on the second or third try, those who fail the examination the first time will often decide to spend one or two years in full-time study before trying them again and may attend a special school for those who have already completed high school but have not yet passed their entrance examinations. If the family is very poor, the child may have to work part time or full time after his first failure.

For a high-school student, serious preparation often begins a year or two before the examination. The student may stop various other kinds of activities and settle down to a serious life of study. He will probably be studying several hours a day after school, and in the summer vacation preceding the February examinations he will spend much of every day in study. Even the sixth-grade students may be attending special classes after grade school lasting well into the late afternoon or evening and may often arrive home as late as 8 or 9 P.M. He will then study on his own at home. It may be necessary to give up movies and any special hobbies during this year of preparation. In other cases, the beginning of such extracurricular studies as music may be postponed until after any crucial examinations, perhaps even until after entering college. If the children have various kinds of jobs to do around the house, they may be excused from these duties. Other children will be urged to be quiet so as not to interfere with the study. The mother may arrange her work so that she is available for answering questions during the child's study period. If the mother herself has had insufficient education to answer the questions and if the father has had more education, then the father will generally try to make himself available for answering questions.

In the year preceding the examination the mother will spend a great deal of time investigating various schools, particularly the expenses, the entrance requirements, and the success of the school's graduates. She will find this out by going to the school directly and by talking with other friends. In addition, she will spend much time consulting with her child's teacher and other parents in order to assess her own child's abilities. Naturally one wants one's child to get into the best possible school, but this involves an element of strategy and risk-taking. While it is possible to take as many as three or four examinations if they are not offered on the same date, it is difficult and sometimes impossible to take more than three or four, and, if the child fails all these, he may be out of luck. Application fees cost money, and one cannot afford to take examinations indiscriminately. In addition, taking an examination is tiring for the student, and if he tries to take three or four examinations during the same season, he may be so tired out from the first two or three, and perhaps so discouraged by the results, that he will not perform well on the later ones. Hence it is very important that the mother assess her child's abilities accurately in order that he may take the most appropriate examination.

Not only must the mother consult with others but she must also make sure that the father and the child approve her choices. Indeed, the child's veto of a certain school is usually final, and, while the mother often persuades a child, in the final analysis he is the one who decides, since without his co-operation and motivation the mother can have little hope of success. She is reluctant to take all the responsibility herself for making this decision and is likely to consult with the father either to elicit his suggestions or simply to make sure he will go along with the decision. They may be very anxious to consult with friends or relatives who have special knowledge about school admissions, and there may be heated discussions during the period of decision-making.

By late January these decisions have all been made, and applications begin. One cannot apply early but only during the two or three days that the school accepts applications. The mother goes in person to make the application, taking with her the health certificate, school records, and entrance fees. Schools announce that it does not matter what time the mother comes to make the application, but there will always be a few mothers who came the previous night and waited in line overnight, perhaps bringing sandwiches and cushions, so that they would be among the very first to make the application. These mothers know that the school says that arrival time makes no difference, but perhaps they hope to impress the school administration with their seriousness of purpose, or that the low number on the application blank may be lucky, or that their children may receive examinations earlier in the day and may be somewhat fresher for taking them. Or perhaps their coming early is simply a reflection of anxiety and feeling of excitement and a desire to get the application over with. While most "new middle class" mothers think it somewhat foolish to wait overnight, nevertheless many start out on the first train leaving suburbia, as early as four o'clock in the morning, on the day when applications are due. Even then, there may be a long line when they arrive, and those who have enough "nerve" to come later in the day may have an even longer wait of several hours before filling out the application. If it is the first time that a mother has gone through the application procedures or if she is going for her only son, she may be among the first in line. If the woman is a "beteran" (veteran) she may be relaxed enough to come much later, but it will undoubtedly be dark before she returns home. Sometimes it is necessary for the child to go along with the mother for the application, though in the case of a college application the child will probably go by himself. This procedure of standing in line may take place three or four times, depending on the number of applications to be made.

If a personal interview is also required, the mother and child will be very much concerned about the impression they will make. It may be desirable to bring along various letters of introduction from people who have some reputation or who have some personal connection with the faculty administration or with the P.-T.A. Even though a child and mother plan carefully what to say during this interview, it is not uncommon for the child to be frightened and so have difficulty expressing himself in a very brief interview. While the mother and child may know that the examination is much more important than the interview, still, in order to be safe, they approach the interview as if it were of crucial importance.

In the period immediately preceding the examination the family restricts its outside activities and every effort is put into last-minute study so that the child will have every possible bit of knowledge at hand. There may be concern in this period that the child will become sick or catch a cold, which might interfere with his performance or even require him to miss the opportunity completely. As a result, any slight sign of a cold is taken very seriously, and the family quickly tries to do everything to cure it as quickly and completely as possible.

During examination season, social contacts sharply decrease. The mothers all seem to avoid meeting each other. If family members do happen to meet someone accidentally, then they try to avoid giving much information, except perhaps to a close friend. Since it is embarrassing to be refused by a school, they often avoid identifying the school, or they may mention the school, but explain that there is little expectation of success, since the child didn't really prepare for that examination properly, and that they are really trying to get him into another school (to which he is almost certain to be admitted). The family purposely underestimates the extent to which they are trying for entrance to a difficult school, in some cases even distorting the facts, pretending not to be interested in a certain examination—only to be discovered by an acquaintance at the scene of the examination. The children also watch very closely who is missing from school on a certain day, because if their friend is missing on the day certain examinations are given, they will be able to tell where the schoolmate is taking the examination. However, on the whole, children are much more open and direct in talking about examination plans than are parents, although the children will, of course, report to their mothers about which children are taking which examinations.

2. A SOCIOLOGICAL INTERPRETATION OF EXAMINATION PRESSURE

a) There are numerous educational institutions in urban areas that are in competition with one another, and this tends to encourage and reinforce the pressure for admission to them. While a few are specialized institutions, generally the populace is able to rank the junior high schools and high schools by one criterion: the proportion of their graduating classes who are placed in, respectively, good high schools and good colleges. Precise figures are published annually in the popular press.

Historically, the best way to obtain competent people for government offices was to select them from certain institutions of higher learning. Indeed, which institution a person attended was used as the main universalistic criterion for employment in government, even more crucial perhaps than the civil service examination itself. To some extent the same tradition still obtains. The high schools are clearly ranked in hierarchical order (in prewar days the top middle schools were numbered, and the number in general corresponded with their rank in popular prestige and respect).

Just as an American football coach is judged on the basis of number of games won, so is the Japanese high-school principal judged by any rise or fall in the proportion of graduates successfully placed in major institutions. For the private high school, there are obviously economic reasons, also, why it is important successfully to place graduates in the best colleges. (In general, it appears that institutional competition is less subdued in Japan; for example, it is very common for hospitals, doctors, dentists, etc., to advertise.)

In addition, schools require that the application be filled out in person (at least in the mother's person), and successful candidates' names are usually posted or announced publicly, as on the radio, rather than being privately announced. In fact, there seems to be a feeling that the longer the line at the time of application, or announcement of results, the better the school. There is no question but that this does a great deal to heighten the tension and excitement surrounding admission.

Since each school's prestige depends in part on its ability to place candidates successfully at institutions of advanced learning, school administrators exert a great deal of pressure on teachers to press the students to prepare adequately for the examinations, and to study harder if they expect to pass them. Teachers are often given extra rewards (praise, presents, and sometimes money) by parents for assisting in examination preparation, and the school often provides classrooms as well as teachers for students who wish to study beyond the regular hours of school. Often teachers will take students aside, advise them to drop extracurricular activities, to study harder, etc., so as to be able to pass the entrance examinations.

Some educators have been known to say that they think the threat of examinations is an important stimulus in promoting education. The Japanese Ministry of Education is strenuously attempting to raise the quality of what is learned in the school system, as witnessed by the agitation for teachers' rating systems and the fairly recent attempts to raise standards of education. Thus, with some pressure for higher standards coming from the central Ministry to the various schools, and from the school to the teacher, the teacher uses concern over examinations as an important inducement for study. The threat of examination is, perhaps, the functional equivalent of the stern discipline of the previous generation.

b) Japanese firms generally make a life commitment to the employee at the time of hiring. They usually prefer to hire someone immediately upon his completion of school, and in many cases anyone hired at a later time in life is subject to a variety of disadvantages, including lower pay scale and slower rate of salary increase. Just as a Japanese professor almost never changes his position from one university to another (unless it is an affiliate of the one where he is teaching), so an employee of one company almost never changes to work at another company. The company gives a great deal of reward for loyalty, and an employee who is so unreliable as to switch from one company to another is slightly suspect, since he may not be as loyal to the new firm. The firm can ordinarily dismiss a man only for gross incompetence, disobedience, etc., and such cases are extremely rare. Instead, an employee would be switched to a less important position within the company, or perhaps his rate of progress would be slower than his peers.

For large firms and government agencies, initial admission is almost entirely on a universalistic basis, on the adjudged basis of competence. They seek to obtain men of considerable competence, since they will be committed to these men for life. Since universities can be fairly clearly ranked, and since the best students will almost invariably try to get into the best universities, the most reliable single factor for judging competence is the university attended. It is usually safe to assume, as the firm does, that there is a fairly clear ranking by schools, not only on the basis of ability but also on quality of training. Each university has a highly crystallized status ranking, and there is much greater agreement in Japanese society on the relative ranking of universities than there is, for example, in America. Because of this there is a "self-fulfilling" accuracy, in that firms pick students from the best schools, and the best students will try to enter the best institutions.

Once a student is accepted in a university, he may not study very hard. Indeed, prominence is given to the peer group and other particularistic relationships within any given institution, and the competition is focused on getting into the institution. Whether this be cause or effect, it is clear that academic ranking within a university is not a very accurate criterion for measuring a student's abilities. Many bright students do not study hard once they have been admitted to such an institution, so firms rely much more on which institution a student has attended than on his relative rank within an institution.

As a result, there is considerable reality to the view of the Japanese applicant that his entire future career depends on the success of a single examination. He will or will not enter a good company, and, once in or out, he is likely to stay there. Even if an American's entire future were dependent upon the results of his admission to college, the performance by which he is judged is spread out over several years so that there is not so much pressure focused on one single time, the entrance-examination time.

It may be argued that in a general way Japan is in the process of transition from an ascriptive to an achievement-oriented society. Japanese organizations are still to a large extent governed on the basis of ascriptive ties. (For example, seniority is a very important basis for advancement of salary and rank within the firm, even though the actual task assignments and informal lines of authority are often based on technical competence.)[3] The importance of achievement has not yet become widespread throughout society and tends to be very heavily

---

3. For the analysis of Japanese firms, I am heavily indebted to the as yet unpublished work of Professor Kazuo Noda of Rikkyo University.

concentrated at certain times, that is, the time of getting into a reputable school. The result is that, in the life span, the time of pressure for achievement is heavily concentrated in the late adolescent years.

It may be suggested that Japan's suicide curve also suggests the concentration of achievement stress in this age group. Unlike other countries, the suicide rate is higher in late adolescence than in middle age, as Professor De Vos shows in more detail elsewhere in the present volume. In the mass media, and in popular folklore, contemporary suicides are often associated with examination failure or fear of failure.[4]

c) Very rarely is the Japanese mother in the "new middle class" able to work outside the home. While for some lower-class mothers it is still possible to engage in "naishoku" ("letting-out work," usually sewing and other handicraft work), this is generally felt to be beneath the "new middle class" mother.

In addition, she typically knows very little about her husband's work, and decisions about the husband's work (where he should work, whether to ask for a raise, whether to change specialties, etc.) are almost completely out of her hands, her opinion in these matters being considered unimportant. The social life of the Japanese man is largely with his fellow workers, and the wife rarely has a chance to go out with her husband, so she participates almost not at all in her husband's social activities.

Thus whatever drive the mother has for achievement cannot be expressed in relationship to either helping her husband's career or furthering her own career. It can be expressed only in one direction: in furthering the career of her child.

The Japanese mother's sphere is almost entirely limited to the home and her children. But her role in planning the child's success and making arrangements for him (in all matters, but particularly the crucial ones regarding school choice and marital choice) is much greater than, for example, that of the American mother. It is she who bears the brunt of the decision about which examinations the child shall take; it is she who is given praise or blame for the child's performance.

Since all her energies are directed toward the child and since she feels that his success is in large part her success, she is motivated to do everything she can to prepare him adequately for the examinations. She is enormously involved in the child's successes, and he cannot help but feel this pressure from the mother.

Children have little opportunity to be away from home. Dating in high school is virtually nonexistent. The child's social circle is very circumscribed, and the Japanese child-training practices are such as to encourage dependency on the mother.[5] This makes him very responsive to his mother's pressures.

4. While it is clear from Professor De Vos's analysis that examinations per se are not the only cause of high suicide rates at this age, it is possible that the high rates in certain rural areas are related to the same fundamental problem: the fact that one's future is thought to depend so completely on the organization that one is or is not able to get into at this age.

5. Ezra F. and Suzanne H. Vogel, "Family Security, Personal Immaturity, and Emotional Health in a Japanese Sample," *Marriage and Family Living* (1961), 23:161–66.

It is not easy for the mother to give valuable assistance to her child when he is studying for examinations. She herself typically has only a few years' education beyond grade school, and, with the recent changes in postwar educational content and practices, it is a real challenge to be able to give proper guidance to her children and to help them adequately with their homework. It may be suggested that some of the strong motive power of the mother in trying to help her child perform adequately stems from the fact that it is a very real challenge to be able to help.[6]

d) The pattern of achievement by examination is so heavily institutionalized that the prestige of the mother in the neighborhood is greatly dependent on her children's successes on examination. Most mothers have high ambitions for their children and are eager to learn ways that will assist them in achieving these goals. Hence, they are willing and even anxious to cultivate contacts with mothers who have been successful in placing their children in good universities. Indeed, some of the finest praise for a mother is in saying that her children are in particularly good educational institutions, and if her child has successfully passed an examination to an important university, she will be listened to on all kinds of topics regarding child-rearing. Her status rises and covers other areas besides that of preparing for examinations. Conversely, a mother whose child has not done well is ashamed in relation to her friends and must assume a much more submissive role.

Aside from informal groups, about the only organization that the "new middle class" mothers attend with any regularity is the Parent-Teacher Association. The Japanese P.-T.A. has a variety of committees with many more functions than has a comparable American P.-T.A., including fund-raising of fairly major proportions, preparing school luncheons, honoring various teachers and administrators, maintaining the beauty of the school and schoolyard, officiating at school field days, etc. For many mothers, it provides one of the few opportunities for getting out of the home. When the mother goes to P.-T.A. meetings, one of the key topics is almost certain to be preparation in anticipation of examinations. In other words, a large part of the mothers' conversation is focused on problems of school achievement. This does a great deal to stimulate mutually the anxieties about examinations. A mother, having relatively few contacts with others, generally does not have a great deal of confidence about her own handling of her children and is eager to listen to the advice of teachers and mothers with older children. This heightens her concern about her child's examination performance and does a great deal to encourage her to want to show the other mothers that her child can do well. Some of the mothers jokingly comment that the various homework assignments are often too difficult for the children and quickly degenerate into a competition between mothers. There is no question, however, that the mothers' concerns about achievement come to be felt by the children.

---

6. Cf. the finding that alternate reward and punishment rather than continual reward increase strength of drives (David McClelland, *Personality* [New York: Dryden Press, 1951]).

e) Yet the facts given above do not entirely explain the intensity of the feeling about examinations. In fact, many jobs are available, even for men who do not pass examinations, and many opportunities are available for promotion later in life. The standard explanation that the Japanese gives as to worry about examinations is that Japan is a small country with few opportunities, one that has many natural disasters, so one must belong to organizations that provide security.

While this argument in its bald form seems to be an oversimplification of the facts, still the general argument has a great deal of meaning for many of these parents. They have gone through an earthquake in their early childhood that destroyed large parts of many major cities. They have endured a depression, a war, and a postwar period of several years of great self-sacrifice. Since, generally, they had been living barely above the subsistence level, any disaster has been a great crisis. As the Japanese say, *"yoyū ga nai* (there is no margin to spare)" no room for comfort, so that one must always be tense and on the alert. Even now, in the greatest period of prosperity, there is a fear that some disaster may again overtake them. Something might happen to the world economy, on which Japan is terribly dependent, and there would be no chance for recovery. There might again be an earthquake, or the annual typhoons might hit their areas. There might be a nuclear war, and, since nuclear weapons have fallen on Hiroshima and Nagasaki, they know how frightening this would be.

A large portion of these "new middle class" families have come in from the rural area during the parents' lifetime. The countryside was crowded and they knew they had to make their way in the city. Yet jobs were very hard to come by in the city, and there was always a fear that one would be without any means of support. Since public welfare was not well developed, it is true that some families in the depression and immediate postwar period fell by the wayside, with no one to look after them. The people who came to the cities were eagerly searching for some permanent tie to an occupational setting that would give them some degree of security. It is true that there were far fewer decent openings than applicants to fill the openings.

Thus, even with the present prosperity, many feel that they need a truly secure tie with the husband's firm. It should be a large, stable, and reliable firm, able to withstand fluctuations of the business cycle and absolutely committed to the employee. Such opportunities for a secure attachment to a firm are most likely to be available through success on examinations.

3. THE IMPLICATIONS FOR MENTAL HEALTH

From the foregoing analysis, it should be clear that the importance of examinations is, in the language of the psychiatrist, "overdetermined" by a number of historical and social structural characteristics of Japanese society. While it is not possible to trace all the implications of this concern about examinations for mental disturbances, two general problems can at least be mentioned and illustrated by case material.

The first problem is extremely simple and flows directly from the concern about examinations: the various types of anxiety and disturbance that follow from the tensions surrounding examinations. As an example of this kind of problem we may take the case of a fifth-grade boy brought by his mother to a child psychiatric outpatient clinic for stuttering.

While the mother ostensibly brought the child into the clinic for his stuttering problem, in one of the early interviews she incidently mentioned that the boy was not doing very well in school and that the teacher thought he might do somewhat better if he did not stutter. Later in the course of treatment she began expressing her worries about the child's future career and expressed particular concern that her son might make a poor showing at the time of the interview in connection with entrance into middle school. Stuttering was somewhat alleviated during the course of treatment, but, even before it had disappeared completely, the week after the child had successfully passed the middle-school examination the mother came to the therapist, thanked him for his help, invited him to a small party, and terminated regular visits to the clinic.

Psychiatrists to whom the case was presented felt that the child's stuttering was dynamically related to the pressure the mother was putting on the child for school performance.[7] The mother had even less education than most mothers in the neighborhood and was greatly worried about her ignorance in her relationships with other mothers. Even before the time of examination she was worried by the fact that her children ranked much lower in the class than did neighbor children.

That her thinking about her child's admission to junior high school was clearly linked to her worry about his later career is indicated by her attempts to place the responsibility of her child's future career on her therapist. At times she even directly raised the question whether the therapist would help find some suitable job for her son in case he was unsuccessful with the examinations.

This mother was deeply involved in her child's successes and failures and would be furious at her son when he was not performing well in school. There is no doubt that the son was extremely worried about his own academic performance as well, but, because of annoyance at the mother's nagging and pressuring him, he was ambivalent about achieving and at times defiantly refused to study. Sometimes the boy would not listen to his mother, and they would become so excited that they could not properly study together. At such times, the mother would withdraw and turn the son over to his father, who would then try to work with the child.

While this particular example involved a case of stuttering, there are many other types of cases that are associated with examinations. There are, for example, acute anxiety episodes, depressive periods following failure, and various types of learning blocks. Clearly, examination pressure was not the single cause

---

7. The author is indebted to an informal seminar of Dr. Theodore Lidz, Dr. Ruth Lidz, Miss Alice Cornelison, Dr. Steven Fleck, and Dr. Hollingsworth for their comments on several case histories.

for the development of disturbances. In all these case histories there was information about various kinds of disturbances long before examination time. But the severity of the disturbance and the particular form it took did seem to be related to the examination pressure.

The second kind of problem to be considered here is the problem of family composition and role allocation within the family. As one example we may take the case of a boy brought to the psychiatric clinic for learning problems. He was the only son, with an older and a younger sister. The older sister, while not outstanding, was performing well within the average range in the school class. The father was a high-school teacher and, as one might expect, was interested in the academic achievement of his children, particularly his son, who would be the successor in the family line.

In fact, the boy's intelligence, as measured in a test at the clinic, was only borderline, but the mother, and particularly the father, found this almost impossible to accept. The father used to have drill sessions with the son, trying to make him learn something, but these sessions almost invariably ended with the child crying. While the mother was disappointed with the child's school performance, she did feel that the father was being too harsh on the boy and trying to push him too hard.

When brought into the psychiatric clinic, the child showed signs of serious emotional disturbance and a great deal of conflict around learning tasks. Yet, no matter how much he tried, the father, anxious that his son be a success and reflect credit on the family as he went through the same school system in which the father was teaching, could not keep from pressuring the child to learn.

Precisely how the examination pressure affects any given child within a family depends on, among other things, the composition of the household. It may be suggested that an only son, as in the case above, is particularly vulnerable. If there are two sons, and one does not perform well, then the pressure is often placed on the other child. At times, depending on how the roles within the family are distributed, the pressure may be placed on the brighter one. If a family has, for example, two sons and decides that one is more capable, then the family is likely to put a disproportionate amount of energy into trying to make this son a success. More time will be spent teaching him, more money will be spent on tutors, and, if he fails an examination to a good public school, the family may even decide to pool its resources to pay for a private school. Since the typical Japanese "new middle class" family has very limited financial resources and cannot give adequate support to several sons, it may concentrate its energies and efforts on the one thought most likely to succeed. In such a case, the boy who is most capable will be suffering from a great deal of tension associated with the responsibility he feels, since the family has spent so much time helping him and has, in fact, made many sacrifices in the hope of his academic success. The other child in such a family may receive much less pressure regarding preparation for examinations and may respond in a fairly relaxed manner even if he fails an examination.

While there are differences in role allocation within the family, still there is generally a great deal of consistency in the amount of pressure placed on all the children within a given family. Families that have numerous contacts or a great deal of money or whose performance on a variety of scores is better than that of others in their social group seem to be much more relaxed about examinations and to place somewhat less pressure on the children. But families that must rely entirely on competitive examinations for their children's future success and that have difficulty meeting normative patterns of achievement within their particular reference group are likely to place great pressure on their children.

Many Japanese parents and educators have remarked that entrance examinations are unfortunate because they force children to lead a very restricted life of study and worry about examinations. For the upper classes and for the wealthy, who can afford to send their children to private schools, the problem is not so serious, but the typical "new middle class" parent, who must rely on universalistic examinations, believes that there is little he can do to buck the system. Even children who do not become seriously emotionally disturbed cannot help being affected by the intense pressure placed on them at the time of entrance examinations.

DEVIANCY AND SOCIAL CHANGE: A PSYCHOCULTURAL EVALUATION OF TRENDS IN JAPANESE DELINQUENCY AND SUICIDE

GEORGE A. DE VOS

THE study of socially deviant behavior is one approach to understanding the social structure of a culture as well as its patterns of socialization and personality formation. Two notable manifestations of increased incidence of deviant behavior in modern Japan during the postwar period are (1) the trend toward a higher rate of juvenile delinquency and (2) an increase in the suicide rate among the youth. These statistically verified general trends stimulate speculations concerning their possible relation to the nature of social change going on in Japan today. Social-class stresses, economic pressures, and shifts in ideology and values are deeply involved, but it seems clear that global theories about such forces beg the question of explaining the processes that create certain statistics of the type uniquely Japanese.

These phenomena must have historical genetic explanations related to the peculiarities of Japanese culture, on the one hand, and to peculiarities of socialization experiences common to Japanese, on the other. The theorist working in the field of culture and personality asks what experiences make a person Japanese and how these experiences are operating in a period of social change. Sociology or social anthropology formulates how the universal dynamics of society influence the individual as well as group processes; dynamic psychology reveals the universals in human psychosocial development. The study of culture and personality operating with concepts derived from both disciplines in one sense is a historical genetic science. From it evolves the study of how the unique features in the history of a particular culture have general effects on the developmental psychology of its members. From the study of several cultures seen comparatively, theoretical generalizations are subsequently deduced.

Within the limits of a brief general account of recent trends in forms of deviant behavior in Japan, it is impossible to explore satisfactorily the relevant theoretical issues. Suffice it to say that in the conclusions to this paper an attempt will be made to point out that the trends noted have some relevance to socialization experiences common to Japanese and to the processes of social change now obviously at work.

There is no doubt that since World War II revolutionary changes have been occurring within Japanese society at an increasingly rapid pace. The amount of change is certainly equal to that experienced by the Japanese in the last decades of the nineteenth century after the Restoration of the Emperor in 1868 and the subsequent self-conscious attempt of the government toward modernizing Japanese society as much as possible within the context of traditional values. The Allied Occupation provided a second opportunity by legal and other means to bring about changes not only in such areas as agriculture and business structure, politics and education, but in the family system and other basic social institutions previously preserved in Japan. The results of such change are now becoming increasingly manifest in the younger generation. Seen in the context of usual American social values, the younger Japanese are concerned positively with individual effort and personal liberty. To see the total picture, however, one must note that various forms of deviant behavior are also on the increase. Specifically, we note that suicide in youth, on the one hand, and various forms of juvenile delinquency, on the other, are of serious import in modern Japan. In this paper some attention will be paid to the increase in both these phenomena before some speculations are raised as to how they may relate to social change or to Japanese national character.

POSTWAR TRENDS IN JAPANESE CRIME AND DELINQUENCY

The radical increase in juvenile crime in postwar Japan, compared with prewar, is a phenomenon seemingly similar to that reported in certain other modern nations. In the statistics of 1936–39, the time during which the Japanese nation was most directly engaged in militarist expansion, it may be noted that the number of individuals cited for criminal activity was actually decreasing. Several reasons were advanced for this decrease. Among those most cited are the influence of international tensions caused by the Sino-Japanese War and the fact that the mobilization of individuals for the war effort siphoned off a good deal of the energy of the youth, who were drafted in large numbers for military service. The sense of danger to the national entity was presumed to be a focus of concern for the younger generation. At the same time that these activities were going on, the government was actively engaged in attempts to colonize Manchukuo. One could presume that, rather than a diversion of energy occurring, actually, individuals of a more aggressive type—who would thrive under less direct police surveillance and who wanted a field of operation for more questionable activities —could find the situation in a developing colony more promising and less controlled. Such selective fields for aggressive activity could also help explain the drop in actual incidence of crime in the homeland. The statistics for the years during the beginning of World War II show a decrease in the incidence of crime, but, by the end of 1942 and in 1943, with the increasing disillusionment about the war effort, the crime statistics start to go up. By 1944 and through 1945 the situation in the urban areas became so chaotic that one could not assume that the police reporting at that time was at all accurate.

The characteristic trends that are most obvious today in juvenile statistics start in the postwar period; that is, crimes of assault and violence become radically more prevalent compared with other forms of juvenile activity (Ministry of Justice, 1958). By 1956, whereas 23 per cent of all crimes committed were by individuals under twenty years of age, 53 per cent of the cases of rape reported, and 39 per cent of the cases of robbery, were by individuals under the legal adult age. These figures show eleven times as high an incidence of rape and ten times as high an incidence of crimes of violence, as compared with the figures for the prewar year 1941. By age, the largest increase of incidence in crime is observable in individuals eighteen and nineteen years old. Also reported is a continually increasing incidence of repeated acts of delinquency. By 1956 one-third of the cases handled by the family courts were concerned with individuals having previous delinquent records. The trend also is apparently toward an earlier age of commission of the first act of delinquency.

Some Japanese theorists, such as Ogawa (1956), would have it that a long-term general trend is occurring in maladjustment patterns, from more socially withdrawn forms, such as running away from home and suicide, to more directly aggressive forms of acting out. He uses a number of statistics to bolster his arguments. However, as discussed below, the increase in the suicide rate cannot be explained by such a theory.

THE ECOLOGY OF JAPANESE DELINQUENCY

Numerous sociological theories concerning the genesis of delinquency emphasize human ecological factors, especially the urban neighborhood environment. The differential association theory of Sutherland and Cressey (1960), the neighborhood research of Shaw and McKay (1929), and the recent writings of Albert Cohen (1955) about delinquent subcultures are illustrative. These theories all seek to suggest that there are forces within the mobile, urban industrial city that produce a high incidence of delinquency within specific neighborhood class segments. The individuals, families, and ethnic groups in these areas change, but the delinquency rates in certain urban areas seem to remain high.

An examination of the increased delinquency rate in Japan, raises the question whether or not it is directly related to the urbanizing industrial changes reflected in residence areas. Statistically (Ministry of Justice, 1958) the delinquency rate in the six largest urban areas is higher than that of the rest of Japan. For individuals between sixteen and twenty, the rate, when traffic offenses are eliminated, is close to 1.5 per cent of the total teen-age population; the rural rate is approximately 0.9 per cent. As closely as can be figured from the poorly handled American statistics, when traffic offenses are excluded, the rate is about 2.3 per cent—the rate for New York City alone is about 2.25 per cent (Police Report, 1960). We estimate on this basis that about 4–7 per cent of Japanese youth and 10–15 per cent of American youth are adjudicated for a delinquent act before adulthood.

Although the urban statistics in Japan are higher than are rural statistics, they do not necessarily reflect ecological patterns similar to those of the American city. The Japanese city pattern seems not to have developed the type of transitional neighborhood found in American large cities. A few areas are pockets of disorganized transient families or individuals, and slums exist, but the atmosphere is not that found in the more extensive American deteriorated neighborhoods. Many segments of urban Tokyo are actually traditional communities. Dore's study (1958) of an urban Tokyo neighborhood, for example, points out the strong continuing function of community sanctions. Japanese research workers have conducted numerous environmental-type studies of crime and delinquency in the urban areas. To illustrate, the Supreme Court in Tokyo (Kashikuma, 1958) conducted a survey of all individuals arraigned before the Court during one year. Maps were constructed that revealed a certain lawful regularity in the incidence of acts of juvenile delinquency occurring in particular areas. However, these areas did not correspond to areas of residence of those committing the delinquent acts. Residence of delinquents is diffused generally throughout the city, although in certain sections here and there a higher incidence of delinquency is appearing. These Japanese surveys contra-indicate any direct relationship between urban residential mobility patterns and delinquency, as is found in the cities of the United States.

New residents from rural regions diffuse through the city rather than congregate in specific areas. The large cities are populated not by distinct waves of ethnic groups but rather by rural immigrants from all over Japan. Once settled, individuals do not readily move to a different area. There is no pattern of high mobility in housing such as there is in the American city. What will occur in the future with the increasingly rapid development of concrete apartment structures throughout Tokyo remains to be seen.

Rather than being a delinquency pattern related to ethnic minorities living in transitional neighborhoods, the Japanese statistics on delinquency, in Tokyo at least, are related to the influence of public transportation patterns, the flow of people through the city, and the development of large amusement-area complexes around each of the major transfer points in the traffic flow of the city.

Many of the youth who have developed more or less delinquent identity patterns congregate in these amusement areas—the residence areas whence they came are scattered throughout the city. These centers are readily reached by public transportation. As they become involved, youth tend to spend an increasingly large part of their lives in these amusement areas. Those who have developed more or less delinquent identity patterns are readily identifiable. They wear characteristic modes of dress and haircuts and use a language of their own, in many ways resembling American slang. Observing the behavior of these youth, one cannot avoid the conclusion that mass-entertainment media, including American films, play some notable role in the way Japanese youth perceive themselves and the way their fantasy of the modern world becomes structured. Films, without self-conscious effort, hold up patterns for emulation. Some American films, especially, suggest possible patterns for violence or sexual behavior. Moreover, films depict lives of ease and wealth. For purposes of gaining audiences, films show success as occurring in a context of violence and for personal heroism. Such films stimulate the interest of the more unattached alienated among the youth to aspire to a similar pattern by some means or other. Nevertheless, as Blumer (1933) points out, rather than being the cause of delinquency, they most probably merely give content, style, and manner to delinquent acts.

There have been careful reports of how some delinquent youth gradually shift from the home area to full-time residence in these entertainment areas. This shift may be individualistic in nature or through participation in a series of gangs. Most recently noted by school authorities is the development of gang formation among juveniles, starting early in the higher grades of the primary school. There are characteristic recruitment patterns among likely candidates. Many of the young pass by stages through a number of gangs that center their activities in the entertainment areas until they find their way either into the adult criminal world or back to some more socially conforming adult pattern (Horie, 1954).

As will be discussed in a separate paper, the adult Japanese underworld is highly organized (Mizushima and De Vos, n.d.). Although things are changing fast, much of this organization is still derived from premodern times and is based on pseudo-kinship ties of familial nature around patterns of personal loyalty. Traditional gamblers and racketeers, as well as new-style gangs, have moved into the lucrative trade of prostitution, which until five years ago was controlled by a group of traditional family organizations on a quasi-legal basis. The new gangs, it must be noted, including the recently appearing juvenile gangs, cannot maintain the older ties of loyalty that are true for the traditional groups. They are more impersonally organized and depend less on formalized codes (Abe, 1957; Iwai, 1954; Berigun, 1955; Takemura, 1957).

The evidence is not clear, but delinquency appears to be predominantly a lower-class phenomenon in Japan, as it is also in the United States. Assessment of the relationship of social class to delinquency is very difficult, since impressionistically the class system in Japan is more in a state of flux than is true for the United States. The opportunities for social mobility in Japan within the expanding industrial development have not been available to all the previous rural populations who aspire to urban middle-class social status. A large-scale movement into the cities is still taking place.

It is usually noted by Japanese social scientists that Japan does not evidence in her cities the type of ethnic racial-minority phenomenon so characteristic in the United States. When the topic is discussed, one gains the general impression that Korean youth are overrepresented in arrests and convictions by police. But, being statistically numerically insignificant, they contribute little to the over-all figures on statistics. The Ainu, an aboriginal racial-cultural minority still found in Hokkaido, are not known for their delinquency, although unemployment and illegitimacy are very high.

The differential rate of delinquency among members of the former outcaste segment of Japanese society, the *burakumin* or *shinheimin* (Eta), has received no dispassionate objective study. The outcaste group was officially abolished shortly after the Restoration of the Emperor in 1888, but obvious discriminatory practices exist today in job opportunities. Marriage with a member of the outcaste meets as strong social disapproval as do white-Negro marriages in the United States. Japanese social scientists until recently have avoided the issue involved as too socially explosive. Estimates suggest that up to 3 million, or 3 per cent of the Japanese are descendants of the *shinheimin* or Eta. In Tokyo patterned discrimination is much less evident, but in the Kansai area of Japan, in its cities of Osaka, Kobe, and Kyoto, the traditional living areas of the former outcastes are well known and an individual's home address is sufficient to classify him. If he goes for a job or is interested in marriage, the family registry can be examined and the place of origin traced back. One hears tragic stories of suicide following the discovery that an applicant for a job or a lover turns out to be ineligible because of his background.

Informal discussions with family-court officials and social workers in the Kansai area indicate that the *shinheimin* are exceedingly overrepresented in delinquency cases coming before the family courts. One official indicated that close to 50 per cent of the cases of delinquency in Kobe were outcastes, although the estimated population for that area is about 15 per cent. A Catholic priest working with an outcaste group in Kyoto relates that family life there is very chaotic, that there is a great deal of desertion and illegitimacy as well as delinquency. The parallels to the American Negro are very close (Wagatsuma and DeVos, n.d.).

In sum, there appears to be a need for further research to ascertain the degree to which social discrimination is related to delinquency in Japan. Such social discrimination not only has direct effects on the individual but through its effects on family life has deleterious effects on the individual's primary group as well.

THE FAMILY AND DELINQUENCY FORMATION

The theory that family relationships of a characteristic nature are highly conducive to the appearance of delinquent behavior in one or more children is supported by a number of careful studies done in Japan (Suga, 1956; Tatezawa, 1954, 1958; NIER, 1959; Õura, 1956). Consistently, delinquents are shown to have been previously truant, even from the earliest school grades, and to have manifested other difficulties of various sorts in the schools. The home situation is most often characterized as insufficient, disharmonious, or involving neglect or direct rejection of the child who has become delinquent. Notable among the prediction studies that have been done in Japan is a replication of the research approach used by the Gluecks in the United States. This study points out the major central predictive value of rating the supervision and the discipline used in the home, the love and affection expressed by both parents, and an over-all index of family cohesiveness (Tatezawa, 1954, 1958). Research reports such as these indicate that, within the primary family at least, the same characteristics that seem to be productive of delinquency in the United States hold for Japan.

The diffuse nature of the ecological pattern throughout the city, however, would suggest somewhat less relationship between poor intra-family environment and social class or community than that which occurs in the United States. Summarizing far too briefly a highly complex situation, we can say that although the over-all social changes may somehow contribute to a higher appearance of delinquency in Japan today, the nature of the urban residence patterns within the Japanese city appears different. Forces within the family environment themselves are similar psychodynamically to those inducing delinquency in the United States. Neverthelesss, the formal patterns of family affiliation and community organization in Japan are somewhat different from those found in United States urban areas.

The question may well be raised as to the relevance of the concepts of national character to patterns of delinquency in various countries. In the research we are conducting at the University of California, we are interested in this question. We have therefore been studying groups of lower-class American youth drawn from the Mexican-American, Negro, and white subcategories found in the prisons of California. This American sample has been matched with non-delinquent controls. In turn, we have used similar psychological measurements on a group of working-class delinquent and non-delinquent youth of similar ages in Japan. Our work is not as yet complete, but I might cite some bits of evidence from the Thematic Apperception Test, one of the psychological devices used. We have found that within both Japan and the United States, respectively, delinquent and non-delinquent youth do not differ from each other significantly in achievement concerns as measured on the TAT. Cultural differences between America and Japan are, however, very significant. The working-class Japanese, both delinquent and non-delinquent, show more achievement concerns than do their American counterparts. As a matter of fact, the Japanese working-class sample resembles to a considerable extent American middle-class protocols. The American lower class, both delinquent and non-delinquent, show more conflict over parental pressure concerning performance than do the Japanese. The Americans are also more concerned with competition. The Japanese more directly express feelings of inadequacy. The Americans repress such feelings and, instead, are prone to put defaults in terms of lack of motivation. Japanese are more likely than Americans to view achievement as being inspired by a beloved dead person or to see achievement in the context of bettering one's economic position in the face of poverty. The Japanese lower class, as well as middle class, generally show an over-all hopefulness about the future and are most notably in high contrast to the strong emphasis on sexual concerns and violence found in both delinquent and non-delinquent lower-class Americans. Such concerns are not nearly so evident in Japanese youth, either delinquent or non-delinquent. There is a greater class difference among American youth in regard to fantasy preoccupations with sex and violence than among the Japanese. In general, our incomplete evidence to date does suggest some personality variables related to affective lability and impulse control related to delinquency, but the evidence from our data is not conclusive. Our evidence brings out no specific Japanese features related to delinquency in Japan.

It must be noted that we are finding systematic similarities in social attitudes between Japanese and American delinquents on the Gough California Psychological Inventory (Gough and Peterson, 1952; Gough, 1957, 1960a, 1960b). It is specifically on the subscales measuring social responsibility and delinquency that both the American and Japanese delinquents show the most marked deviations from the average population norms. Gough believes that his inventory reflects personality only indirectly through social attitudes. Nevertheless, the items used in his subscale do reflect self-assessment of self-control and other essential personality characteristics.

To remain objective, one must rule out the possibility that there is some magic personality key that will reveal delinquent acts to stem from some few definable personality variables. On the other hand, one cannot rule out consideration of personality variables simply because over-all comparisons with certain instruments do not show systematic differences between the total population of delinquents and matched controls. Within the total delinquent population there are, in all probability, a number of discrete etiological syndromes that lead to delinquent behavior, but they are lost in an over-all inclusive classification that puts together all forms of delinquent acts, regardless of the variation of motives involved. Discussion of etiology becomes possible only when subtypes are singled out in a more meaningful manner (Nakada, 1953; Hasegawa, 1957).

Some previous levels of investigation of personality or physiological variables are not without suggestive evidence. On levels of investigation dealing with the physiological functioning of the brain or autonomic nervous system (Makino, 1953) done in Japan, there is considerable evidence that there are differences in the over-all incidence of abnormalities between delinquent and non-delinquent population.

For example, studies with the electroencephalogram turned up significantly more abnormal propensities of a peculiar type in delinquent groups. Delinquents under condition of hyperventilation or stimulated by drugs show a higher group incidence of immature theta waves than do carefully matched normal groups of the same age (Satake et al., 1957).[1]

There is suggestive evidence in the variety of minor studies done in Japan that certain delinquents at least, that is, individuals committing certain forms of aggressive acts toward persons either with or without stealing and other crimes against property, tend to have trouble internalizing controls enabling them to conform to social norms. In such individuals impulsive or volatile reactive affective behavior is less under continuous ego control (Makino, 1953; Kitagawa and Yamazaki, 1954).

1. Results in France are turning up highly similar evidence in EEG according to Mr. Michard, director of an interdisciplinary French study on delinquent youths being conducted at Vaucresson near Paris.

Comparing rural with urban samples in regard to delinquent acts of all kinds, it seems apparent that impulsive acts of aggression are proportionately higher in rural areas, whereas over-all rates of crimes against property and certain forms of deliberate assault for monetary gain are lower. One may infer that in rural areas, in a minority of delinquents at least, impulsive behavior breaks through in spite of stronger community sanctions. In contrast, the stimulating nearby atmosphere of the impersonal entertainment areas makes antisocial acts of city youths proportionately less a matter of faulty ego control and more a matter of progressive attitudinal estrangement from family and normal community controls. Unfortunately, no studies demonstrate conclusively that we are safe in considering such interpretations as final or conclusive.

RECENT TRENDS IN JAPANESE SUICIDE[2]

One would assume from reading Japanese periodicals and publications today, whether newspapers or journals, that the postwar phenomenon in regard to suicide is something entirely new for Japan. In actuality, a relatively high suicide rate has been characteristic for Japan since statistics were first reported in 1882 (*Japanese Empire Statistical Year Book, 1882*). Moreover, the characteristic suicide curve in regard to age found today also appears in the first statistics. The Japanese suicide curve has a U-shape found in no other suicide curve reported for any Western country; that is, the rate of suicide among individuals below thirty and above sixty is relatively higher than the rate for individuals in the middle years. Another feature of Japanese suicide compared with world statistics is a fairly high rate of suicide in women. Roughly, for every three males who commit suicide in Japan, there are two females (National Institute of Mental Health in Japan, 1958). The nearest approximation in European countries is a ratio of two to one in such countries as Switzerland, Denmark, and Germany. The rate in the United States is four males to one female. Another feature of the high female rate in Japan is the fact that historically and until recently the number of women under twenty committing suicide was higher than the number of men for the same age period.

Whereas the relative nature of the curve itself has not changed and the rate has always been high, there is no argument against the fact that the recent statistics point to an increasingly high rate of suicide until by 1958 it had reached the astounding statistic of 80 per hundred thousand in men under thirty (Watanabe, 1957). The rate in Japan in 1920 for individuals from twenty to thirty years was approximately 36. By 1950 it was approximately 40. The closest recent rates to this for those under thirty in Europe is 31 for Finland and 27 for Austria. The Danish rate is 25. After age forty, the rate in Danish males jumps to 62.

---

2. The best brief review of Japanese suicide in English is by Iga (1961). The best single-volume statistical treatment of suicide in Japanese is that of Okazaki (1960*b*).

By 1959 suicide in Japan had become the single most common source of death for individuals under thirty (Ministry of Welfare, 1960). Suicide, as a matter of fact, has long been second, but with the radical decrease of the death rate from tuberculosis it has now become the single highest cause of death. Also noteworthy in Japan, from the standpoint of culturally prevalent forms of suicide, is the number of group suicides, in which an individual, usually the male head of the family, will kill first his entire family and then himself, or in other situations where the man is absent and a mother will kill first her children and then herself. The reason often given for such group suicides is that the family has reached a state of impoverishment that is not to be endured. The double love suicide is also relatively a feature of Japanese culture, but it is perhaps more outstanding for its dramatic qualities than for its over-all contribution to the suicide rate (Isomura, 1959). Yet, in such acts as the group suicide or the double love suicide, one finds imbedded attitudes concerning primary relationships that are related to aspects of Japanese character.

For the sociologically oriented social scientist, the high suicide rate in Japanese youth can very readily be related to the tremendous pressure going on in Japanese society for youth to find long-range accepted occupational roles (Sato, 1958). The youth have been put under strenuous pressure to accomplish. There is intense covert competitiveness in the educational system. Students are put under severe psychological pressure in terms of the familial expectations to succeed. They run into what Merton would term a tightly strictured "opportunity structure" in Japanese society, with its overproduction of the educated according to the positions available. The fact that such social conditions exist, however, is not sufficient to explain the suicide rate. Similar social conditions have come to exist elsewhere without producing high suicide rates. A recent explanation by a Japanese social scientist studying suicide is that today Japan as a nation seems unclear as to where it is going (Nishimoto, n.d.). In other words, young Japanese lack a sense of purpose. There are no assigned roles available for the youth in terms of national objectives. Such interpretations as these are not sufficient, since this state of confusion about national goals is not unknown in other countries. Why suicide results from the type of frustration or difficulty experienced by Japanese youth cannot be explained solely in terms of such sociological considerations.

It seems necessary to go further back into the socialization process to understand the proneness to suicide. But, first, it is also necessary to recognize that suicide has been traditionally in Japan a condoned form of behavior. (Kato, 1954; Nakano, 1957; Nakahara, 1960). As such, it does not have the type of sanctions of horror and rejection that have been more characteristic in reaction to this act in the West. Therefore, it must be acknowledged that suicide as an act is more available psychologically to Japanese youth than perhaps to individuals of a number of other countries. It has been pointed out that in both China and Japan suicide was a means of protest against rigidities in the social system. It has been so used by women as well as men in situations in which no other form of rebellion seemed possible.

The viability of this attitude, derived from the feudal period, however, must be related to personality internalizations that still make it psychologically relevant today. To put more emphasis on the psychological aspects of the act is not to counter the very compelling theory of Durkheim in regard to forms of suicide seen sociologically (Durkheim, 1950; Halbwachs, 1930). Rather, what is necessary in the light of modern-day dynamic psychology is to understand the genesis of motivational factors that underlies suicide. Suicide, like delinquency, is selectively induced in certain individuals and not in others. It is our contention that the proneness toward suicide as a solution is related to early childhood relationships, especially of a particular type fairly common in Japan. The related papers of Vogel, Caudill, and Doi in this volume touch on various aspects of the intense mother-child relationship, occurring not only during infancy but also throughout much of the childhood period. This form of socialization has to be related to the later intense preoccupation of Japanese with their social role; for, on a conscious level at least, many suicidal acts are related to some failure in either assuming or fulfilling an occupational social role as well as to other more intimate personal relationships that have gone badly in one way or another. The suicide act may thus be seen in reference to what is termed the "object cathexis" of individuals in an over-all psychoanalytic theory of socialization. Assuming the intensity of the primary relationship to the mother, we may conclude that for some individuals there is a difficulty in shifting the basic attachment found in this highly charged continuing relationship and that the attachment is not given up psychologically even when the mother is no longer present. We would assume that the youth finds it difficult to shift his attention to social outlets other than those that the mother herself has previously thoroughly espoused.

The Japanese individual frequently views the ultimate meaning of his life as fulfilling a goal set by the parents (De Vos, 1960). The feelings related to this sense of life purpose are similar to those related to religion by those who strongly adhere to a religious code. The individual sustains himself through adversity by fulfilling a role for which he has been destined by family attitudes and expectations. The mother especially is seen by the son as sacrificing herself to this end. The Japanese youth, however, must seek to accomplish in a real world, not, as in a Western religious sense, through adherence to an individualist moral code supposedly entirely under his own control. A Japanese youth may be driven to accomplish social goals and tasks unequal to his capacities. In numerous instances the early relationships to the mother may be characterized by an ambivalence of hate and love. If so, a great deal of inner turmoil will take place in regard to acting properly in pursuing a future life goal. Social failure can cause a feeling of deep guilt and depression, since symbolically it can mean an attempt to injure a parent whose wishes have so deeply become an internalized part of the self. It also symbolizes a possible final loss of love of the mother. Such a loss of a primary love object on the part of anyone takes away the sense of meaning from life. Suicide readily occurs in such a circumstance whether in the United States or in Japan. What is unique about Japan is the social reinforcement by the culture of the intense parent-child relationship. American culture norms by contrast tend to wean the child from any such psychologically symbiotic relationship to a parent. The suicidal act in certain instances may be an attempt to break away from the parent psychologically in a rebellious act, but at the same time it suggests a reunion with a love object, as in the case of the double suicide. The Japanese self-concept is not viewed clearly as separate or coterminous with the biological body. The family is traditionally an entity of which the individual forms a part. Even though modern values emphasize individual independence, the Japanese feel very strongly that, as John Donne put it, "no man is an island." There is not enough sustenance in individualist existence to make it self-sustaining.

Occupational achievement and success symbolically keep an individual bound to life. Japanese preoccupation with success and achievement and the relation of this to the internalization of guilt have been demonstrated in a previous paper (De Vos, 1960). Failure, conversely, is construed by some as being cut off from a life purpose and leads to an empty, pointless life.

It is assumed by those who study the effects of urbanization that the pattern I have been describing characterizes the urban industrial scene. It would be assumed that the suicide rate, therefore, would be highest in the cities. It would, therefore, surprise some to find out that the suicide rate in Tokyo is by no means the highest in Japan. The highest rates occur in the mountain provinces of central Honshu (Okazaki, 1960b). Leading all occupations insofar as suicide rates are concerned is that of agriculture. Whatever is causing an increase in the suicide rate must therefore have been operative not only in the city but throughout Japan. It must be pointed out, as we have done in our survey of achievement concerns in Japanese rural villages, that the Japanese farmer is very much concerned with getting ahead. He has always self-consciously considered himself of middle-class status and has had aspirations characteristic for the middle class generally. Bellah (1957) and others have well documented the almost puritanical work ethic of rural Japanese. Certainly in our Thematic Apperception Test data gathered from rural villages, the stories concerning achievement would rival any produced by Horatio Alger. They are amazingly similar in many respects to those produced by the American middle class. Also found sporadically in these stories, in a manner not usual in American stories, is the view that work and success are in atonement for guilt felt toward self-sacrificing parents.

CONCLUSION AND DISCUSSION

In this too brief report there has been a purpose in bringing together discussion of increasing evidence of two forms of social deviancy in Japan, those of delinquency and suicide, which are usually discussed separately in most theoretical or research efforts. Theoretical explanations offered for the incidence of one or another form of social deviancy sometimes are mutually contradictory, or, when general explanations are offered, they are often so broad as to avoid the very real issues involved. Explanations aimed only at the over-all sociological forces on one level of analysis or the psychological features involved in behavior on another level are not sufficient. Only some form of interdisciplinary framework, such as that afforded by the specialization of culture and personality within anthropology, can systematically cope with multi-caused phenomena that must be examined on a number of levels at the same time. Sociological, historical, and psychological determinants contribute differentially to various forms of social deviancy when they are examined separately.

In Japan the cultural-historical availability of specific behavioral patterns plays more of a role in the case of suicide perhaps than it does in the case of delinquency today. Adult crime and criminal organization, as compared to juvenile delinquency, on the other hand, still show more the influences of the past. Second, underlying the continuity of certain of these traditions are motivations that can best be understood on the psychological level of analysis. Many of these motivations are found in peculiarities of socialization practices as well as in forms of social relationship that continue within the family.

Suicide in Japan attests to such motivational continuity. Patterns of socialization have a continuity of their own that are only indirectly affected by changes that have occurred in the economic-political spheres of the social structure. Tensions in the economic-political sphere will be reacted to selectively by individuals who have been differentially affected by earlier socialization. Many Japanese youth experience forms of relatedness in infancy and childhood that cause them to react by suicide to situations of stress.

In our study of delinquency we are coming to the conclusion that although there are cultural-psychological differences between Japanese and Americans, such as in the manner or degree that they are preoccupied by sex or violence, comparative research evidence suggests the presence of a social-psychological as well as sociological universals. Factors in family experience and personality orientation that predispose a Japanese youth toward delinquency are dynamically similar to those found in American youth so predisposed. Rejection or neglect on the part of a parent may cause similar results in either culture. Patterns of mass communication, transportation, and entertainment allow for escape from community sanctions by unattached predisposed youth into an environment where delinquency can flourish. In a consideration of processes contributing to present-day delinquency, universals in human nature, on the one hand, and in social processes, on the other hand, seem more pertinent than do peculiarities in past tradition or uniquely Japanese socialization experiences. Even here, however, the differential effects of traditional culture must be considered. The effects of these social forces do pattern out differently in Japan than they do in the United States. In Japan, delinquency appears to be less related to class or ethnic groupings or neighborhood environments than it does in the American pattern. The new Japanese urban working class derived from rural regions reveals attitudes similar in some aspects more to the American middle class than to the American working class.

Urbanization may not follow the same patterns in various parts of Asia as in the United States. Not only is the pattern of urbanization in Tokyo different from that reported for American cities, but evidence of other differences in urbanization is beginning to be prepared for Asian cultures in which kinship and family play more important roles. For example, the Batak pattern of urbanization in Sumatra or that of Bombay in India well illustrates that urbanization or industrialization may have differential effects. These differences call for theories of economic and cultural change based on comparative anthropology, not on classical economics.

To remain focused on Japan, no one can gainsay the ultimate effect of modern industrialization on the texture of Japanese social institutions. The increased individualism of the youth and the loss of respect for the family system and the social authority of elders are very much in evidence, although no systematic controlled studies have as yet been able to ascertain the direct effect of these changes in social attitudes upon the rates of delinquency and the like. In fact, delinquents who have been interviewed were seemingly more likely to be from rather traditionally oriented families than from families whose behavior has been modified by modern trends.

Statistical evidence suggests that stresses in the Japanese society are at their severest in adolescence and early adulthood. More has to be done than to make direct inferences from statistics, however. The processes of change involved within the individual need more direct examination. How much the effects of social change are mediated by their indirect effects on socialization experiences at various stages of the life cycle is a matter to be examined in detail in future work. It is with this sort of multilevel approach that work in culture and personality justifies itself as having a role to play in the development of social science.

BIBLIOGRAPHY

ABE, JUNKICHI
 1957 "Hikō Keisei ni Kansuru Shakaishinrigakuteki Kenkyū" ("A Sociopsychological Study of Delinquency Formation"), *Tōhoku Kyōsei Kagaku Kiyō* ("Tōhoku Correctional Bulletin"), 2:183–211. Sendai.

BELLAH, ROBERT N.
 1957 *Tokugawa Religion*. Glencoe, Ill.: Free Press.

BERIGUN, DURREL
 1955 *Yakuza no Sekai* ("The Outlaw World"). Tokyo: Nijuseiki-sha.

BLUMER, HERBERT
 1933 *Movies and Conduct*. New York: Macmillan.

BURG, MOSES
1961 "A Psychocultural Analysis and Theoretical Integration of the Dynamics of Japanese Parent-Child Suicide." *Tōyō Daigaku Shakaigakubu Kiyō* ("Bulletin, Department of Sociology, Tōyō University"), No. 2:127–154.

COHEN, ALBERT
1955 *Delinquent Boys*. Glencoe, Ill.: Free Press.

DE VOS, GEORGE
1960 "The Relation of Guilt toward Parents to Achievement and Arranged Marriage among the Japanese," *Psychiatry*, 23:287–301.

DE VOS, GEORGE, and KEIICHI MIZUSHIMA
1962 "The School and Delinquency: Perspectives from Japan," *Teachers College Record*, 63:626–638.

DORE, RONALD P.
1958 *City Life in Japan*. Berkeley: University of California.

DURKHEIM, ÉMILE
1950 *Le Suicide*. Glencoe, Ill.: Free Press.

FENICHEL, OTTO
1945 *The Psychoanalytic Theory of Neurosis*. New York: W. W. Norton & Co.

GOUGH, H. G.
1957 *Manual for the California Psychological Inventory*. Palo Alto, Calif.: Consulting Psychologists Press.

1960a "Cross-cultural Studies of the Socialization Continuum," *Amer. Psychol.*, 15:410–11 (abstr.).

1960b "Theory and Measurement of Socialization," *J. Consult. Psychol.*, 24:23–30.

GOUGH, H. G., and D. R. PETERSON
1952 "The Identification and Measurement of Predispositional Factors in Crime and Delinquency," *J. Consult. Psychol.*, 16:207–12.

HALBWACHS, MAURICE
1930 *Les Causes de Suicide*. Paris: Librairie Felix Alcan.

HASEGAWA, HIROSHI
1957 "Seishōnen no Rinkanjiken ni kansuru Kenkyū II" ("A Study of Group Rape in Juveniles"), *Tōhoku Kyōsei Kagaku Kiyō* ("Tōhoku Correctional Bulletin"), 2:257–262. Sendai.

HAYASHIDA, SHIGEO
1957 *Jisatsu Ron* ("Essay on Suicide"). Tokyo: Sanichi-shobō.

HIGUCHI, KŌKICHI
1953 *Sengo ni okeru Shōnen Hanzai no Seishin Igakuteki Kenkyū* ("Psychiatric Study of Post-War Juvenile Delinquency"). Tokyo: Ministry of Justice.

HORIE, YURIKO
1954 "Han-in-sei Kankyo ni tsuiteno Kenkyū" ("A Study on Criminal Environment"), *Katei Saiban Shiryō* ("Family Court Report"), 35:233–70. Tokyo: Family Bureau, Japan Supreme Court.

IGA, MAMORU
1961 "Cultural Factors in Suicide of Japanese Youth with Focus on Personality," *Sociology and Social Research*, 46:75–90.

ISOMURA, EIICHI
1959 *Shinjū-kō* ("Essay on Double Suicide"). (Million Books.) Tokyo: Kōdansha.

IWAI, HIROAKI
1954 "Hanshakai Shūdan to Shakaiteki Kinchō" ("Antisocial Groups and Social Tensions"). In: NIHON JIMBUN KAGAKUKAI (ed.), *Shakaiteki Kinchō no Kenkyū* ("Studies of Social Tensions"), pp. 81–122. Tokyo: Yūhikaku.

KANBE, TADAO, and ISHII KANICHIRO
n.d. "Wagakuni Seishōnen no Jinseikan to Jisatsukan" ("Japanese Youth's View of Life and of Suicide"). In preparation for publication in *Jisatsu ni Kansuru Sōgōteki Kenkyū* ("Interdisciplinary Studies on Suicide"). Kyōto Sōbun-sha.

KARAKI, JUNZŌ
1954 *Jisatsu ni tsuite* ("On Suicide"). (Atene-bunko ["Athena Library Series"].) Tokyo: Kōbundo.

KASHIKUMA, KOJI et al.
1958 *Tokyo-to ni okeru Hikōshōnen no Seitaigakuteki Kenkyū* ("Ecological Study of Juvenile Delinquents in Tokyo"), *Katei Saiban Shiryō* ("Family Court Report"), No. 58. Tokyo: Family Bureau, Japan Supreme Court.

KATŌ, MASAAKI
1947 "Jisatsu ni itaru Michi" ("Way to Suicide"), *Tōkei* ("Statistics"), 8, No. 9.
1954 *Jisatsu* ("Suicide") (Ijō Shinrigaku Kōza ["Abnormal Psychology Series"], No. 3) Tokyo: Misuzu Shobō.
1958 "Jisatsu" ("Suicide"), *Seishin Eisei Shiryō* ("Annual Report on Mental Health"), No. 6. Japan: National Institute of Mental Health, Ministry of Welfare.

KITAGAWA, KAZUO, and YAMAZAKI TOMIO
1954 "Shōnen Gōkan no Kenkyū" ("A Study of Juvenile Rape"), *Katei Saiban Shiryō* ("Family Court Report"), 35. Tokyo: Family Bureau, Japan Supreme Court.

MAEDA, SHINJIRŌ
1955 "Jisatsu-ron" ("On Suicide"). In MAEDA, SHINJIRO, *Hanzai Shakai-gaku no Shomondai* ("Problems in Criminial Sociology"), 261-321. Tokyo: Yushindō.
1957 "Toshi to Nōson ni okeru Jisatsu" ("Suicide in Urban and Rural Areas"). In: MAEDA, SHINJIRO, *Hanzai no Toshika* ("Urbanization of Crimes"), 209–221. Tokyo: Yūhikaku.

MAKI, TADAKATSU
1937 *Nihon Jisatsu Kō* ("Essays on Suicide in Japan"). Ōsaka: Kansai Shuppan Club.

MAKINO, KAZUO
1953 "Mondai Shonen no Jiritsu-shinkei Kinchō to Seikaku tono Kankei" ("Relation between Tension of Autonomic Nervous System and Character in Problem Juveniles"), *Kyōsei Igakkai-shi* ("Japanese J. Correctional Med."), 2, No. 4: 1–11.

MENNINGER, K. A.
1938 *Man against Himself*. New York: Harcourt Brace & Co.

MINISTRY OF JUSTICE
1958 *Juvenile Delinquency in Japan*. Tokyo.

MINISTRY OF WELFARE
1949–52 *Jinkō Dōtai Tōkei* ("Vital Statistics of Japan"). Tokyo: Kōseishō Daijin Kanbō Tōkei-chosa-bu ("Division of Health and Welfare, Ministry of Welfare's Secretariat").

MIZUSHIMA, KEIICHI, and GEORGE DE VOS
n.d. "The Organization and Social Functions of Japanese Gangs." (In preparation.)

NAKADA, OSAMU
1953 "Hōkanin no Hanzai-shinrigakuteki Kenkyū" ("A Psychological Study of Ar-

sonists"), *Katei Saiban Geppō* ("Monthly Bulletin on Family Court"), 5, No. 6: 51–92. Tokyo: General Secretariat, Japan Supreme Court.

NAKAHARA, HIROMICHI
1960 *Seppuku* ("Suicide by Disembowelment"). Tokyo: Kubo-shoten.

NAKAMURA, KOKYŌ
1922 *Jisatsu oyobi Shinjū no Kenkyū* ("Study of Suicide and Double Love Suicide"). (Nihon Hentai Shinri Sōsho ['Japan Abnormal Psychology Series'], No. 2.) Tokyo: Arusu-Shobō.

NAKANO, TETSUO
1957 "Wagakuni ni okeru Jisatsu" ("Suicide in Japan"), *Shakai Kairyō* ("Social Reform"), 2, No. 3: 4–10.

NATIONAL INSTITUTE OF MENTAL HEALTH
1958 "Jisatsu" ("Suicide"), *Seishin Eisei-Shiryō* ("Annual Report on Mental Health"), 6:71–84. Tokyo: Ministry of Welfare.

NATIONAL INSTITUTE FOR EDUCATIONAL RESEARCH (NIER)
1959 "Keihin Chitai ni okeru Hikō oyobi Seijō Chūgakusei no Hikaku Kenkyū" ("Comparative Study of Delinquents and Normals in the Secondary Pupils in the Keihin Area"), *Kokuritsu Kyōiku Kenkyūjo Kiyō* ("Bulletin of National Institute for Educational Research"), 13. Tokyo.

NISHIMOTO, SŌSUKE
n.d. "Kyōto-fu no Mikaihō Buraku to Jisatsu" ("Unliberated *Buraku* in Kyōto Prefecture and Suicide"). In preparation for publication in *Jisatsu ni kansuru Sōgōteki Kenkyū* ("Interdisciplinary Studies on Suicide"). Kyōto: Sōbun-sha.

OGAWA, TARŌ
1956 "Sengo Jūnen no Shōnen Hanzai" ("Juvenile Delinquency in the Ten Years after the War"), *Keisei* ("Penal Administration"), 67, No. 11: 8–13. Nihon Keiji Gakkai ("Japanese Assoc. of Criminology").

ŌHARA, KENSHIRŌ
1961a "Jisatsu no Yōin ni Kansuru Kenkyū—Seishin Igaku no Tachiba kara" ("A Study on the Factors Contributing to Suicide, from the Standpoint of Psychiatry"), *Nihon Seishin Shinkei Igaku-shi* ("Japanese J. Psychiatry and Neurol."), 63, No. 2: 107–166.

1961b "Rōjin no Jisatsu" ("Suicide in Old Age"), *ibid.*: 1253–68.

ŌKAZAKI, AYANORI
1958a *Jisatsu no Kuni: Nippon no Kiroku* ("Country of Suicide: The Record of Japan"). Tokyo: Tōyō Keizai Shimpōsha.

1958b "Jisatsu to Tasatsu to no Kanrensei" ("Relationship between Suicide and Homicide"), *Jinkō Mondai Kenkyūjo Nenpō* ("Annual Report, Institute of Population Problems"), No. 3. Tokyo: Institute of Population Problems, Ministry of Welfare.

1958–59 "Jisatsu no Jisshōteki Kenkyū" ("Statistical Study of Suicide"), *Jinkō Mondai Kenkyū* ("Journal of Population Problems"), No. 74–77: 1–36. Tokyo: Ministry of Welfare.

1960a "Seishōnen no Jisatsu Mondai" ("Suicide Problems of Youth"), *Seishōnen Mondai* ("Youth Problems"), 6, No. 6.

1960b *Jisatsu no Shakai Tōkeiteki Kenkyū* ("Social-Statistical Study of Suicide"). Tokyo: Nihon Hyōron Shinsha.

ŌSAKA CRIME PREVENTION COUNCIL
1960 *Shōnen no Jisatsu no Jittai* ("The Actual Conditions of Youthful Suicide").

(Hikō Hakusho ["Delinquency White Paper"]). Ōsaka: Ōsaka Prefecture Police Center.)

ŌURA, KINZŌ
1956 "Hikō Shōnen to Katei" ("Delinquent Juveniles and Their Families"). *Katei Saiban Geppō* ("Monthly Bull. on Family Court"), 8:98–132. Tokyo: General Secretariat, Japan Supreme Court.

POLICE DEPARTMENT
1957 *Annual Report*. San Francisco.
1958 *Annual Report*. Chicago.
1960 *Statistical Report*. New York City.

SATAKE, RYŪZŌ, et al.
1958 "Nōha ni Kansuru Shimpozhiamu" ("Symposium on EEG of Delinquents or Criminals"), *Kyōsei Igakkai-shi* ("Japanese J. Correctional Med."), 6, Special Issue: 111–86. (See esp. "General Introduction" and "Changes in the Distribution of Pattern by Photo-Metrazol Activation.")

SATŌ, YASUKO
1957 "Jisatsu no Tōkeiteki Kansatsu" ("A Statistical Observation of Suicide"), *Jinkō Mondai Kenkyūjo Nenpō* ("Annual Report, Institute of Population Problems"), 2: 41–44. Tokyo: Institute of Population Problems, Ministry of Welfare.
1958 "Jisatsu Keiko ni tsuite" ("On Suicidal Tendencies"), *Jinkō Mondai Kenkyū* ("Journal of Population Problems"), 71:24–33. Tokyo: Ministry of Welfare.

SHAW, CLIFFORD, HENRY MCKAY, et al.
1929 *Delinquency Areas*. Chicago: University of Chicago Press.

SONOHARA, TARŌ
1954 *Jisatsu no Shinri* ("Psychology of Suicide"). Tokyo: Sōgensha.
1958 "Jisatsu" ("Suicide"), *Gendai Shakai Shinrigaku Kōza* ("Modern Social Psych. Series"), 5:143–163. Tokyo: Nakayama-shoten.

STATISTICS BUREAU OF THE PRIME MINISTER'S OFFICE
1950 *Nihon Tōkei Nenkan* ("Japanese Statistical Yearbook"). Tokyo.

SUDŌ, SHUNICHI
1959 *Kōkōsei no Jisatsukan ni tsuite* ("High School Students' Views of Suicide"). (Report of the Institute of Education, Fukushima University, No. 22.) Fukushima.

SUGA, SHINICHIRŌ
1956 "Hikō Shōnen no Katei oyobi Shakaiteki Haikei" ("Family and Social Background of Juvenile Delinquents"), *Kyōiku Shakaigaku Kenkyū* ("Japanese J. Educ. Soc."), 9:46–52.

SUTHERLAND, EDWIN H., and DONALD R. CRESSEY
1960 *Principles of Criminology*. 6th ed. New York: Lippincott.

TAKEMURA, HISASHI
1956 "Shōnen-Hanzai no Shakaigakuteki Kenkyū" ("A Sociological Study of Juvenile Delinquency"). *Hōmu Shiryō* ("Judicial Report"), 11, No. 4. Tokyo: Ministry of Justice.
1957 "Hōken Isei to Hanzai to no Kankei" ("Crime and the Remaining Traces of the Feudal Regime"), *Katei Saiban Geppō* ("Monthly Bull. on the Family Court"), 9, No. 7: 1–14; 9, No. 8: 1–36; 9, No. 9: 1–25. Tokyo: General Secretariat, Japan Supreme Court.

TATEZAWA, TOKUHIRO
1954 "Hikō no Yosoku" ("Prediction of Juvenile Delinquency"), *Katei Saiban Shiryō*

("Family Court Report"), 35:271–334. Tokyo: Family Bureau, Japan Supreme Court.

1958 "Hikō no Yosoku Kenkyū" ("A Prediction Study of Juvenile Delinquency"), *Katei Saibanshō Chōsakan Jitsumu Hōkokusho* ("Research Report, Research and Training Inst. for Family Court Probation Officers"), No. 2.

U.S. PUBLIC HEALTH SERVICE

1950 *Vital Statistics* (Special Reports, 37.)

WAGATSUMA, HIROSHI, and GEORGE DEVOS

n.d. "The Outcaste Tradition in Modern Japan: a Problem in Social Identity." (In preparation.)

REFLECTIONS ON DEPENDENCY PHENOMENA AS SEEN IN NISEI IN THE UNITED STATES*

CHARLOTTE G. BABCOCK

STRUGGLE to develop the full use of his mental capacity and mastery of himself, sufficient to reach socialization within his society, characterizes the life task of a human individual. Mental health and ill health and, similarly, adequate and inadequate socialization, are present but vary in form and degree in the individuals of each society. Aspects may differ, but similarities and differences, referable both to the biological organism and to human socialization processes as they are involved in the development of personality, exist in individuals of each society. Culturally expressed characteristics will be transmitted to the young child as soon as he can respond to early socialization patterns. Expressions of these become phenomena of the conscious, preconscious, and unconscious structure of the human psyche. They are absorbed both with and without awareness by each person from his specific culture. For the most part, awareness of the characteristic patterns occurs only when they are called to the person's attention by culture differences that he observes.

Nisei in the United States were the first-generation children of Japanese-born and -reared parents, who tended to maintain the culture of Japan as they remembered it. The Nisei found themselves exposed to the culture of Japan as interpreted by their parents, to the culture of some portions of the United States as seen through their parents' eyes, and as soon as they were mobile, to the determinants of the American pattern that they encountered. The young of Homo sapiens are dependent upon parental care for a much longer period than are the young of other mammals. Likewise, socialization processes, and societal organizations of men, rest partially on the use of dependency and interdependency, not only throughout the life of the individual, but also from generation to generation. Each culture develops its ways of handling dependency phenomena, of which some are universal and others are unique. Thus, Nisei were reared in a situation that permitted them experience with two cultures, each of which has its own distinctive features in the handling of these common dependency phenomena. World War II put many of the Nisei under severe stress. In the period 1945–49, 342 families who were evacuated from the west coast of the United States and relocated in a midwestern metropolis were studied by a research team com-

---

* This paper was prepared for publication while the author was in residence as a Fellow, 1961–62, at the Center for Advanced Study in the Behavioral Sciences, Stanford, Calif.

prised of social psychologists, social anthropologists, and a psychiatrist (Babcock and Caudill, 1958; Caudill, 1952; Caudill and De Vos, 1956; De Vos, 1954, 1955; Jacobson and Rainwater, 1953; Nishi, 1946). Data for this paper are derived from that study, in addition to the continued work of the author with individual Nisei from 1945 to 1955.

Dependency may be described as an on-going process, active throughout the life span. By his biology, every individual must receive from sources either outside or within himself substances vital to his physical, his emotional, and his intellectual existence. If one takes as a basic postulate (Freud, 1953, 1957; Waelder, 1960) that an individual has drives (*Triebe*), with source, strength (intensity), and direction deriving from the soma and an aim and object, the organism must then develop, in its continuing growth, ego clusters and patterns of function in response to those drives. For gratification of a drive,[1] the infant requires an adult who, via identification with the infant's helplessness and his need, provides the appropriate object (himself or other). Without such an object for gratification of the drive, death will occur. Thus there is set up a condition for satisfaction (the gratification of the drive via the object) that we may call "dependency." Soon, the characteristic of anticipation appears, so that the infant expects that the object will somehow appear at the proper time. There occurs in the infant a feeling connected with the experience that the "unpleasure" (Freud, 1955) can be reduced by receiving something from the object, a feeling that at a later date will have its mental representation. An attitude gradually develops within the infant, so that he and his caretakers begin to note his "dependency needs." *These "dependency needs" are not instinctual needs; they are conditions for feeling loved and for loving.* Because such conditions are universal (in quality, not quantity), it is easy to confuse them with the drives to which (via the object) they become attached.

An example may serve to highlight these comments. An infant is hungry. He responds to the biological drive arising from his soma with an intensity roughly appropriate to the degree of his hunger. The aim of his drive is to restore his balance of comfort, which appropriate suckling will accomplish for him. His object, in his earliest hours known only as that which fits his need (his mother will be perceived as *his* mother only after some weeks of life), is that person who provides the food. Repeated experience makes it an anticipated characteristic of his object that the object will (by some way still unknown to him) appear at the proper time. As a result of the gratification of the drive, the feeling develops in the infant that the tension of the hunger can be reduced by receiving something from the object. At a later date, the growing individual discovers not only that he has been satisfied by what he has received from the object but that this experience has become internalized and synthesized into his own psychic representation of this experience. The memory about the nostalgia

---

1. *Drive, wish, need condition,* and *requirement* should be clearly separated in the reader's mind to avoid confusion.

for specific foods, invested with interactive meaning because they were given to one by one's mother when she was the object that provided the gratification of the primary hunger drive, becomes a mental representation. It may later itself become an internal source of the gratification, as is well known from the study of fantasy and dream phenomena. Or, in an adult, for example, even in the presence of the correct immediate perception and accuracy of present reality testing, a mental representation that is determined by past experience as well as by the present may determine the attitudes toward and handling of drive phenomena and their derivatives in the current life.

To return to the example of hunger drive, the pleasure of eating uncooked protein exists in most cultures. In restaurants in some cultures one orders *rare beef*, in others, *sashimi*. The attitudinal reaction of one person toward another's choice of uncooked protein may be determined by all the factors we have just mentioned: by the strength of his drive and its aim; by the attitudes and resources of his internal and external object, from which he obtains gratification; and by his own present and earlier learned reactive attitudes, which are derived from both his current state of perception and knowledge, and which also are complexly determined by his unique automatic responses to inner psychically or somatically perceived experience (Waelder, 1960). Thus throughout life the dependency phenomena, that is, the conditions for being cared for and caring, being loved and loving, are highly complex sets of configurations. These configurations are consequent upon the dynamic interaction between, on the one hand, special varieties of current infantile need, and, on the other, gratification or frustration of the needs. These needs impinge upon a variety of mediating mechanisms of the ego and bring into play defensive, adaptive, or creative ego functions, which result in aggregates producing behavior that may or may not be demonstrable as patterns in covert and overt behavior.

Dependency phenomena characterize the life of any individual. It is their process attribute that guarantees changes in the dependency patternings appropriate to the vicissitudes that the drive and its ego components encounter as time passes in the life span. The individual whose ego needs were met with adequate resources in his infancy and childhood will accomplish the management of his dependency needs in any culture with less anxiety and more competence and creativity than will an under- or overstimulated person of the same culture. Whether the person is healthy or ill, his behavioral components will be both sequeled by and determined by the cultural units that impinge upon the genetic organization of the individual. These cultural units include the family, the peer group, his local institutions, and the national and international elements of society that come within the perceptual range and the reality availability of the individual for use in the service of id, ego, superego, and ego-ideal functions.

In a preceding paper, Takeo Doi (see also bibliography, below) has reported a contribution to the understanding of personality structure through the use of the *amae*. In an earlier publication he elaborated the concepts involved in a clinical syndrome, *shinkeishitsu*. "*Shinkeishitsu*" is a term, defined by Morita,[2] that comprises neurasthenia, anxiety neurosis, and obsessional neurosis, which have in common a basic symptom, *toraware*. In the abstract of his article, "Psychopathology of *Shinkeishitsu*" (1958), especially regarding the psychodynamics of its "*toraware*," Doi pointed out that the apparent reciprocal effect of a patient's attention does not account for the symptom *toraware*, which means "to be bound" or "to be caught" in an ambivalent-obsessive state. Doi believed that frustration of the conscious, preconscious, or unconscious wish to *amaeru*,[3] that is, "to depend and presume upon another's love or indulge in another's kindness" is the primary driving force for *toraware*. The process that leads from the state *amaeru*, "to depend and presume upon another's love or indulge in another's kindness," to the state *toraware*, "to be bound," is as follows: One is prevented from being able "to depend and presume upon another's love or indulge in another's kindness" because of repression and isolation.[4] Yet the desire to *amaeru* persists and leads to the development of distorted interpersonal relationships, the feelings of which are then displaced onto or reflected back on one's self or one's own body, thus producing the end result of "to be bound," that is, *toraware* (Doi, 1958).

From his case histories, Doi takes the view that psychological decompensation has occurred in his patients primarily as a result of the state of the frustrated

---

2. According to Dr. Katsumi Kaketa, the most significant and greatest influence on the history of psychoanalysis in Japan was brought about by Professor K. Marui, who studied in the United States under Adolph Meyer and returned to become professor of psychiatry at Tohoku Imperial University in 1919. Professor Kaketa, who is now general secretary of the Japan Psychoanalytic Association and professor of psychiatry, Juntendo Medical School, Tokyo, says

"As it is so with all research, Prof. Marui and his disciples carried out extensive study of neurosis in Japan from the viewpoint of Freud's theory of neurosis and emphasized that it was evident that Freudian theory was in agreement in principle with the neurosis in Japan. However, since the standpoint was from what may be called an orthodox Freudism the criticism to his views was quite strong. The criticism was especially strong from Prof. S. Morita of Jikeikai Medical School and his school whose standpoint was a "Shinkeishitsu" (nervosity) theory built on the background of Zen-Buddhism ideology. As a psychologist Prof. K. Sata became a severe critic and questioned the scientific basis of psychoanalytic theories. The debate on neurosis and nervosity between Morita theory and psychoanalytic theory became a repeated theme" (Kaketa, 1956).

Morita therapy for the treatment of the neuroses consists essentially of a period of total isolation, with prohibition of all contact and activity, a period of communication with the doctor through the writing of a diary upon which the doctor comments in writing, combined with the performance of simple manual tasks designed to bring the patient in contact with nature, and ultimately some conversations with the doctor concerned with the attitudes of the patient. Morita therapy is probably better known in the United States through both scientific and popular articles concerning it than are the contributions of Japanese psychiatrists to psychoanalysis. (For further information see De Vos, 1955; Freud, 1955; Goodman, 1957.)

3. Caudill thinks that Doi implies that the defenses are postulated to rise from fear or from lack of expectation that the wish will be fulfilled. (Cf. Erikson, 1959, on lack of basic trust.)

4. Another translation of *amaeru*, which is an intransitive verb, might be: to induce (someone) (into being or) to be taken care of, or to be pampered or cuddled.

desire to *amaeru*. He says that "despite his or her past life, each of the patients seems to rely too much upon others, . . . these patients are always troubled with a feeling of dependence dissatisfied or prevented." He points out that this complex is present in other cases of neurotic illness as well as in those classified as *shinkeishitsu*. When the symptom was understood and the patient's dependency wish and need made conscious, improvement occurred. Doi comments that

> in Japanese society parental dependency is fostered and its behavior pattern is even institutionalized into its social structure, whereas the opposite tendency prevails in Western society. . . . [O]nly in the society where the motivation of *"amaeru"* is so important as to need a word for it, can the consciousness of "toraware" occur as its deformation, thus enabling Morita to conceive of "shinkeishitsu" as an inclusive term [Doi, 1958].

Dr. Doi's paper stimulated me to look once again at the dependency patterns I had encountered in a group of Japanese-American patients.[5] These people were relating themselves to two quite different cultures: that of their Japanese-born and -reared parents, who lived in times of a great transition from a hierarchical feudal society to a modern society in Japan, and that of the culture of the United States, where the Nisei were born. Each of these cultures had unique and common avenues for the handling of universal dependency phenomena. Nisei individuals whose case histories provide data for this paper were born in the United States between the years 1911 and 1930. They were referred for treatment because of such feelings as inadequacy, anxiety, and depression. In some degree all suffered from psychological, somatic, and social discomfort. These patients had been reared on the West Coast of the United States; most had finished high school there and were active in or contemplating college work when, after Pearl Harbor, their families were implicated in the evacuation and relocation of the Japanese from the West Coast to the middle and eastern United States in the years 1941–45 (Bloom and Reimer, 1949; Leighton, 1945; Nishi, 1946; Okubo, 1946; Smith, 1948; Thomas and Nishimoto, 1946; War Relocation Authority, 1946).

At the time that these Nisei were being reared, their Issei parents were consciously and unconsciously stimulated by and reacting to a new culture. Often the culture of the United States was reacted to with vacillation and inconsistency in the child-rearing practices used by the Issei. Many times they intensified those attitudes and activities regarded as important in their own childhood but, in contrast to some immigrant generations, they rarely became "more American than the Americans." Thus it could be predicted that the personality structure and interpersonal problems relative to the fulfillment of dependency need and

---

5. Clinical data (1945–55) obtained from Japanese-American Study Sample (Caudill, 1952) or by referral from persons aware of the study. One hundred and sixty-two Japanese-Americans were seen for diagnosis and disposition (1–5 interviews); fifty-two Nisei (first-generation Japanese born in the United States) cases were taken into psychoanalytic psychotherapy or psychoanalysis (6–400 interviews).

reflective of dependency conflict would portray in some measure the differences between the Japanese and American cultures.

Clinical data from the case record of a single twenty-six-year-old Nisei man well represents the dependency conflict.[6] The patient was the middle of three sons; his mother, age forty-nine and in an arranged marriage, had wanted only her first child, the oldest son.[7] The patient suffered from passive rage and depression and marked constriction of his adaptive functions; overt and covert anxiety, mainly psychic but with some somatic signs, paralyzed him. He had been frankly obsessional in his childhood. Like many of the Issei mothers in our series, the problems of his mother had been seriously increased by her displacement from the Japanese to the American culture. For the patient, this intensification was reflected in both the degree and the fact that he was rejected by the mother. She had accomplished her goal, to have a son, and wanted no more children. If she must have another child, she wanted a daughter, who could be taught to take over the duties of the house. She was a clean and obsessive housekeeper but a reluctant and unhappy woman, who felt that she "was sent rather than that she came" to the United States. In his boyhood, the patient was assigned to do the dishwashing, the floor-scrubbing, and often the cooking. His older and younger brothers worked with the father. The father was an efficient and able importer of art wares, quite distant with his sons. It became clear to the patient during his adolescence that he would shortly be expected to shift for himself.[8]

An excerpt from an analytic hour highlights the patient's conflict. Now a graduate student in a university, he reported that he had been speechless, unable to communicate, and terrified in a seminar. The professor found the patient's passivity and silent watching of him and his classmates frustrating and near the close of a class attacked the patient as a non-contributor and as unworthy of having been admitted to the graduate school. The patient described his reaction as follows:

"I haven't had anything to eat since yesterday morning and I still feel nauseated; I just went home and sat still; I don't even feel angry, just helpless. I only came down here today because you commanded me to do so. I am not worth anything. He is the Emperor; I can see every detail of his angry face; I think he hates me and he wants me to beg for his favor. I can't write that thesis; I can't do it; and I never can go to class again; it will be too humiliating. Last night I didn't even undress, but I shaved this morning because I had to come here. I know you didn't command me to come here, but you gave me the appointment and it makes me come. Everything we had to do at home was from a command. I never dared ask anything . . . the price of anything, how

---

6. No attempt will be made in the following presentation to give the psychoanalytic formulations of this case. Transference manifestations and the techniques for handling these and other problems of therapy are deleted from this paper.

7. In our sample the Issei men were five to twenty years older than the Issei women, many of whom were picture brides. At the time data were collected, the Nisei men and women ranged from eighteen to thirty-five years of age.

8. Many second sons in the Japanese culture of his parents' era were expected to do so.

much money there was, what things we could have to eat . . . I never demanded anything. I suffer from silence . . . my mother made me be silent, and sit under the table; he wants me to sit under the table, too. I can't go back . . . but I've got to. I feel miserable . . . I am just nothing. Once when I was hungry at my father's store, I kicked the glass in the back door. My father was very angry and said I brought great shame on the shop, the imported china in it, and us, how could I? Mother was along and she chimed in; and the next day was the anniversary of my grandfather's death. And she said, "Grandfather will be very ashamed of you and will punish you"; so she burned the incense and said to the ghost, having put some bananas and cookies up for it [on the god-shelf], that I had been a very bad boy and brought great shame on the house and she hoped he would bring down a *bachi* [punishment] on me. I was terrified and couldn't move and I went and sat under the table for a long time. And after they went to bed, I went and got a piece of the banana and ate it; I thought I would be dead in the morning. . . . I am good in class; I sit still, I watch him all the time [patient had very high grades on all of his written work], but he looks at me as though I were so insignificant. I just shrink away. I am worthless, I am nothing. I feel embarrassed in his presence. It is frightening. I can't ask him any questions and my classmates all signal that they want to talk all of the time. I don't know their names."

In a therapy hour afterward, the following dreams were reported:

"I was in a restaurant; father and Joe were out. In the back of the restaurant were three toilets. I went in to try one, and tried to lock the door. I wasn't quite sure whether I wanted to use the toilet or to masturbate. A noise disturbed me. I came out and saw three girls and noticed that they were very pretty. They wanted to inquire why I was there. I wanted to make friends, at least with one of them. I sat down behind the counter; they walked out, laughing. That was all there was."

"I was at home in the kitchen at the sink and there were dirty dishes. Mother was angry and expected me to finish making the supper. There were a couple of pans and I wanted to get everything into one pan. I was doing this and then it was cooked and greasy. Then I was getting some water mixed in, and I did this for the longest time. I was taking the meat out of a bowl and putting it in another. It was cooked in some soy sauce, and in small pieces."

"Two men with guns were trying to break into the house. I was terrified. I tried to barricade the doors and then I hid behind a table with a gun in my hand."

These examples contain multiple-determined material, rich in associations and meaning that cannot be described here. However, they show that dependency was a conflict to this young Nisei man. Day after day the content of his therapy hours contained frank conscious and unconscious evidence of rejection in infancy and childhood, a state that had continued into his early twenties, was still unremitting, and was often self-provoked. Thus he had a deep and terrifying feeling of helplessness and an overwhelming fear of asking for or receiving help, even though consciously and unconsciously he wished to do so. Reared within the values of his Japanese parents, he perceived himself not only as a second son, but also as less loved, of less value than the older brother, and, subject to ignominious comparison, was expected to bear these attacks upon him without retaliation. No one supported his masculinity. Driven by the needs of the parents to fulfil their life patterns by subordinating the individual for the sake of collateral orientation (Caudill, 1952, 1961; Caudill and Scarr, 1962) in family relations, he reacted to his dependency deprivation with great fear and further deprivation. This is illustrated by his food revulsion, which was typical, his denial of dependency need, and his paralysis of motility ("I haven't eaten anything since yesterday and I still feel nauseated"), the dream in which the cleaning-up after the meal precedes the clumsy and potentially self-destructive preparation of the food, a fantasy that gives evidence of his negative identification both with his mother and with the role that she projected for him. The passivity ranging from quiet to a sense of being paralyzed, yet with active watching, is demonstrated by the sitting in silence in the face of danger from mother, father, ghost of grandfather, and the teacher, and, in the dream, from the invaders (be they three pretty girls or two men with guns).

But the defenses are not only those that manifest the fear of and denial of need. The patient experiences, compatible with the demands of the parents (the Emperor), worthlessness, humiliation, and shame. He even attempts "suicide," by an oral route, with the banana from the god-shelf. Beneath this is the reassurance, hinted at by the rebellious testing-out of the grandfather's ghost, that he is a man; the girls are pretty and the men are armed. The dream of food preparation is only a retreat from the heterosexually tinged dream, a defense against the assertion of his maleness. And, indeed, there was also the hostile provocation of the professor, by staring impassively and unmoved until his unresponsiveness brought down the frustrated teacher's outburst. Thus, in addition to the fear and thwarted dependency, there is the tremendous anger, in danger of overwhelming him but kept in check by intense guilt ("I am a bad boy"), whose surface manifestation is shame and humiliation.

Faced, then, with his Caucasian peers, who are less inhibited and more adequately equipped for activity, the defenses that reflected his dependency conflict and were fairly effective at home broke down at school. If he conformed at home, he had a place and could make his own food, but the angry, staring, guilt-provoking demand to be "fed" (cf. *amaeru*, an intransitive verb) in the classroom not only thwarted the dependency that is met by passive resistance and conformity but brought down so much of an attack upon him that he could no longer supply his own needs, much less ask for help. As in the reprimand from the father on the occasion of being hungry, and in the classroom, where he is also very "hungry," the patient was told that he brought shame upon the household. Whether aggressive, as in the first instance, in response to unsatisfied needs for (oral) dependency fulfilment, or passive in response to essentially the same order of needs, in the second, he was "destined" to bring tyranny upon his head. In the former it came from the parents, acting through their internalized Japanese cultural attributes; in the latter, from the American parental surrogates. Before the onslaught of the non-directly active father-professor, he retreated into anxiety approaching panic. His passivity, sometimes successfully defensive, was now massive and hostile, a far distance indeed from the relaxed, warm, flexible state of inactivity and sensual pleasure so characteristic of both food and bathing gratifications in Japan (Briggs, 1954; Caudill, 1962; Caudill and Scarr, 1962; Goodman, 1957; Lanham, 1956; Vogel, 1961). While his passivity expressed anger, it did not resolve his dependency conflict.

The Nisei in this series experienced shame and guilt over dependency wishes, particularly if they or others gave voice to them. But the fear was not always so terrifying. Many men in the series had been away from home in military service, but this was a well-structured situation, and their dependency needs were met by the structure. They reacted on their return to civilian life with overpassivity, as seen in this patient, or in some instances with overcompetitive aggressiveness. The women, however, had become more independent; they were pushed to and did display more leadership in their tasks of relocation of people and in their work roles than did the men, but relocated Issei parents, in deep value and culture conflict intensified by World War II, were often oblivious to the intensity of the dependency needs of their daughters.

It is our impression that the Japanese in America, on the whole, and the Nisei in particular, made an excellent adjustment to the culture of the United States. In many ways, behaviorally, they more elegantly and industriously lived up to the "great American ideal" than did the Caucasian middle-class people themselves (Caudill, 1952). Success was too often at the expense of conflict over dependency wishes, as is reflected in the example cited here and in other defenses not specifically illustrated, such as the reactive shame, guilt, and depression series of phenomena or the reactive competitive achievement striving, which often went to the point of greater rigidity than the values of the Japanese parent demanded.

For the most part, the men handled dependency need, as described here, by denial, passive withdrawal, painful guilt imposed by the superego, and intense anger masochistically concealed or passively expressed. Often the dependency process remained infantile and inhibited. While these defenses were present in them, the women were less immobilized and were effective in their use of the characteristics of the American culture.

Both men and women could be said to have made a working adaptation to the culture of the middle-western United States by reason of the high use of intellectual capacity, skilled imitation of peers, and concentrated watching for ways to achieve and acquire. The men did this by more passive means without angering the parent-surrogate upon whom they were dependent, while the women were more ingenious in the use of their equally able intellects and were freer to be less compliant and more aggressive, though not without pain and guilt. The Nisei women learned from Caucasians relationship skills to use with Caucasians with greater ease. In a sense, they had less to lose than did the sons—less of status in the Japanese value system, less of tenderness from the mother, though sometimes more from the father. Being less cherished than her brothers, the woman often had less internalization of the Japanese culture. She had less reason and opportunity to identify with the often outmoded and frequently uncommunicative mother. Though they may have been cherished in their little-girlhood, these Nisei as women were pushed out. The Caucasian world, particularly of the relocation period, appreciated their skills, their attractiveness and self-assertiveness, and offered them something that was not so available at home. Fear of the mother, and guilt for the anger at her because she failed to recognize the potential of the woman, were enormous and inhibiting, particularly in the expression of heterosexual affection and behavior, but the drive to achieve was less impaired. In many of the men, particularly for sons younger than the first-born son, fear of and anger at both parents for failure to give adequate support to their dependent state in childhood was paralyzing of expression of feeling and sometimes of activity, as is illustrated by the male patient described.

Dr. Doi comments, in his formulation of the psychodynamics of *toraware* ("to be bound"), that this results from frustration of *amaeru*, the need "to depend or presume upon another's love or indulge in another's kindness." Opportunities for the Japanese-Americans to *amaeru* seem to have been less than for the Japanese in Japan. Both Dr. Doi and Dr. Caudill point out the acceptance of the helplessness that the patient feels when he comes needfully to the doctor and cite many instances in which the patient says directly and simply "I am in your hands" (Caudill, 1958, 1959a, 1959b, 1961; Doi, 1958).

Possibly there are attitudes in Japan that foster the direct expression of dependency wishes under stress (i.e., the influence of the historically significant hierarchical attitude in the culture and the experience of the rewards as well as the punishments of a defined subservience, of the gratification of oral drives freely in the childhood of many Japanese patients, with much loving pleasure on the part of the parent until the child enters school). A Caucasian patient says with anxiety and every evidence of constriction and perhaps only after many weeks or months of therapy, "I had the thought that I want to be held in your arms and cuddled." As with the Japanese patient, when the patient finds that the wish is acceptable to the therapist even though the activity may not be indulged in, improvement occurs. Perhaps in Japan *amaeru* is more likely to exist alone as a thing in itself as contrasted with its being a regressive expression of, for example, passive phallic strivings. Similarly, among certain European Jews, a man may *amaeru* in a Turkish bath, but most Americans of Gentile extraction limit themselves to haircuts and some tonic and would feel anxious in the bath, which would seem regressive to them. The oral and sensual dependency is perhaps to be glimpsed more easily in Japan than in the United States.

In therapy the Japanese-Americans repeatedly use the phrase, "I can't do it." It is a statement both of the feeling and of the fear of inadequacy, anger, and abandonment. However, this statement covers a feeling of great need to have dependent wishes met or to be able or allowed to meet them. This ego need was almost totally pre- or unconscious in the Japanese-American patients under discussion here. In Japan there may be more culturally acceptable adult behavioral derivatives of the passive wishes than appear to be readily available in the United States.

In the Japanese-American the feeling of being bound is also very high, but the accompanying hostility seems to be more urgent. In the men passivity is more pervasive than in the women, but in both the hostile feelings of anger aroused by frustration are felt intensely; the woman, by virtue of the culture patterning, is more rejected by her kinship experiences and less by the Caucasian society. These factors may help her to make more ego syntonic use of her aggressive drives. Compared with American middle-class patients, the phrase "I can't do it" carries, for the Japanese-American patient, the implicit "but I have got to, regardless," which stems from the internalized parental superego, with its sternness and insistence on work discipline. The concept of Japanese-born parents that restricts the ego to a limited focus concerned with its reality testing and intellectual functions, such as the realistic appraisal of daily problems, and a great determination to keep striving for success no matter what the obstacle may be, makes the asking for nurturing difficult. For the Nisei men, "but I've got to, regardless," lets him be passively conforming in a culturally syntonic way so that he can achieve in the American society. The passivity leaves the man in great conflict over his partially conscious dependency wish and his ego need for support. Since he suppresses overt hostility as too threatening, he must express the dependent need only indirectly, with seething and bitter internalized rage, masochistic in himself and controlling of the environment. Many middle-class Caucasian Americans, both men and women, respond to "I can't do it" with an ever more devastating breakdown in panic, psychosis, or suicide; they seem to be less protected by the "but I've got to do it, regardless" attitude. In contrast, Nisei men and women both fight against their conflict. On the whole, the Nisei women we studied were more successful in the resolution of this conflict at less personal cost than were the men. It is often said that middle-class American men and women (and again generalizations are never more than partly true) are less able to express their dependent needs and conflicts both directly and indirectly and to obtain fulfilment than people of some other cultures. Dr. Caudill has suggested that derivatives of pregenital experience may be used more frequently as defenses of the ego against the anxiety of oedipal conflict in Japan, or that derivatives of the oedipal conflict may be used more frequently against the anxiety of unresolved pregenital conflict in the United States, the dependent behavior being used defensively to mask deeper oedipal problems (Caudill, 1962). If this is so, many factors, economic, societal, or political, common to all cultures but differently experienced and expressed, are, in addition to the internal personal ones, determinants of which cultural solution of conflict will appear in any given individual. Intra-psychic conflict, which enhances or retards sublimatory processes essential for maturation of work and other pertinent adult activities, is also reflected in individuals in any culture.

However, when the conflict over dependency need is primary in a sick, urban middle-class Caucasian American, the phrase, "I can't do it" tends to have an even more ominous cast, as suggested above, than it had for any of the Japanese-Americans in the series in therapy. At the conscious level, to "be dependent" tends to be more weighted with anxiety and tension and is a greater deviant from the norm in the Caucasian American group. Before experience with the Nisei group was accumulated, the therapist was concerned because she heard the phrase, "I can't do it" repeatedly from Japanese-American patients as though she were hearing it from Caucasians of similar age range, education, and goal direction.[9] However, as experience was accumulated, it became clear that the "I can't do it" was indeed a statement of fear, helplessness, and the great personal pain of inadequacy, as reflected through the internalized eyes of the Japanese parent and the society, but that it also was a statement of rebellion against having to fulfil the life-process nature of dependency demands expressed in "I don't want to do it, but I can." Because the Japanese has developed skill with face-saving devices, and because the young Nisei had internalized some of the cross-culturally determined defenses of the ego of his parents in the United States, he was to use the now internalized command, "but I've got to, regardless," and translate it into some kind of ego activity more useful than destructive.

Furthermore, such activity was compatible with the individual's evaluation of his capacities rather more than with the introjected and projected role assigned to him by the Japanese parental and cultural patterns. To some extent, "I can't do it," said in despair, anger, and misery, and experienced as nauseating, was a way for some Japanese-Americans to express anger at having to do something about the dependency conflict while, at the same moment, saying, "but I can." It may be that the early and continued pre-oedipal emphasis on mastery of body controls and related tasks produces a foreshortening of the period of dependent gratifications on the American scene as compared with the effects on these phenomena of the earlier and some of the present Japanese child-rearing patterns. Under severe stress, internally or externally derived, many Caucasian patients tend to regress to a level at which the ego is relatively helpless, and, still hungry, the "I can't do it" feelings may threaten life itself. For the Japanese-reared person, the dependency feelings seem to be more acceptable. In the presence of stress the individual regresses and experiences shame but is not so deterred that he cannot ask to be fed (*amaeru*). Perhaps, then, in the patterns of some Japanese-Americans one sees, deeply engrained in the characterological handling of dependency, the imprint of both cultures. "I can't do it, but I've got to" may represent a pattern somewhat midway between the open expectation of dependency fulfilment in some Japanese in Japan and the denial of that wish in some middle-class Caucasians in the United States.

9. Suicide and suicidal threat occur in Japanese-Americans as well as in Caucasians, but the point under discussion here is significant because of quality differences.

BIBLIOGRAPHY

BABCOCK, CHARLOTTE G., and WILLIAM CAUDILL
1958 "Personal and Cultural Factors in the Treatment of a Nisei Man." In: GEORGENE SEWARD (ed.), *Clinical Studies in Culture Conflict.* New York: Ronald Press Co.

BLOOM, LEONARD, and RUTH RIEMER
1949 *Removal and Return.* Berkeley: University of California Press.

BRIGGS, D. L.
1954 "Social Adaptation among Japanese American Youth: A Comparative Study," *Sociol. & Social Res.* 38, 293ff.

CAUDILL, WILLIAM
1952 "Japanese American Personality and Acculturation," *Genet. Psychol. Monogr.,* 45, 3.

1958 *The Psychiatric Hospital as a Small Society.* Cambridge: Harvard University Press.

1959a "Observations on the Cultural Context of Japanese Psychiatry." In: M. K. OPLER (ed.), *Culture and Mental Health.* New York: Macmillan Co.

1959b "Similarities and Differences in Psychiatric Illness and Its Treatment in the United States and Japan," *Seishin Eisei* ("Mental Hygiene"), 61–62, 15.

1961 "Around the Clock Patient Care in Japanese Psychiatric Hospitals: The Role of the Tsukisoi," *Amer. Sociol. Rev.,* 26, 204.

1962 "Anthropology and Psychoanalysis: Some Theoretical Issues." In: T. GLADWIN and W. C. STURTEVANT (eds.), *Anthropology and Human Behavior.* Washington, D.C.: Anthropological Society of Washington. (In press.)

CAUDILL, WILLIAM, and GEORGE DE VOS
1956 "Achievement, Culture and Personality: The Case of the Japanese Americans," *Amer. Anthrop.,* 56, 1102.

CAUDILL, WILLIAM, and HARRY A. SCARR
1962 "Japanese Value Orientations and Culture Change," *Ethnol.,* 1, 53.

DE VOS, GEORGE
1954 "A Comparison of the Personality Difference in Two Generations of Japanese Americans by Means of the Rorschach Test," *Nagoya J. Med. Sci.,* 17, 153.

1955 "A Quantitative Rorschach Assessment of Maladjustment and Rigidity in Acculturating Japanese Americans," Genet. Psychol. Monogr., 52, 51.

DOI, TAKEO
1956 "Japanese Language as an Expression of Japanese Psychology," *Western Speech,* 20, 80.

1958 "Psychopathology of *Shinkeishitsu,* Especially Regarding the Psychodynamics of *Toraware,*" *Psychiat. et Neurol. Jap.,* 60, 733.

1960a "Psychopathology of *Jibun* and *Amae,*" *ibid.,* LXI, 149.

1960b "The Theory of Narcissism and the Psychic Representation of Self," *Jap. J. Psychoan.,* 7, 7.

ERIKSON, E. H.
1959 "Identity and the Life Cycle," *Psychol. Issues* (monograph), 1, 18.

FREUD, S.
1953 "Three Essays on the Theory of Sexuality (1905)." In: JAMES STRACHEY (ed.). *The Complete Psychological Works of Sigmund Freud,* p. 7. London: Hogarth Press.

1955 "Beyond the Pleasure Principle (1930)." In: *ibid.*, p. 18.
1957 "Instincts and Their Vicissitudes (1915)." In: *ibid.*, p. 14.

GOODMAN, MARY ELLEN
1957 "Values, Attitudes and Social Concepts of Japanese and American Children," *Amer. Anthrop.*, 59, 979.

JACOBSON, ALAN, and LEE RAINWATER
1953 "A Study of Management Representative Evaluations of Nisei Workers," *Soc. Forces*, 32, 35.

KAKETA, KATSUMI
1956 "Psychoanalysis in Japan," *Psychologia*, 1, 247.

KONDO, AKIHISA
1953 "Morita Therapy: A Japanese Therapy for Neurosis," *Amer. J. Psychoan.*, 13, 31.

LANHAM, BETTY B.
1956 "Aspects of Child Care in Japan: Preliminary Report." In: DOUGLAS HARING (ed.), *Personal Character and Cultural Milieu*, p. 564. Syracuse: Syracuse University Press.

LEIGHTON, A. H.
1945 *The Government of Men.* Princeton: Princeton University Press.

MORITA, SEIMA
1928 *The Nature and Therapy of "Shinkeishitsu."* Tokyo: Tohoda.

NISHI, SETSUKO M.
1946 *Facts about Japanese-Americans.* Chicago: American Council on Race Relations.

OKUBO, MINE
1946 *Citizen 13660.* New York: Columbia University Press.

SMITH, BRADFORD
1948 *Americans from Japan.* Philadelphia: J. B. Lippincott Co.

THOMAS, D. S., and R. S. NISHIMOTO
1946 *The Spoilage.* Berkeley: University of California Press.

VOGEL, EZRA F., and SUZANNE H.
1961 "Family Security, Personal Immaturity, and Emotional Health in a Japanese Sample," *Marriage & Fam. Living*, 23, 161.

WAELDER, ROBERT
1960 *Basic Theory of Psychoanalysis.* New York: International Universities Press.

WAR RELOCATION AUTHORITY, UNITED STATES DEPARTMENT OF INTERIOR
1946 *Wartime Exile: The Exclusion of the Japanese-Americans from the West Coast.* Washington: Government Printing Office.

Index

INDEX

A

Abegglen, James, 92n.
Academic performance, 146
Acculturation, of Japanese in America, 180–81
Adopted son. See *Mukoyōshi*
Agricultural cooperatives, 77–78, 82, 103
Agricultural periods since 1868, 105–108
Aichi Prefecture, 93
Ainu, 17, 157, 139
Allied Occupation of Japan. See Occupation of Japan
Altaic language, 5, 8–9, 17–19, 21
Amae (passive lovability), 132 ff., 174; as an aspect of dependency, 136; and *on*, 137–38; terminology related to, 134
Amaeru (to coax), 120, 175, 179, 181, 183
Arensberg, Conrad, 93
Ascriptive status, 141, 146, 147
Atotori (heir), 68
Attitudes: toward challenge, 182; of collaterality, 115; toward family, 52, 55 ff; flexibility of, 98; hierarchical, 181; toward primogeniture, 56 ff.; toward suicide, 162; toward the *yōshi* system, 37, 63–66

B

Balint, Michael, 135
Beardsley, Richard K., 6, 37
Bellah, Robert, 91, 164
Benedict, Ruth, 136, 137
Blood types, 17, 21

Bronze and iron, prehistoric, 9
Bunke (branch house). See *Honke-bunke*
Buraku (basic community), 73 ff.; administration as a sub-autonomous unit, 86–88; common interest associations of, 75, 77, 88; communalism of, 90; democratization of, 86 ff.; self-interest of, 87; shopkeeper type, 93 ff.

C

Career, determined by examination, 145–46
Change: agricultural, 103–104, 105–108; through common-interest associations, 79; economic, 91, 100 ff.; social, 47 ff., 55 ff., 103 ff.
China: family system of, 38, 95; influence on Japan, 3, 21–22, 27, 31; suicide in, 162-63
Chōnan (eldest son), 56 ff., 68, 92
Chōnin (town dweller, burgher), 94
Chū (fealty), 137
Collaterality, value orientation toward, 115
Common-interest associations, 74 ff., 88 ff.; of *buraku*, 75, 77, 87; democratization of, 83; entrepreneurs in, 97; and kinship, 81, 82; outside of *buraku*, 103; types of, 75–77; See also Agricultural co-operatives; Co-operative associations

Communalism, in *buraku*, 70

Constitution of 1946, 51–52, 53–54, 102, 103
Co-operative associations, 77–78, 82

D

Dekasegi (job away from home), 95
Delinquency of juveniles, 153 ff.; cross-cultural features of, 157, 159–60; and family conditions, 158–61; and mass entertainment media, 157; and national character, 159–60; and suicide, 160, 165–66; urban-rural comparison of, 161
Democratization: of *buraku*, 86 ff.; through common-interest associations, 83; in the family, 51, 55
Dependency, psychological, 172 ff.; defined, 172; *See also Amae*
Dependency feelings: acceptance of, 183; conflict in, 182; suppressed among daughters, 180
Descent rules. *See* Inheritance; Succession
Dialects, Japanese, 18
Differential socialization of sons, 91
Doctors, as projective test respondents, 119 ff.
Dore, Ronald, 106, 156
Dōzoku (lineage group), 39 ff., 42 ff.; co-operative functions, 45–46; decline of, 42; and *ie*, 39, 42–43, 45
Durkheim, Émile, 163

E

Economic change, 91
Educational institutions, hierarchy of, 145
Electroencephalogram patterns of delinquents, 160
Embree, John F., 93

Emotions, 119, 127, 149, 174 ff.; patterns of, 115 ff.; and physical pleasures, 129–30; uncontrolled, 160; *see also* Feelings
Emperor-worship, 138
Employment criteria, 145–46, 149
Entrepreneur orientation, 91 ff.; in conflict with farmer interests, 97; among junior sons, 92 ff.; in politics, 96–97
Eta, 157–58
Examinations, school entrance, 140 ff.; preparation for, 141–42

F

Family, 34 ff., 43, 47, 51 ff., 66, 73, 91, 143, 151; composition of, 43, 49, 79, (charts, 48, 50); cycles of development of, 49; and delinquency, 158–61; democratization of, 51, 55; extended type of, 73; functions in entrance examinations, 143, 151; legal and constitutional provisions for, 51, 54, 103; nuclear type of, 43, 47; perpetuation of, 34, 35, 43–44, 53–54, 55, 66; stem type of, 91, 98; *See also Dōzoku; Honke-bunke; Ie;* Kin terms; Primogeniture
Feelings: about bathing, 122–27; about heterosexual interaction, 121–22; about minor illness, 118–21
Firth, Raymond, 39
Foster son. *See Mukoyōshi*
Freud, Sigmund, 138, 173
Functional groups. *See* Common-interest associations; *Buraku*

G

Glueck, Sheldon and Eleanor, 158

Gratification of impulse, 116

H

Haniwa (fired-clay images), 12
Hierarchy: of family, 47; of schools, 145
Himiko, Queen, 5
Hiyameshi-kui (dependents), 47
Hokkaido, 57, 101
Honke-bunke (main family-branch family), 42–46
Honshu, 37
Horse-riding invasion, 4, 12
Household. *See* Family
Hoynden, Yoshio, 74

I

Ie (house, family line), 42–46, 95; hierarchy of, 47; perpetuation of, 43–44, 49, 56; *See also Dōzoku;* Family
Impulse, expression of, 116
Income, farm, 110
Inheritance, 17–19, 27, 55, 95; *See also* Primogeniture; Succession
Issei (first generation emigrants), emotional patterns of, 176

J

Jacobs, Norman, 92n.
Japanese language: comparisons of, 5, 8–9, 17–19, 20; morphology of, 18–19; vocabulary of, 19–20
Jimmu, Emperor, 12-14
Jisannan (junior sons): entrepreneurial orientation of, 92; flexible qualities of, 98
Jomon, culture periods, 6, 8, 17

Juvenile delinquency. *See* Delinquency of juveniles

K

Kansai region, 158
Kin solidarity, 73, 81, 82
Kin terms, 25 ff.; Chinese influence on, 27, 31; Eskimo system, 31; in historical records, 26 ff.
Kluckhohn, Florence, 115
Kō (filial piety), 137
Komae, Tokyo, survey in, 52 f., 62 ff.
Korea, 13, 15, 19–20, 81, 139, 157
Koseki (household membership register), 26, 43
Kroeber, Alfred L., 107
Kyōdai (siblings), 123
Kyushu, 57

L

Landlords, 44, 108
Land reform, 101–102, 111
Law code of 1948: family provisions in, 51, 55; property provisions in, 55
Law codes, historical 28–29
Legends and myths: Chinese, 14; Japanese, 4, 13–16; Korean, 13–14; Manchurian, 14

M

Malayan language and Japanese, 26
Marriage: with adoption, 35–37; in China, 38; under the Civil Code, 55
Maruyama, Masao, 138
Mass entertainment media, 157
Miyagi Prefecture, survey in, 74 ff.
Mother-child relationship, 118, 120, 129,

132, 136, 141–44, 147–48, 150–51, 163–64, 177, 180
Mukoyōshi (foster son-bridegroom), 35 ff., 37, 63–66

N

Nagura-mura, Aichi Prefecture, 93 ff.
Nakamura, Hajime, 136
Narcissism, 135
National character and delinquency, 159–60
New middle class, 140 ff., 141n.
Nisei (children of emigrants), 172 ff.
Nōhon shugi (farming as a way of life) movement, 109
Nurses, as projective test respondents, 119 ff.

O

Occupation of Japan (1945-1952), 55, 101, 154
Ohkawa, Kazushi, 108
On (obligating gift), 137
Opinion survey. *See* Attitudes
Otaba, Tokyo, survey in, 52 f., 62 ff.
Outcastes. *See* Eta

P

Paleolithic discoveries, viii
Parent-Teacher Association, 77, 143, 148
Parental dependency, 136
Parsons, Talcott, 91
Passive object-love, 135
Personal relations, emphasis on, 137
Polynesian language and Japanese, 20
Population increase, 106, 108–109
Pottery: Jōmon, 8; Yayoi, 9

Preceramic period, 7, 17 f.
Primogeniture, 34 ff., 55–63, 103

R

Regions: Hokkaido, 57, 101; Kansai, 158; prehistoric, 6, 17–18; Tohoku, 56; Tokyo, 52 f., 62 ff.
Role allocation, 151, 180, 183
Rosovsky, Henry, 108
Rural common-interest associations, 73 ff.; entrepreneurs in, 93; familism in, 52; *See also* Buraku; Change

S

Sashimi (sliced raw fish), 174
Seinendan (Young People's Association), 74, 76
Shingaku movement, 91
Shinkeishitsu (neurotic patterns), 132, 175
Situational ethics, 137
Social change. *See* Change
Socialization, differential, 91 ff.
Standard of living, village, 104–105
Stem-family. *See* Family; *Ie*
Succession to family headship, 17–19, 27, 64, 95; patrilineal, 34 ff., 43, 47, 55, 68, 95; *See also* Inheritance; Primogeniture
Suicide, 147, 161 ff., 179, 182; linked with juvenile delinquency, 165–66
Sumanai (unending, unpardonable), 133
Suye-mura, 93

T

T.A.T. *See* Thematic Apperception Test
Taxation, 86, 88

Thematic Apperception Test, 159, 164
Tohoku region, 56
Tombs, 4–5, 6, 10, 11 ff.
Toraware (be bound, be caught), 132, 175, 181
Toyama, Tokyo, survey in, 52 f., 61 ff.
Tsukisoi (practical nurse-companion), 116 ff.

U

Underworld, 157
United States: Catholics and *amae* in, 136; delinquency in, 156, 157, 164–65; immigrant adjustment in 176, 180–81; voluntary associations in, 80, 82

V

Value orientations, 115; *See also* Democratization; Family; Primogeniture

Voluntary associations. *See* Common-interest associations; United States

W

Wa Kingdom, 4, 5, 13, 15–16
Weber, Max, 91
Writing system in Japan, 11, 21

Y

Yamato dynasty, 3 ff., 16
Yayoi culture (prehistoric) 4, 5, 9–10, 17 ff.
Yōrō Code, 27
Yōshi (adopted family member). *See Mukoyōshi*
Yūryokusha (influential person), 87

For Product Safety Concerns and Information please contact our EU representative GPSR@taylorandfrancis.com
Taylor & Francis Verlag GmbH, Kaufingerstraße 24, 80331 München, Germany

www.ingramcontent.com/pod-product-compliance
Lightning Source LLC
Chambersburg PA
CBHW051644230426
43669CB00013B/2430